Fodor's
aspen and snowmass

fodor's travel publications
new york • toronto • london • sydney • auckland
www.fodors.com

contents

On the Road with Fodor's   iv

Don't Forget to Write *v*

- introducing aspen/snowmass   2
- perfect days   18
- eating out   22
- shopping   56
- downhill skiing   78
- other sports   110
- here and there   128
- nightlife   146
- cultural activities   158
- where to stay   170
- practical information   198
- index   223

maps

aspen/snowmass region *vi–vii*

aspen dining *26–27*

snowmass dining *50*

aspen exploring 132–133

snowmass exploring 144

apsen lodging 178–179

snowmass lodging 196

ON THE ROAD WITH FODOR'S

EVERY VACATION IS IMPORTANT. So here at Fodor's we've pulled out all stops in preparing Pocket Aspen and Snowmass. To direct you to the places that are truly worth your time and money, we've rallied the team of endearingly picky know-it-alls we're pleased to call our writers. Having seen all corners of Aspen, they're real experts. If you knew them, you'd poll them for tips yourself.

Gavin Ehringer is a freelance writer and photographer from Colorado who specializes in equestrian events, winter sports, and travel. His work has appeared in publications including Fodor's Skiing USA, People Weekly, the Rocky Mountain News, Snow Country, and Encyclopedia Britannica.

Brent Gardner-Smith is a journalist and writer who has lived in Aspen since 1982. Formerly with the Aspen Skiing Company, he is currently news editor for Aspen.com, the main Internet community portal.

David Gibson is a staff writer for Aspen magazine.

Cindy Hirschfeld, a freelance writer and editor living in Aspen, is the author of the best-selling Canine Colorado: Where to Go and What to Do with Your Dog. Cindy also writes and edits regularly for Skiing, Backcountry, Hooked on the Outdoors, and SnoWorld magazines and contributes articles to the Aspen Times and Sojourner, an Aspen-based publication. In her "spare" time she teaches skiing at Snowmass.

Jeanne McGovern is a freelance writer and editor who fled Southern California for the Colorado Rockies more than 15 years ago. For the past 10 years, she has called Aspen home. The former executive director of the Aspen Writers' Foundation, McGovern now works for the *Aspen Times* and *Sojourner* magazine, as well as other local, regional, and national publications.

Don't Forget to Write

Keeping a travel guide fresh and up to date is a big job. So we love your feedback—positive and negative—and follow up on all suggestions. Contact the Aspen editor at editors@fodors.com or c/o Fodor's, 280 Park Avenue, New York, New York 10017. And have a wonderful trip!

Karen Cure

Karen Cure
Editorial Director

aspen/snowmass region

aspen and snowmass

Aspen offers visitors much more than the great skiing and celebrity sightings for which the town is justifiably famous. A rich history as a boom-and-bust mining town, lovingly restored Victorian homes, spectacular scenery, and a vibrant arts scene turn this glamorous ski resort into a year-round destination.

In this Chapter

THE MAKING OF ASPEN 4 • GLITTERATI GULCH 7 • SKIERS' PARADISE 9 • IT'S NOT JUST WINTER ANYMORE 12 • CULTURAL CAPITAL 15

By David Gibson

introducing aspen/snowmass

ASPEN'S REPUTATION PRECEDES IT. It is a place known as much for its Hollywood stars as for its starry nights, as much for its social scene as for its skiing, as much for its multimillionaires as its mountains. And while skiing and people-watching may be the headline activities at this fabled resort, Aspen is a year-round destination, a town that is rich not only in natural resources but in history and culture. With galleries, museums, international conferences, and festivals celebrating music, art, and food and wine, there is so much going on that, even in winter, many people come to "do the scene," and don't even ski.

Popularity has its price, however. Aspen is one of the few places in the world that has spawned its own verb: for mountain towns facing the prospect of rapid growth, being "Aspenized" is perhaps worse than being swallowed by an earthquake. There is no denying that Aspen is not the quaint little mining town it once was. But in many ways, what sets Aspen apart from other ski resorts is what it is not. It is not provincial. It is not backward-looking. It is not a theme park. It is not a cultural, culinary, or consumer wasteland.

If you look beyond the soap-opera lifestyle of the glitterati and the media hype, you'll find that Aspen is a real community, inhabited by real people with very strong ideas. Here, your waitress may hold a Harvard law degree, your lift op may be a former navy pilot, and the guy next to you at the sushi bar may have left his Silicon Valley start-up for less stressful climes. But these people aren't hiding from the real world; they live here for the same reasons you spend your annual two weeks here.

They just think you're about 50 weeks shy of perfect bliss.

THE MAKING OF ASPEN

In 1879 the first prospectors made their way from the booming mining town of Leadville across the Continental Divide into the Roaring Fork Valley. By the end of that summer, a mining camp known as Ute City (named after the indigenous Native American tribe, who also gave the state of Utah its name) was in full swing, along with the nearby camps of Ashcroft and Independence, which exist today only as ghost towns.

Ute City was a silver camp, and ore was found in great abundance in both Aspen Mountain and Smuggler Mountain. At the time, the United States operated on a dual currency standard of gold and silver; a miner with determination and a little luck could literally pull money from the ground. Jerome B. Wheeler, an ambitious scion of an East Coast mercantile family, invested heavily both in the silver mines and in the newly renamed town of Aspen. The town's improved infrastructure, as well as Wheeler's aggressive salesmanship, made Aspen an attractive investment for outside capital. Soon two railroads found their way into the valley, ensuring ready markets for silver and easy transportation for laborers looking to make their fortune in the West's newest boom town. By 1893 Aspen had a population estimated as high as 17,000, making it the third-largest city in Colorado. It boasted gas streetlights, municipal water and power, multiple newspapers, three banks, a streetcar line, and a busy red-light district. Wheeler himself had added an opera house and a luxurious (by Wild West standards) hotel, known now as the Hotel Jerome.

But disaster soon struck. In 1893 the United States demonetized silver. Aspen's economy, built around a single commodity, soon

Geography

Aspen and Snowmass are located within the valley of the Roaring Fork River. At an altitude of 7,908 ft, Aspen marks the southernmost point in the valley flat enough for concentrated settlement. Snowmass lies in a smaller, higher valley to the northwest.

Aspen is sandwiched between Aspen Mountain to the south and Red Mountain to the north. Barring a foggy night, navigation is simple. Highway 82 becomes Main Street as it enters town from the north (the only route of entry during the winter), and the town is laid out in a simple grid pattern, with the downtown core occupying roughly 25 blocks to the south of Main.

Snowmass's main landmark is its ski mountain, again located to the south. However, the village is laid out in a system of Macchu Picchu–style terraces, and the only straight road is occupied by the Snowmass Village Mall, to the west of the mountain's base. From there, everything's either up, down, or best reached by taxi.

---

collapsed. Wages fell, and with them fell the population to less than 3,000 within the decade, and to mere hundreds by the 1940s. Aspen languished in what is known locally as "The Quiet Years." Still important to the local economy, mining was marginally profitable thanks to technological advances, though ranching and farming had become the chief methods of subsistence in the valley. But there was another industry on the horizon—like silver before it, a gift of the mountains.

Skis had served as the most reliable form of winter transport before roads and railways made their way into the valley, indeed skiing had been a recreational pursuit in the valley since mining days. Ski racing had even served as entertainment in the few hours of free time afforded the miners. In the late 1930s a group of investors formed the Highland Bavarian Lodge and began towing skiers up Mount Hayden. Soon a volunteer "Citizen's Brigade" had cut the first ski run on Aspen Mountain and christened it Roch's Run, in honor of Andre Roch, the world-famous European mountaineer who first suggested its route.

Meanwhile, the U.S. Army's 10th Mountain Division was training in Leadville in anticipation of what was to be a heroic role in World War II. The Division consisted of mountain men, Ivy League ski club racers, and European alpinists who had fled their homes as the Nazi regime spread. The soldiers spent much of their free time skiing in Aspen. One of them, an Austrian-born naturalized-American ski instructor named Freidl Pfeifer, foresaw the skiing mecca that Aspen was to become. He returned to Aspen after the war and, in partnership with Chicago industrialist Walter Paepcke, formed the Aspen Skiing corporation. In 1947 the world's longest ski lift opened on Aspen Mountain.

The evolution from abandoned mining town to thriving ski resort had begun, and in 1950 the staging of the Fédération Internationale du Ski (FIS) World Alpine Championships thrust Aspen into the skiing spotlight. Racers from around the world attended, and tales of this quaint American ski town spread abroad. Success begat expansion, and other ski areas opened, including Snowmass Resort 12 mi away.

At the same time that Aspen was earning a reputation as a premier ski resort, the town was also becoming a cultural mecca. During the summer of 1949, in a makeshift circus tent set up in a hog pasture on the edge of town, Aspen had celebrated the Goethe Convocation, a summerlong festival of music and lectures in honor of the "spirit of man" as invoked by Johann Wolfgang von Goethe. Albert Schweitzer and Arthur Rubinstein were just a few of the notables in attendance. The festival was the brainchild of Walter Paepcke and his wife, Elizabeth, who had persuaded her husband to invest in the decaying town.

Troubled by the intellectual vacuousness he saw in his fellow businessmen, Paepcke saw Aspen as the perfect place to create a new Athens; a city dedicated to the enrichment of "Body, Mind, and Spirit." At first, his efforts were resented by the local populace, but from that Goethe Convocation sprang the Aspen Music Festival, the Aspen Institute, and the International Design Conference Aspen. Aspen was suddenly an arts town, and one of the first ski towns blessed with a year-round economy.

During the '50s and '60s, Aspen was just an American small town with an unusual cottage industry. By the '70s, however, the addition of three more ski mountains—Highlands, Buttermilk, and Snowmass—had turned Aspen into something of a destination. Rents were still cheap, though accommodations were not luxurious, and soon writers, artists, ski bums, and other escapees from the rat race began to make up a noticeable slice of the population. Guido's restaurant, which still sits at the corner of Cooper and Galena, posted a sign by the entrance that read "Hippies use side door." There was no side door.

But a secret, particularly one involving real estate, can't be kept forever, and in the 1980s Aspen saw a boom rivaled only by the boom that created it a century before.

GLITTERATI GULCH

Phil Donahue and Marlo Thomas didn't start the Aspen craze, but a photo of them still hangs in Aspen Highlands' Merry-Go-Round restaurant, their rainbow-striped ski gear clearly dating the shot to the early '80s. Many other celebrities were making the trip to the high country then, and photographers and gossip columnists were trailing right along behind. Soon celebrity-watching America had filed away "Aspen" in its collective consciousness, right alongside "Bel Air" and "Monte Carlo."

Aspen had its own champion years before, when a young, almost embarrassingly positive folk singer named John Denver decided to make the valley his home. Right there in his Greatest Hits album is "Starwood in Aspen," on which he sings about his "sweet Rocky Mountain paradise." John Denver, one of America's most persuasive environmental crusaders, lived to see Starwood change from a few houses on a mesa to a gated community of multimillion-dollar homes, inhabited by the likes of former Playmate Barbi Benton and a crown prince of Saudi Arabia. But even Starwood is a has-been neighborhood these days.

This wasn't the first time a star had attracted attention to Aspen; Gary Cooper owned one of the first houses on Red Mountain in the late '40s. But Cooper skied and drank wine in the Hotel Jerome with a small group of iconoclasts ranging from war heroes to Olympians—he just happened to be an actor. And at the time, Aspen was not someplace the average American would ever think of going. Average Americans didn't ski.

But soon came the plastic boot and the metal-edged ski, which made skiing easier, as well as a host of manmade fabrics, which made it more comfortable. Ski areas, Aspen included, began marketing to the general consumer: a ski vacation was a family vacation and a romantic getaway; it was something everyone could enjoy. Thanks in part to its star power, Aspen soon became the premier North American ski resort, and people came in droves. Those with money bought property, and then those with more money bought it from them. And as property grew scarce, prices went up—way up. Today the average new single-family home in Aspen costs more than $3 million.

The wealthy, to quote a bumper sticker from Little Annie's Eating House, "didn't come all the way to Aspen just to lay up." Beginning in the '80s, the town followed the real-estate agents to the money. Restaurants with high-ticket items began to replace the burger shacks. Nightclubs served champagne instead of longnecks; they pulled Waylon and Willie off the jukebox in favor of Lisa Lisa and Cult Jam. Aspen was catering to the monied class from L.A. and New York, and it soon began to resemble a higher-altitude, more compact version of those cities. By the mid-'90s, boutiques such as Chanel, Fendi, and Gucci were popping up. Even the Planet Hollywood chain, the least subtle of all star-powered businesses, opened a footprint in downtown Aspen. Locals were disgusted and refused to set foot inside; the restaurant closed in just three years.

Prosperity has been a mixed blessing for Aspen. On the plus side, the demands of wealthy residents fuels an incredible arts scene, supports a strong infrastructure, keeps employment rates high, and guarantees the availability of artisanal cheeses in the supermarkets. But it also guarantees high rents (only slightly lower than New York and San Francisco), $14 cheeseburgers, and an hour's drive to buy a pair of underwear. In early 2000 the Board of County Commissioners imposed a moratorium on new residential projects over 3,500 square ft until a suitable plan to mitigate the impact of those homes was worked out. Twice in 1999 the airport was closed to private traffic because there was no place to park another Gulfstream.

But there's also a good chance you'll sit next to Sally Field in an Aspen restaurant one day. And you know, she really is as nice as she seems in the movies.

SKIERS' PARADISE

Aspen considers itself the cultural capital of the Rockies. It swears no better food will be found between New York and San Francisco. It is peopled by an enlightened, ennobled race of free-thinking Utopians. But don't let the locals fool you; they live here because of the skiing. And if you love to ski, there may be no place better in the world to do it.

Aspen/Snowmass comprises four mountains, each with its own personality: Aspen Mountain (also known as Ajax), Buttermilk,

Aspen Highlands, and Snowmass. Three hundred and eleven runs—from the parking lot–like Panda Peak at Buttermilk to the near-vertical bowls of the Y-Zones at Aspen Highlands—encompass every type of terrain that can be conquered on skis or snowboards. And the snow itself is exceptional: airborne snow from the Pacific dries out over the deserts of Nevada and Utah, falling here in snow that is only 1% water. It's fluffy, and it doesn't pack down or ice up as easily as coastal snow. Aspen averages over 300 inches of snowfall a year, with most of it falling in February, March, and April. But even early-season skiing can be great, thanks to an aggressive snowmaking campaign waged by the Aspen Skiing Company.

SkiCo, as it is known locally, operates all four area mountains on land that is partly private and partly leased from the White River National Forest. SkiCo is well aware of Aspen's position in the pantheon of ski resorts, and it places a premium on customer service. Any reasonable request will probably be met with a nod and some quick action. SkiCo has not placed much importance on customer savings, however. Lift ticket prices fluctuate in the mid-$60s, making them the most expensive in North America. Shrewd vacationers will buy multiday passes early (before the snow even starts to fall), which can reduce prices to the sub-$40 level. The SkiCo party line is that you get what you pay for.

But much of what you get in Aspen has nothing to do with what you pay for. The natural beauty of this valley is breathtaking (though the altitude may have something to do with that). Magnificent peaks, such as Pyramid, Capital, and the Maroon Bells, tower over the tops of the ski mountains, and from practically every run are views of the Continental Divide, a row of mountains stretching from horizon to horizon like giant waves on a frozen sea. The straight white trunks of aspen trees and the deep green of conifers line every run, and, for the more adventurous, grow in the middle of the run. Weasels, foxes, and even porcupines are occasionally sighted from the chairlift, and the beautiful blue-and-black magpie is as common as the cities' pigeon. The gray jay has been known to steal French fries from more than one unsuspecting patio diner.

The patio dining is, of course, dependent on sunshine, but there's plenty of that to go around. The Roaring Fork Valley is blessed with an average of 300 sunny days a year. Next to boots, bindings, and boards, the most important piece of equipment for an Aspen skier is a tube of sunblock.

Skiing in Aspen is, above all, convenient. The mountains are linked by a free shuttle service, with the longest possible trip taking barely 15 minutes for the haul from Aspen Mountain to Snowmass. And if you don't feel like carrying your skis, each ski area has a ski-concierge service that will make sure that your skis are waiting at whatever mountain you choose to ski the next day. Most of the lifts in the valley are high-speed, four-person chairs, giving you more time on the snow and less in the air. But be forewarned: you'll tire that much more quickly.

Crowds are rarely an issue. Five minutes in the lift line is considered a sacrilege in these parts. With the possible exception of the Christmas/New Year holiday, lines only form at two points in the space–time continuum: at the Silver Queen Gondola on a powder day, and at Fanny Hill at Snowmass on weekend mornings. East Coast and California skiers will be amazed to find they can ski directly to the next chair. European skiers will be amazed to find common-courtesy rules apply, and a lift op actually makes sure we all take turns. You won't even have much of a wait getting fitted for rental equipment; it seems as if the only crowds in Aspen are in the restaurants.

In addition to downhill skiing, Aspen also has less conventional snow sports. Powdercat tours off the back of Aspen Mountain offer all the benefits of heli-skiing at a fraction of the price; they are considerably safer, too. Backcountry experiences are also available from the top of Snowmass and Aspen Highlands with just a little hiking and the proper backcountry equipment. But be sure to bring a guide unless you'd like to make this your last ski vacation.

The athletically inclined may wish to conquer cross-country skiing, one of the world's most aerobically taxing, but most peaceful, sports. Several cross-country trails exist in the valley, though experienced XC'ers may want to tackle some of the hundreds of trails in the surrounding mountains. Here again, backcountry knowledge and the proper equipment are crucial. Some of the most enjoyable times to be had in Aspen are in the many mountain huts in the high country, where cross-country skiers are joined by telemarkers, skiers on randonnée gear, and the occasional snowshoer. The firewood is there already; you only have to haul the food and wine.

IT'S NOT JUST WINTER ANYMORE

There is a very common phrase among transplants to Aspen: "I came for the winters, but I stayed for the summers." They've discovered that Aspen has more to offer than just snow.

In the past decade, Aspen has turned itself into a year-round resort. At least, mostly year-round; it does take a while for the mud to dry out in the early summer, and after the leaves fall everyone just sort of waits for the lifts to open. But summertime in Aspen is glorious. There's plenty to do for the arts buffs, but more on that later. There's also plenty to do for the merely buff.

The great outdoors is the place to be during a Colorado summer. The skies are almost always cobalt blue (remember those 300 annual days of sunshine?), and temperatures rarely make it into the 80s before dipping into the 40s at night. Do not let perfect weather fool you into going out unprepared, however. Snow is not out of the question any day of the year here, and late-afternoon thunderstorms sometimes happen early, dropping temperatures by 30 degrees in the space of an hour. Lightning is

The Aspen Tree

Jerome B. Wheeler, town father and shameless promoter, christened Aspen in honor of the beautiful trees that gird the mountains surrounding it. The quaking aspen (Populus tremuloides) has a straight, white trunk with black, eye-shaped scars where branches have been shed. The leaves are a bright yellow-green, pointy and lobeless, turning to a brilliant yellow in the fall.

The aspen reproduces by cloning from its roots, so what appears to be a forest may actually be one plant. This reproductive system makes aspens especially prolific after clear cutting or burning, but modern, disaster-adverse forestry has actually reduced aspen populations in Rocky Mountain forests.

This cloning system also means that the millions of leaves in an aspen colony will change, not only to the same color, but simultaneously, creating unbroken miles of gold in September or October. The largest and most accessible groves are only a few miles east of town on Independence Pass.

also a common occurrence, claiming victims in the Colorado High Country every year. From the proper indoor vantage point, however, a Colorado thunderstorm puts on a show that rivals any of nature's spectacles.

Hiking is part of the lifestyle here. In other communities, people may congregate at a mall or on the steps of city hall, but in Aspen the summer meeting place is Smuggler Mountain, which forms the east end of the little box canyon. In the leisurely (though not easy) hour it takes for a round trip to the observation deck, you'll see kids and septuagenarians, Labradors and Jack Russells, mountain bikes and perhaps even a unicycle (honest) trudging up or flying down the gravel road. There is a great view of town from up top, but "doing Smuggler" is more of a twenty-minute get-your-heart-rate-up experience than a true hike. Even the more scenic hikes up the Ute Trail (off Ute Avenue) or up Aspen Mountain or Buttermilk are usually performed more in the interest of looking good than looking.

For the views, dozens of three- to four-hour hiking trails dot the mountains around Aspen and Snowmass. Trails at Cathedral Lake and American Lake, on the way to Ashcroft, are strenuous but beautiful, and the Rim Trail is perhaps the best way to see the Snowmass valley. And if you're being social on Smuggler, do yourself the favor of dropping over into Hunter Creek valley after the trip up. Though most trails in the area are clearly marked and well trodden, it never hurts to have a map on hand.

Aside from a good pair of hiking boots, every local seems to own a mountain bike. Some are only used for in-town transportation, but many more make trips along the same trails used by hikers. Novice bikers beware: trails can be slippery, rocky, rutted, or snowy at any time of year, and a great deal of expertise and preparedness is required for all but a few trails. Any local bike shop can recommend a trail suited to your riding ability and equipment. Several local guide services offer more adventurous trips to the same backcountry huts used in winter. Road bikers are also a common sight in the valley, particularly on the scenic ride to the Maroon Bells, or the masochistic ride to Independence Pass.

All that winter snow means rivers, and rivers mean fish. The Frying Pan and Roaring Fork rivers are teeming with trout, as are many of their tributaries. Any angler with a license can wade in and cast, but for the least frustrating results, hire one of the local guide services. They not only know where the fish are, they know what they'll bite. For a more relaxing trip, consider fishing from a guided dory, and float your way downstream.

Floating is the premise behind a couple of other sports that are popular in the valley: rafting and kayaking. Rafting, which requires little or no experience, is a must for any summer visitor. Is the water cold? Yes. Will you get wet? Yes. Will you have the time of your life? Most likely. Those not comfortable around water can take a leisurely float down the middle of the Roaring Fork, and the more adventurous can tackle the Colorado as it flows through Glenwood Canyon. Most valley guide services also run a shuttle to the Arkansas River on the other side of Independence Pass. The Arkansas contains within its banks some very extreme rapids, as well as some that are just gnarly enough to give you some bragging rights back home. If rafting is old hat to you, kayaking may be your sport; even rank amateurs can stuff themselves into a tandem version of one of these tippy boats and see what the river is like from the water's level.

Not all Aspenites are extreme-sports maniacs, though. Some prefer cruising the canyons for wildlife, lying on a sun-warmed boulder, or gathering wild mushrooms after a rain (though this last is perhaps the most potentially deadly of all summer activities). The glimpse of a bald eagle while basking in the sun may be just as rewarding as a four-hour hike through fields of wildflowers, and considerably easier on the knees. Perhaps the best advice for vacationing in Aspen—any time of the year—is to do exactly what you want to do, and nothing more.

CULTURAL CAPITAL

Aspen has a long history as a center for culture, and this legacy is perhaps best represented by one building: the Wheeler Opera House. The Wheeler was built when Aspen was little more than dirt streets and miners' cottages, but its builder and namesake, Jerome B. Wheeler, envisioned a future in which Aspen would be a glorious representation of the American dream. Looking around today, he would be very surprised at the way his vision turned out, but most likely very happy with the state of the arts in the little utopia he helped establish.

There was little evidence of high art or philosophical discussion outside the opera house in those early days, but a "rediscovery" of Aspen in the 1940s by a group of wealthy intellectuals turned culture not only into a thriving pastime, but a second industry.

The 1949 Goethe Convocation led to the founding of the Aspen Institute for Humanistic Studies, which now oversees over a hundred conferences worldwide every year, on topics of political, corporate, and academic interest. A number of those conferences take place at The Meadows, a Bauhaus-designed campus in the west end of town. Though many of the conferences are private affairs, the institute regularly hosts lectures for the public on a variety of topics. Closer to town, the Given Institute, a branch of the University of Colorado, offers public lectures dealing mainly with medicine and health. Even that venerable old opera house gets in on the act, when the Aspen Center for Physical Studies hosts talks by prominent physicists. At any of these gatherings, you'll find leading academics seated next to wealthy socialites, with a surprisingly large sprinkling of tourists and ski instructors thrown in.

A similar mix assembles for the Aspen Music Festival each summer. The festival, begun in 1949, has hosted some of the world's leading composers and performers, from Aaron Copland to Midori, and Philip Glass to James Levine. In 2000, the festival unveiled a new music tent (actually a state-of-the-art permanent structure) that will assure Aspen's prominence among summer music festivals for years to come. Winter Music, the festival's winter program, hosts dozens of concerts in the acoustically perfect Harris Hall, only steps away from the new tent. The Aspen Music School, one of the world's top teaching programs, brings hundreds of students to the mountains every summer.

Aspen also attracts big-name popular acts to the Wheeler (Lyle Lovett is almost a local by now), and occasionally to smaller venues and hotels, but by far the biggest pop events in the valley happen in June and over Labor Day weekend. Then Jazz Aspen/Snowmass brings in the likes of Ray Charles, Ziggy Marley, and Johnny Lang, as well as a variety of up-and-coming acts. Held in a field in Snowmass, it not only boasts some great lineups but one of the world's most beautiful venues as well. Also active in the summer is the Thelonious Monk Institute Jazz Colony, which brings established and newly discovered stars of the most American music form to Snowmass for the summer. Look for legends of the future in small venues in Snowmass and Aspen.

Performing arts play a big role in Aspen as well. Aspen has its own ballet company and regularly brings in guests. Theatre in the Park operates throughout the summer with three different programs, as well as programs for kids. A variety of locally produced and surprisingly professional musicals and dramas take the stage at the Wheeler each year.

Visual art is ubiquitous in Aspen, though often overshadowed by the valley's own beauty. That natural beauty is the inspiration for dozens of local artists, who display their masterpieces in Aspen's many galleries. Most local galleries feature works by nationally known artists as well, and gallery openings are excellent opportunities to rub elbows with the rich and famous. Aspen also supports its own art museum, which mounts well-respected shows throughout the year, as well as the annual International Design Conference Aspen, which brings leading designers together just in time for a June cold snap. Creative bonding keeps them warm.

There are many other arts for which Aspen is known: the art of fine cuisine, the art of the deal, the art of plastic and reconstructive surgery. But Aspenites will never surrender their claim to the cultural riches to be found in the mountains today.

It's hard not to have a perfect day in Aspen, with all its cultural offerings, excellent recreational opportunities, and culinary adventures. Whether you're craving a vertical drop, a ballet performance, or a soak in the hot tub, Aspen has all the ingredients needed to create your perfect day.

In this Chapter

A PERFECTLY LUXURIOUS DAY 19 • A PERFECT WINTER DAY 20 • A PERFECT SUMMER DAY 21

By Gavin Ehringer

perfect days

THERE IS NO SINGLE RECIPE FOR A PERFECT DAY IN ASPEN. Variations abound depending on the season, your personal taste, or perhaps the size of your budget. But whether your fancy leads you to a vigorous bike ride through the mountain passes or a rejuvenating massage in a local spa, Aspen delivers.

A PERFECTLY LUXURIOUS DAY

Sleep late. Today is a day to indulge yourself. Don't worry that you'll miss the amber glow of sunrise upon Ajax Mountain or the first chair at Snowmass. Save those for tomorrow.

Instead, put on your Sunday best for a late-morning brunch at the restaurant at the Little Nell. The hotel itself defines Aspen style and elegance, so take a few minutes to stroll the lobby. Admire the opulent floral arrangements and perhaps relax with Sunday's *New York Times* in front of the limestone fireplace before sitting down in the white-linen formal dining area for a breakfast of lemon soufflé pancakes or eggs Benedict.

As morning gives way to noon, take a long hour walking downtown Aspen, stopping in at some of the many small art and photographic galleries in the redbrick pedestrian malls along Hyman and Cooper Avenues. From the landmark Popcorn Wagon on the corner of Hyman and Mill Streets, it's a 4-block walk north to the Aspen Art Museum. Housed in an historic power mill on the banks of the Roaring Fork River, the museum mounts exhibitions from some of the world's great museums.

Following the Rio Grande Trail footpath, you walk along the river to South Spring Street, heading back through town for a 2 PM appointment at the Aspen Club & Spa. There, you opt for the three-hour Alpine Vitality treatment, which includes a massage, herbal body therapy, and facial.

Return to your hotel around 5:15 PM, and take a short nap—yes, a nap. Then, dress for a 6:45 PM dinner at Piñons. Finish off the evening with a ballet performance at the Wheeler Opera House.

A PERFECT WINTER DAY

It's tough not to have a perfect winter day in Aspen. But some perfect days are better than others. Here's one that can't miss: start with a light breakfast of fresh-baked muffins, juice, and coffee at the heaven-sent Paradise Bakery. By car, head to Ashcroft (follow Hwy. 82 west to Castle Creek Rd.), a ghost town located 13 mi from Aspen. There, you link up with the Ashcroft Ski Touring Center for Nordic ski instruction.

After being outfitted with rental equipment and taking a three-hour guided tour amid the spectacular 14,000-ft peaks that surround the Ashcroft Valley, have lunch on the sundeck at the Pine Creek Cookhouse, a trailside log cabin that's anything but rustic. Lunch entrées include spinach crepes and Rocky Mountain Rainbow Trout.

After the short ski back to the touring center, you return to town around 2 PM—just in time to change clothes and get geared up for the après ski scene at Mezzaluna. Put on the chic resort wear you've bought during your stay, as Mezzaluna is known as the place to be seen. The decor is Los Angeles–hip, with pink marble tables and quirky modern art paintings on the back wall.

After downing $2 happy-hour beers and splitting a $5 wood oven pizza among friends, you're ready for the main course—true northern Italian trattoria cuisine at Campo di Fiore. The tables here are small and close, and conviviality among diners is the norm. Chat up visitors from England, Germany, and Brazil while enjoying, say, the Osso Buco con Risotto Milanese (a veal shank served atop saffron risotto).

Though exhausted, you rally for one final perfect event: a concert by the Afro-Cuban All Stars at the Wheeler Opera House.

A PERFECT SUMMER DAY

Start with the premise of Walter Paepcke's "Aspen Idea," that Aspen is a place to nourish the body, mind, and spirit. In the morning, you consider the possibilities: golf at the Aspen Golf Course, or mountainbiking along the Roaring Fork River. But instead you opt to try fly-fishing with a guide from Aspen Outfitting Co. They provide everything you need, including access to 10,000 linear ft of private stream front on the Roaring Fork River.

After catching your limit of trout, tip your guide extravagantly and head back to town. By now your stomach is screaming for a Hanging Valley Meatball Pie, a pizza topped with sliced Italian meatballs that's a specialty of New York Pizza. Maybe this isn't exactly what Paepcke had in mind when he said nourish the body, but, boy, is the pizza good.

You spend the afternoon riding horseback from the T Lazy 7 Ranch to the Maroon Bells, a mountain basin said to be the most photographed place in America. The photos, you decide, don't do it justice.

Early in the evening, you dress for a concert with the Aspen Festival Orchestra, which will perform in the new Bayer-Benedict Music Tent. Afterward, you indulge in a late dinner of lobster soup, followed by roasted salmon wrapped in pancetta at Aspen's newest culinary rage, Conundrum, whose menu was created by award-winning chef George Mahaffey.

Unlike some ski resorts, Aspen and Snowmass have an abundance of first-rate restaurants. Prices tend to be high, even for simple fare, but the quality of the food, the views, and the people-watching can make dining in Aspen a memorable experience.

In this Chapter

Prices 24 • How and When 25 • ASPEN 25 • American 25 • American/Casual 28 • Austrian 30 • Barbecue 30 • Cafés 30 • Chinese 32 • Contemporary 33 • Delicatessens 41 • Fast Food 41 • Italian 42 • Japanese 44 • Mediterranean 46 • Mexican 46 • Pizza 47 • Seafood 47 • Steak 47 • Swiss 48 • Thai 49 • Vegetarian 49 • Vietnamese 49 • SNOWMASS 49 • American 49 • American/Casual 51 • Contemporary 52 • Italian 52 • Pan-Asian 54 • Seafood 54 • ELSEWHERE 54 • American/Casual 54 • Austrian 55 • Contemporary 55

By David Gibson

eating out

CLOSE YOUR EYES AND THINK of the phrase "ski resort food." Not a pretty picture, is it? Tasteless burgers, bland chili, lowest-common-denominator pasta specials—it's as if most resorts count on you being so hungry from skiing that you won't care about how the food tastes. Lucky for you, Aspen is inhabited by snobs.

Not content to be the glamour capital, culture capital, and skiing capital of the Rockies, Aspen has made sure that it's known as the culinary capital as well. In 25 square blocks are more than a dozen world-class restaurants, serving exciting food prepared by lauded chefs in elegant dining rooms. And the wine cellared beneath this town is probably worth almost as much as the silver pulled out from under it a hundred years ago.

"Colorado cuisine" is the main attraction here; it's a genre similar to "California cuisine" of the '80s. The emphasis is on freshness (those chefs standing around at the airport aren't waiting for relatives; they're waiting for asparagus), and local ingredients serve as the star of a dish whenever possible. So you'll see smoked trout from Basalt, tomatoes from Hotchkiss, and peaches from Palisade on menus throughout town. You'll also see elk from New Zealand, caribou from Australia, and farm-raised venison from Texas. But rest assured that the Colorado lamb was raised locally—and you'll be hard-pressed to find better lamb, or chefs more passionate about preparing it, anywhere outside of Aspen.

Aspen chefs have trained all over the world, and that global influence comes out in the cuisine. Mediterranean flavors abound at the Ajax Tavern, French rustic grounds Renaissance's flights of fancy, Syzygy's dishes have a earthy Alpine feel, and Central American flavors even sneak into the mix at the inventive (if stuffy) restaurant at the Little Nell. Pure ethnic food here is sorely lacking, however, so get your fix at your local major metropolitan area.

Prices

This may hurt a little.

Aspen restaurant prices, on the whole, are just a step down from Manhattan's, and its wine prices are sometimes even higher. At the toniest of locales, the $150-a-head tab may not come as much of a shock, but you might be taken aback at the jeans-and-sweatshirt places where the menus feature $25 entrees. Even lunch is expensive here; the $8 sandwich is standard noontime fare, and that's if you're taking it to go.

Bargains can be had, however. Restaurants designed to surround a bar tend to have prices in the lower end of the spectrum. Mexican restaurants also tend to be priced a bit below average. And there is a McDonald's, but even it doesn't run those specials you see on television.

Keep in mind that dining is as much a part of the Aspen experience as skiing or hiking. So put back that "Where's your Aspen?" T-shirt you were buying for Uncle Ned, and spend the 18 bucks on a foie gras and mission figs appetizer. It's your vacation, after all.

CATEGORY	COST*
$$$$	over $55
$$$	$35–$54
$$	$15–$34
$	under $15

*per person for a three-course meal, excluding drinks, service, and 8¼% sales tax

How and When

Most Aspen/Snowmass restaurants strongly suggest reservations. And most (thanks to ill-behaved diners who reserve at three different restaurants for the same meal) overbook. In other words, you can expect to wait during busy times of the year, reservations or not. Everyone, it seems, wants to eat at 8:30, so a little flexibility in your schedule will often get you into places that have been booked for weeks at prime times.

Restaurants here have no established dress code; this is not, however, a license to wear your Sea World sweatpants to dinner. If you don't see chicken wings on the menu, chances are you won't get in wearing a baseball cap. And while ski or exercise gear is welcomed (nay, encouraged) at lunch, wearing it after dark is a faux pas.

Finally, a word on tipping. No matter how many hours you devote to the United Way each week, your moral worth in Aspen is determined by the size of your gratuity. Poor tippers are not only remembered, but occasionally berated.

ASPEN
American

$$$–$$$$ **JIMMY'S AMERICAN RESTAURANT AND BAR.** Jimmy's has taken the American food concept and run with it, and in the process created a cosmopolitan setting for what is essentially comfort food. The steaks here are exceptional, but you do yourself a disservice by not trying homestyle fare such as meat loaf and pork chops. Jimmy's also serves a variety of fresh fish, jumbo lump crab cakes, and wonderful burgers (including buffalo burgers). And don't forget to order a side of macaroni and cheese. The room and service give this restaurant a fine-dining appeal, and the prices are right in line with that appeal. The bar is always hopping (Jimmy's boasts one of the finest tequila and mescal selections in the United States), and an early

aspen dining

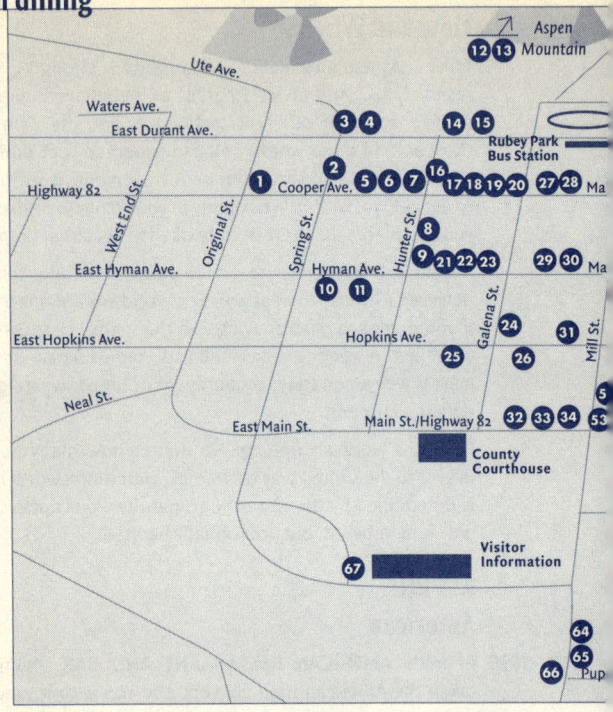

Ajax Tavern, 14
Aspen Underground, 67
Bagel Bites, 64
Benedict's, 12
Bentley's at the Wheeler, 38
Big Wrap, 16
Blue Maize, 8
Boogie's Diner, 18
Butcher's Block, 2
Cache Cache, 45
Café Ink!, 15
Campo De Fiori, 46
Cantina, 32
Caribou Club, 31
Century Room at the Hotel Jerome, 56
Charcuterie and Cheese Market, 5
Chart House, 59
Cloud Nine Café, 71
Conundrum, 53
Cooper Street Bar and Restaurant, 20
Crystal Palace, 41
Explore Bistro, 61
Farfalla, 33
Guido's, 27
Gwyn's, 13
Hard Rock Café, 24
Hotel Jerome Bar, 55
In and Out House, 60
Jack's at the Sardy House Hotel, 63
Jacob's Corner in the Hotel Jerome, 54
Jimmy's American Restaurant and Bar, 44
Johnny McGuire's Deli, 1
Kenichi, 25
La Cocina, 48
L'Hostaria, 11

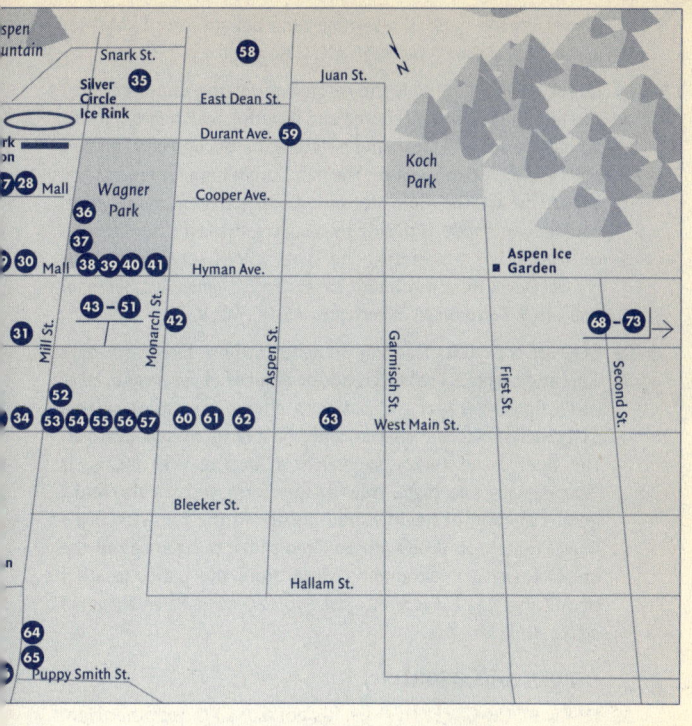

Little Annie's, 23
Little Nell, 4
Little Ollie's, 9
Lucci's, 19
Matsuhisa Aspen, 57
Main Street Bakery, 62
The Meadows Restaurant, 68
Mezzaluna, 7
Milan's, 51
Mirabella, 42

Mother Lode, 39
New York Pizza, 30
Olives, 35
Pacifica Seafood Brasserie, 36
Paesanos, 65
Pine Creek Cookhouse, 72
Piñons, 52
Popcorn Wagon, 37
Poppies Bistro Café, 69

Poppycock's, 6
R Bistro, 50
Red Onion, 28
Renaissance, 49
Rusty's Hickory House, 70
Skiers Chalet Steak House, 58
Steak Pit, 43
Su Casa, 40
Sushi Ya Go-Go, 66
Syzygy, 22

Takah Sushi, 29
Trattoria Toscana, 17
Thai Tini, 47
Ute City Bar and Grill, 21
Variations, 3
Vinh Vinh, 34
Wienerstube, 10
Woody Creek Tavern, 73
Zélé, 26

dinner on the deck is a summertime delight. *205 S. Mill St., upstairs, tel. 970/925–6020. AE, MC, V. No lunch.*

$–$$$ LITTLE ANNIE'S. This is the restaurant for the unpretentious.
★ The food here is well prepared and flavorful, with hearty, down-home fare such as steak and potatoes, barbecued chicken and ribs, and daily fish specials. The hamburger here represents the apex of the art. The room, decorated with golf memorabilia from courses worldwide, is decidedly casual, with plastic tumblers on red-checkered tablecloths, and Tootsie Rolls served with your check. Don't miss the Bundt cake. *517 E. Hyman Ave., tel. 970/ 920–1098. Reservations not accepted. AE, DC, MC, V.*

$–$$ BOOGIE'S DINER. This sun-drenched atrium, filled with pink
★ vinyl and chrome, evokes a roadside diner of a bygone age. Here you'll find meat loaf and potatoes, cheese fries, tuna salads, patty melts, mac and cheese, and a host of 1950s-style classics. The open-faced turkey sandwich, a favorite with locals, is Thanksgiving on a plate. True to Aspen form, you can also find a good selection of healthy food, including the tofu-rich Pep's Power Plate; top it off with an Oreo shake to balance out the meal. There are astounding views from the patio, weather permitting. *534 E. Cooper Ave., tel. 970/925–6610. Reservations not accepted. AE, MC, V.*

American/Casual

$$ HARD ROCK CAFE. Trust us, it's not like all those other Hard Rocks; we have enough local celebrities and sports heroes that the decorations are almost relevant. The food, however, is just what you'll find in Las Vegas or New York, with the same distracting videos playing. Don't look for stars here; there are better places to eat. This is worth the trip if you're into memorabilia or traveling with kids. *210 S. Galena St., tel. 970/920–1666. Reservations not accepted. AE, DC, MC, V.*

$$ HOTEL JEROME BAR. Known to locals as the J-Bar, it's been serving Aspenites and tourists since the 1890s. The main attraction is the room itself, decked out with antique prints, mounted animal heads, a pressed-tin ceiling, and the original bar built by Chinese laborers who came to work in the silver mines. The menu here is sandwich-based, but with an unexpected flourish here and there, such as Gorgonzola and caramelized onions on the burger. The nachos are an engineering feat, not to be missed by the truly hungry. *330 E. Main St., tel. 970/920–1000. Reservations not accepted. AE, DC, MC, V.*

$–$$ BENTLEY'S AT THE WHEELER. Location, location, location. Bentley's is more bar than restaurant, but the soaring windows make for great people-watching at one of Aspen's prime corners, and the food isn't half bad. Buffalo wings, fish-and-chips, and sandwiches are winners, and it's one of the few places in town to find a steak under $20. But asthmatics beware: it's impossible to escape cigarette smoke coming from the bar area. *328 E. Hyman Ave., tel. 970/920–2240. Reservations not accepted. AE, D, DC, MC, V.*

$–$$ RED ONION. More about history than food (and maybe more about beer than either), the Onion has been an Aspen watering hole from the days when the upstairs was a brothel. It's still a popular meeting place for locals and tourists alike. The food is standard pub fare, but the menu also features an admirable Mexican selection. Summertime dining in front of the restaurant offers some incredible people-watching. *420 E. Cooper Ave., tel. 970/925–9043. Reservations not accepted. AE, MC, V.*

$ COOPER STREET BAR AND RESTAURANT. No bones about it, this place is a dive. But if you're looking for a cheap burger, some delicious wings, and a cheap pitcher of beer, this is the place for you. It's also an excellent place to go if you're not terribly talkative; the two-story restaurant features billiards, shuffleboard, pinball, and plenty of video games. Cooper Street is also the home of the official International Dial-a-Shot map. Ask your bartender for details. *508 E. Cooper Ave., tel. 970/925–7758. Reservations not accepted. No credit cards.*

$ **POPCORN WAGON.** Your first encounter with the Wagon will be
★ after midnight, when no other restaurant is serving. But chances are, you'll find yourself craving a chili cheese dog at three in the afternoon, and make a second visit. This is Aspen's cheapest meal, and the crepes and gyros are utterly fantastic. There's no indoor seating, so it's best visited on a sunny day or by those who can eat very quickly. Oh, and they have popcorn, too. *305 S. Mill St., tel. 970/925–2718. No credit cards.*

Austrian

$$ **WIENERSTUBE.** This is where Aspen eats breakfast. The eggs Benedict are outstanding, and the pancakes (blueberry or not, you choose) are some of the best around. The lunch menu includes a variety of sausages, served in true Austrian style. The waitresses, dressed in dirndls and speaking in Teutonic accents, add credibility to the whole experience. The 'Stube also features a tempting selection of Viennese pastries. *633 E. Hyman Ave., tel. 970/925–3357. AE, D, DC, MC, V. No dinner.*

Barbecue

$$ **RUSTY'S HICKORY HOUSE.** You won't come any closer to a barbecue shack this side of Kansas City. The ribs are smoked and smothered, and the sauce is tasty, if not very spicy. The menu is just what you'd expect: ribs and chicken, with some tasty barbecue sandwiches, notably the pulled pork sandwich. The Hickory House also serves Aspen's only Southern-style breakfast, grits and all. You haven't really lived until you've started your day with ribs and eggs. *730 W. Main St., tel. 970/925–2313. D, MC, V.*

Cafés

$–$$ **MAIN STREET BAKERY.** This homey little bakery serves light entrées for breakfast and lunch, but you'll be better served by their delectable cookies, pastries, and cakes. Summer patio dining makes it the perfect early brunch spot. *201 E. Main St., tel. 970/920–6446. AE, MC, V. No dinner.*

The Aspen Food & Wine Classic

Epicurean publication Food & Wine throws a little party in Aspen in early June of every year. And, boy, can they throw a party.

The timing is perfect: the slopes are closed, but the trails haven't dried out, so every Aspenite who's not in Cozumel volunteers to help put the party on. They're joined by wine lovers from the world over, as well as chefs, vintners, restaurateurs, and people who merely like to be tipsy by 11 in the morning. Julia Child comes every year, as does every star-chef-of-the-moment. You can follow a "Wines of Spain" program with "Thai Cuisine for the Home Chef" and a tasting of 12 single-malt Scotches. And that's just before lunch. Each day also features Grand Tastings, in which passholders wander through a football field–sized tent (it's actually a rugby field) full of wines and spirits (and occasionally food) from every corner of the globe. It's an oenophile's Epcot.

A word of caution: weather in June can change on a minute's notice. More than one linen-clad Chardonnay sipper has neared hypothermia when an afternoon hailstorm dropped the temperature by 30 degrees. So bring a sweater, or stay very near the grappa table.

For more information, call 970/925–9000 or 877/900–WINE, or visit the magazine's Web site at www.foodandwine.com.

$–$$ POPPYCOCK'S. The lunch counter and casual atmosphere make this hole-in-the-wall café feel like it could be anywhere. Breakfast is served all day (the hearty oatmeal pancakes can get even the droopiest diner going), with a selection of sandwiches and salads added at lunch. Best to stick with breakfast items. *609 E. Cooper Ave., tel. 970/925–1245. MC, V. No dinner.*

$ BAGEL BITES. This is Aspen's only bagel shop, and it sure beats buying frozen at the supermarket. You'll find a dozen varieties of bagels and all the basic accoutrements, such as cream cheese and lox, as well as more creative spreads like Santa Fe cream cheese and a zesty veggie spread. Bagel Bites also assembles some tasty and inventive bagel sandwiches for lunch. *300 Puppy Smith St., tel. 970/920–3489. No credit cards. No dinner.*

$ CAFE INK! Coffee-oriented cuisine fills the menu here: bagels, pastries, and breakfast sandwiches to go with your joe in the morning, and panini sandwiches for your midday pick-me-up. Cafe Ink! also provides an excellent selection of coffee and fruit juice drinks, and some groovy couches where you can relax away your caffeine buzz. *520 E. Durant Ave., tel. 970/544–0588. No credit cards. No dinner.*

$ ZÉLÉ. This sleek little coffee house has some big ideas. Here you'll find not just coffee and pastries, but soups, smoothies, and sandwiches, served on one of Aspen's prime corners. The outside patio offers breathtaking scenery in both human and geological genres. *121 South Galena St., tel. 970/925–5745. No credit cards.*

Chinese

$–$$ LITTLE OLLIE'S. ★ This is about as ethnic as Aspen gets. The cuisine in this very informal restaurant is designed to appeal to American tastes and isn't so different from the Chinese you'd find in any strip mall. It is, however, quite tasty, and the dishes are inexpensive and the portions generous. Lunch specials, available weekdays, come in well below the $10 mark. Ollie's also delivers, for those times when the sofa is feeling just a little too comfortable. *308 South Hunter St., downstairs, tel. 970/544–9888. No credit cards.*

Contemporary

$$$$ CARIBOU CLUB. The Caribou is Aspen's swankest private club, and in many ways is the perfect embodiment of modern Aspen. The decor is completely over the top, with overstuffed sofas, antler furniture, and impressive original art scattered throughout its subterranean maze of rooms. You won't be able to get in here without pulling some strings, but the food, a menu full of big yet elegant meat and fish dishes, adds substance to what otherwise seems like a tongue-in-cheek joke. The wine list is, undoubtedly, one of the best in America, and a dinner in the private wine room is an unforgettable experience. *411 E. Hopkins Ave., tel. 970/925–2929. Reservations essential. AE, MC, V. No lunch.*

$$$$ CENTURY ROOM AT THE HOTEL JEROME. The Century Room,
★ located in Aspen's first hotel, is an experience not to be missed for anyone interested in historical Aspen. Glance at the turn-of-the-20th-century details and you can almost conjure up the silver barons who dined in this warm and inviting space a century before. But while the room may be frozen in time, the food is a modern synthesis of the rustic and the sublime. Game features prominently here, with elk, caribou, and a gigantic buffalo steak all lovingly spiced and cooked to perfection; accompaniments are thoughtful and delicious. The wine list shows the same thought, and the staff is more than qualified to recommend some unusual pairings for some unfamiliar dishes. *330 E. Main St., tel. 970/920–1000. AE, DC, MC, V. No lunch.*

$$$$ CONUNDRUM. "Conundrum" refers to a local creek, but there
★ is a mystery here: how did they think of that? Chef George Mahaffey, winner of a James Beard Best American Chef award, serves up creations such as a gazpacho martini with spicy oysters, a braised veal cheek with horseradish potatoes, and—

get this—a butterbean cappuccino. The food is excellent, surprising in both flavor and texture; Conundrum is a true food-lover's restaurant. You won't leave bored. *325 E. Main St., tel. 970/926-9969. AE, DC, MC, V. No lunch.*

$$$$ LITTLE NELL. Luckily for Aspen, SkiCo's premier lodging
★ clientele wasn't going to settle for a humdrum hotel dining room, and we got instead the fabulous restaurant at the Little Nell. Every dish here, from the salmon at breakfast to the last creative dessert at dinner, is wonderfully and lovingly prepared. Service is formal for every meal, and, with the exception of a quick ski lunch, don't expect to get in and out quickly. Dinner is a particular star here, with several kinds of fish, from cod to John Dory, as well as a beautiful rack of lamb and a grilled elk chop with foie gras beignets. The wine list, as well as the wine knowledge of every waiter, is astoundingly deep and broad. *675 E. Durant Ave., tel. 970/920-6330. AE, D, DC, MC, V.*

$$$$ PIÑONS. If any restaurant can be said to have started "Aspen Cuisine," this is it. The room is elegant yet rustic, and the food shares this philosophy. Some menu items are so popular with the restaurant's devotees that they stay on the menu for years, but chef/owner Rob Mobilian always has a new classic to tempt diners. The lobster strudel and Freddy salad are must-haves, as is the delicious foie gras–topped beef fillet. Some would say that you haven't eaten Colorado lamb until you have eaten it at Piñons. The service is impeccable, and the wine list is one of the most classically complete in Colorado. *105 S. Mill St., tel. 970/920-2021. AE, MC, V. No lunch.*

$$$$ POPPIES BISTRO CAFE. Ask 20 Aspenites where to find the most romantic meal in Aspen, and 19 of them will tell you Poppies (the other one probably works at the Jerome). Its out-of-the-way location makes it feel like a vacation within a vacation, and the cozy atmosphere, loaded with Victorian charm, just begs you to play Casanova. The classic bistro cuisine is only slightly updated from what you might find in France. Try the tasty steak au poivre in a cognac cream sauce or, for an appetizer, the spicy Anaheim peppers stuffed with lobster and goat cheese. The wine list is extensive if not creative, and the service is efficient and unobtrusive. Poppies is definitely worth a cab ride to West End, but it is enjoyed most following an afternoon summer concert at the music tent. *834 W. Hallam St., tel. 970/925-2333. AE, MC, V. No lunch.*

$$$$ RENAISSANCE. Chef Charles Dale claims a French rustic influence for Renaissance, but the menu sparkles with creativity. Here you'll find a crispy Chilean sea bass with crispy artichokes, seared foie gras with caramelized pears, and a date-marinated rack of lamb. Dale also offers two tasting menus per evening, one vegetarian and the other decisively not; either is a culinary journey. For best results, let the steward bring wine pairings with each course. *304 E. Hopkins Ave., street level, tel. 970/925-2402. AE, D, MC, V. No lunch.*

$$$$ SYZYGY. Influenced by cuisine from Asia to Austria, Syzygy offers tremendous food in a fine dining setting that was once sleek but now looks a bit dated. Both the service and food are exceptional, however. On the menu you'll find elk tenderloin with ancho chili, fabulous tuna preparations, and creative specials every night, such as axis deer with lavender foam. The wine list is exceptional, featuring a superb selection of lesser-known vintages from New Zealand, Chile, and Australia. If you're confused by the choices, simply ask the master sommelier, who also serves as the maître d'. *520 E. Hyman Ave., upstairs, tel. 970/925-3700. AE, D, DC, MC, V. No lunch.*

$$$–$$$$ AJAX TAVERN. ★ Within the warm mahogany walls of this slopeside restaurant, you'll find some of the best food that Aspen has to offer. The menu, Mediterranean in influence, runs from a simple (and outstanding) chicken BLT at lunch, through an astounding and inventive variety of pastas, to a braised short rib that will dare you not to groan in bliss. The wine list is excellent, with a particular emphasis on lesser-known California varietals. The spacious patio, which abuts Aspen Mountain, is an unbeatable venue on a sunny day. *685 E. Durant Ave., upstairs from the gondola plaza, tel. 970/920–9333. AE, D, DC, MC, V.*

$$$–$$$$ **CACHE CACHE.** ★ This tasteful room is among Aspen's most elegant, the service is casual but flawless, and the food is simply heavenly. Cache Cache advertises "the flavors of Provence," but continually pushes the limits of that definition with creative dishes such as its rotisserie chicken with Kalamata olives and capers, a hearty beef daube, and an unmatched osso buco. The chef also has a particularly graceful touch with salads; don't miss the duck salad with candied walnuts or the gravlax and warm potato salad. The wine list is extensive, particularly in Champagnes and legendary French bottlings. The bar menu offers a budget-conscious way to sample this outstanding cuisine. *205 S. Mill St., tel. 970/925–3835. Reservations essential. AE, DC, MC, V. No lunch.*

$$$–$$$$ **JACK'S AT THE SARDY HOUSE HOTEL.** Though only a block from the downtown core, Jack's seems a world apart. Housed in the historic Sardy House, one of Aspen's grandest buildings, the small dining room and neighboring foyer are full of tasteful antiques that give an air of comfort and sophistication, and a roaring fire adds plenty of warmth. Unlike most local restaurants, there are no lines running out the door here, or crowds at the bar waiting for a seat. The refined atmosphere carries over into the menu, where creative updates of classic dishes, such as macadamia-crusted ruby trout or prosciutto and fontina-stuffed chicken breast, are the stars. Select your wines from an extensive and well-rounded list. Jack's also has an excellent breakfast and weekend brunch. *128 E. Main St., tel. 970/920–2525. AE, DC, MC, V. No lunch.*

$$$–$$$$ **THE MEADOWS RESTAURANT.** Simply elegant and never crowded, this restaurant serves three excellent meals a day,

Dining on the Slopes

Not to say that you can't find a grilled cheese sandwich and some heat-lamped French fries on the slopes these days, but it's getting increasingly difficult. The real story with high-altitude dining is fine dining. Pull out your four-mountain trail map for a tour:

On Aspen Mountain, the trend began with **Ajax Tavern** (☞ above), which toned down its Mediterranean menu for a hearty sit-down ski lunch. **Gwyn's** (☞ below), halfway up the hill, offers elegant surroundings and a killer Asian-inspired menu, as well as an interesting wine list. Up top in the Sundeck building, **Benedict's** (☞ below) offers scrumptious homestyle food with a Rocky Mountain flair. **The Sundeck** (in the Sundeck building on Aspen Mountain) offers a scramble-style cafeteria with a wok station, a rotisserie station, and a salad bar, as well as a full cocktail bar.

On Aspen Highlands, the fine dining continues with **Cloud Nine Café** (☞ below). The view of Pyramid Peak is terrific. Two quick lunch options are the **Merry-Go-Round** at midmountain, and the **Thunderbowl Café** at the base, both of which serve traditional ski fare.

Buttermilk hosts three restaurants. **Bump's,** at the base, serves cafeteria-style, but with some wonderful salads and sandwiches, including a barbecued salmon. **Cliffhouse,** sitting on a cliff at the mountain's top, offers a Mongolian barbecue. On west Buttermilk is the charming **Cafe West,** known for its crepes.

Snowmass is the home of the first on-mountain fine-dining restaurant in the valley, **High Alpine** (☞ below). The views here are vast and the food is spectacular. **Finestra** (☞ below), at the top of Sam's Knob, offers hearty Northern Italian fare and another wonderful view. For faster food, visit the French-inspired **Café Suzanne,** or the standard **Ullrhof** and **Sam's Knob** cafeterias. For something a little different, check out the **Mexican Café** at the base of Two Creeks, or the higher-than-high **Up For Pizza.**

mostly to guests of the hotel, but also to Aspenites looking to get just a little bit out of town. Thanks to its West End location, the Meadows has some of the best views in Aspen, and its Alsatian-inspired cuisine is most interesting. For something truly divine, try the vanilla-pasted monkfish or lobster on a crab bread pudding. Look for some Rhone gems on its extensive wine list. *845 Meadows Rd., tel. 970/544–7830. AE, D, DC, MC, V.*

$$$–$$$$ **OLIVES.** With Olives, Chef Todd English has brought his world-renowned Mediterranean-inspired cuisine to the Rockies. The food is creative and zesty, and features twists on the classics, such as snapper served on flageolet beans with a crispy squid, and rib-eye in a red wine oxtail braise, as well as English's signature pizzas. The room is spacious yet warm, and among the most beautiful in Aspen. The cost-conscious can sample the signature cuisine at the spacious bar. *315 E. Dean St., in the St. Regis Hotel, tel. 970/920–7356. AE, D, DC, MC, V.*

$$–$$$$ **JACOB'S CORNER IN THE HOTEL JEROME.** In this airy room you'll find the same style of food as the neighboring Century Room, but with a lighter touch for lunch year-round and dinner in the summers. The constantly evolving menu includes plenty of fish (in the form of crab cakes and an always delicious trout) as well as a wonderful selection of game, beef, and fowl. There is, of course, full access to the Jerome's wine cellars. During summer, lunch and dinner are served on the tree-shaded patio, giving Jacob's Corner the title for best al fresco dining in Aspen. Jacob's Corner also serves a wonderful, but not inexpensive, breakfast. *330 E. Main St., tel. 970/920–1000. AE, DC, MC, V.*

$$–$$$$ **UTE CITY BAR AND GRILL.** Long a favorite with tourists (perhaps because of its central location), the Ute City building has hosted a variety of restaurants since it ceased being a bank. Now it is home to the internationalist chef Maurice Courtier, who brings his fine-dining experience down a notch for wild game, pastas, and seafood in a room that hearkens back to old Aspen. It's a great location for a shopping lunch or a quick bite

from the bar, as well. *501 E. Hyman Ave., tel. 970/920–4699. AE, DC, MC, V.*

$$$ GWYN'S. Walk past the cafeteria here (although that's good, ★ too) for what may be the best on-mountain meal you've ever had. You'll first notice an incredible view of town from the north-facing windows, but you'll almost forget it when the food arrives. There's some definite Far East and Hawaiian influence here, but it stays grounded in preparations such as Mu Shu barbecue duck and calamari rellenos. Gwyn's offers a great breakfast as well, with pan-seared trout topping the list. You'll have to learn to ski to eat here (alas!), and summer visitors are simply out of luck. *Aspen Mountain, at the base of Ruthie's Run, tel. 970/920–6308. AE, D, DC, MC, V. Closed late Apr.–late Nov. No dinner.*

$$$ MILAN'S. This casually elegant subterranean space offers a menu influenced equally by Northern Italian and classic Continental cuisine. Pastas, available in appetizer or entrée portions, are well-balanced, and the main courses, from barbecued Norwegian salmon through veal saltimbocca and into rack of lamb, are hearty and flavorful. Especially good is the roast loin of elk, served with herbed forest mushroom and lingonberry sauces. *304 E. Hopkins Ave., upstairs, tel. 970/925–6328. AE, D, MC, V. No lunch.*

$$$ R BISTRO. Upstairs from Renaissance, but served out of the same kitchen, the R Bistro (more commonly referred to as the "R-Bar") offers some of the same cuisine as its tonier downstairs neighbor. The atmosphere is casual, and entrées tend to be less fancy and more hearty (check out the double-thick pork chop), though Renaissance menu items are available. The full wine list is available, as are cocktails at the bar. Plus, the prices are a bit more reasonable than at the bistro. *304 E. Hopkins Ave., upstairs, tel. 970/925–2402. AE, D, MC, V. No lunch.*

$$–$$$ BENEDICT'S. Sitting high atop Aspen Mountain, this cozy spot offers what might best be described as creative comfort food.

Diners (mostly skiers, though foot traffic is allowed via the Silver Queen Gondola) can enjoy potato leek chowder or a duck stew, followed by a pheasant sausage sandwich, grilled salmon, or elk meat loaf. The view from the deck is amazing, but the restaurant as a whole suffers from the noise created by the Sundeck cafeteria, which occupies the neighboring wing of the building. *Sundeck building on Aspen Mountain, tel. 970/429-6900. AE, D, DC, MC, V. Closed late Apr.–late Nov. No dinner.*

$$-$$$ ★ **BLUE MAIZE.** This small, unassuming restaurant is home to some of the most innovative cuisine in the Rockies. Influenced primarily by Southwestern and Latin American flavors, the kitchen assembles such creations as brie and mango quesadillas, elk tenderloin in cranberry-pasilla sauce, and wonderful mixed-grill fajitas. The elk sashimi appetizer is astoundingly delicious in its simplicity. The room is funky and colorful, with a distinctly casual service style. *308 S. Hunter St., upstairs, tel. 970/925-6698. AE, MC, V. No lunch.*

$$-$$$ **MEZZALUNA.** It's hip, it's happening, and it's crowded. Mezzaluna serves food with Italian and Far East influences, but not in a fusion-happy sort of way. Flavors are crisp and distinct in the innovative salads, wood-fired pizzas, and fresh fish, fowl, and meat preparations. There's not a lot of room to move around in here, the bare floors and marble tables make for a noisy experience, and the service is decidedly casual, but it gives the place an undeniable energy. Lunch on the sunny patio is fantastic in the summer. *624 E. Cooper Ave., tel. 970/925-5882. AE, DC, MC, V.*

$$-$$$ **VARIATIONS.** The concept here marries great views of Aspen Mountain with a constantly changing menu of international influence. On any given day, this may be a French-Indian restaurant, and a month later, classic Italian; the chef seems unafraid of mixing genres. Variations has done an admirable job in keeping its prices low, which begins to make up for its unpredictability. *709 E. Durant Ave., in the Aspen Club Lodge, tel. 970/925-6760. AE, MC, V. No lunch.*

Delicatessens

$-$$ PAESANOS. Aspen's answer to a Long Island Italian deli features
★ a stocked deli case, pizzas, and stromboli, as well as a variety of pasta dishes and hot sandwiches prepared in an open kitchen. The matzo-ball soup, by the way, is outstanding. *300 Puppy Smith St., tel. 970/920–0069. AE, MC, V.*

$ BUTCHER'S BLOCK. Just like in a real city, the Butcher's Block offers a variety of sandwiches and desserts to go. They roast their own beef and chicken, and offer up plenty of soups and salads. The deli is also a great place to pick up aged meat cuts, fresh seafood, and fine cheeses. *424 S. Spring St., tel. 970/925–7554. MC, V. No dinner.*

$ CHARCUTERIE AND CHEESE MARKET. You'll find a good variety of cheeses here, and even liver and egg salad, but you'll have to read the entire menu since every sandwich has some sort of special name. They're imaginative, but sometimes annoying, and good on the whole. Be sure to request every condiment and dressing; the staff doesn't assume anything. *665 E. Cooper St., tel. 970/925–8010. AE, MC, V. No dinner.*

Fast Food

$ ASPEN UNDERGROUND. This quick lunch and early-dinner place offers great burritos, quesadillas, and soft tacos, but falters a bit when it comes to more "gourmet" wraps. They do, however, let you design your own, and they keep their prices on the low side. This is a great meal to go. *455 Rio Grande Place, tel. 970/925–6050. No credit cards.*

$ BIG WRAP. This specialty wrap place offers tortilla-enrobed meals
★ in such variations as Thai, barbecue, Greek, and (go figure) Mexican, as well as soups and salads. The ingredients are fresh, and a foil-wrapped lunch fits pretty neatly into the pocket of your ski jacket or backpack. Big Wrap delivers for lunch within the

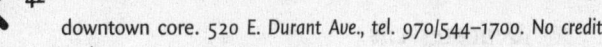

downtown core. 520 E. Durant Ave., tel. 970/544–1700. *No credit cards.*

$ IN AND OUT HOUSE. No mystery here: walk in and take out a hero, grinder, sub, or whatever you call it in your hometown. These guys don't bother getting too creative; they just serve up some great sandwiches. They'll also deliver within Aspen. 233 E. Main St., tel. 970/925–6647. *No credit cards. No dinner.*

$ ★ JOHNNY MCGUIRE'S DELI. This is a sandwich shop with personality. So much, in fact, it seems sort of un-Aspen. Johnny's offers a variety of hot and cold specialty sandwiches on their house-baked bread, and loads them up with everything from wasabi mayonnaise to pineapple. Basic sandwiches aren't a problem here, but sometimes the sandwich guys look a little sad if you just ask for a roast beef on wheat. Delivery is available, but you'll have more fun reading the walls while waiting for your sandwich to be made. Great breakfast starting at nine. 730 E. Cooper Ave., tel. 970/920–9255. *No credit cards.*

Italian

$$$ L'HOSTARIA. Though the food in this subterranean space is as good as any Italian in the city, the reason to visit L'Hostaria is its atmosphere. The tables are large and well-spaced, and a sleek and elegant decor encourages better digestion than the bustle of its competitors. The fresh pastas here are wonderful, and entrées such as stewed rabbit and veal Milanese work well with a big glass of Chianti, of which the restaurant has more than a few. For an interesting change of pace, check out the carpaccio bar, which features some wonderful cured meats and fishes. 620 E. Hyman Ave., tel. 970/925–9022. *AE, MC, V. No lunch.*

$$$ MOTHER LODE. This place has been serving food in Aspen since Aspen was practically a ghost town. The elegant rooms reek with Victorian charm, and the art on the walls alone is worth the price of admission. The menu includes such classics as fettuccine in meat sauce and grilled Marsala veal chop, but also creative dishes like lamb and apple salad and fennel-seared ahi tuna. The wine list is not large or special, but then, it is not very costly. *314 E. Hyman Ave., tel. 970/925–7700. AE, D, DC, MC, V. No lunch.*

$$–$$$ **FARFALLA.** Farfalla is a casual restaurant that was as trendy as trendy could be in the early '90s. The pretty crowd has moved on (they never ate much, anyway), but their loss is our gain. These days the wait for a table is considerably less than before, and the food is probably better. Wood-fired pizzas are always a favorite, at the bar or at a table, and the pastas are the equal of any in town—check out the house-made tortellini of asparagus and goat cheese. Farfalla has a great Italian wine list, as well as a killer selection of grappas. *415 E. Main St., tel. 970/925–8222. AE, DC, MC, V.*

$$ **CAMPO DE FIORI.** The tables are too close together, the waiters are foreign, and the atmosphere is unbearably noisy. In other words, it's an authentic Italian trattoria. The well-seasoned food is perfectly prepared, and the wine list sparkles with all the stars of Italy. The decor here is simple and rustic, with murals covering every available space. If you're looking to be seen and don't need to stretch out while dining, no place beats Campo. Outdoor dining is available (and recommended) in the summer. *205 S. Mill St., tel. 970/920–7717. AE, MC, V. No lunch.*

$$ **LUCCI'S.** Lucci's is a holdover from the days when a family could go out to a place where everyone could find something they liked, and Mom and Dad didn't get soaked on the check. Lucci's offers classics like lasagna, manicotti, and shrimp scampi at reasonable prices, and at least you'll leave full. Aspen's only early-bird special is one of the best deals in town. *508 E. Cooper Ave., downstairs, tel. 970/925–8866. MC, V. No lunch.*

$$ **TRATTORIA TOSCANA.** This quaint little trattoria takes its name
★ from the Northern Italian menu it serves. Intimate and casual, it is a bustling café at lunch and a surprisingly romantic nightspot.

The menu is small but features creative pastas and wonderful entrées from roast chicken breast to osso bucco. The wine list is primarily Italian, with a good selection of bottle sizes. *525 E. Cooper Ave., tel. 970/925–6162. MC, V.*

Japanese

$$$$ KENICHI. This trendy fish spot has come into its own in the last few years, retaining its loyal clientele and building up new business with its creative take on sushi. The rest of the menu swells with pan-Asian cuisine, from steak to a sumptuous daily dim sum. Big parties love the private tatami rooms, and everybody seems to love the sake. *533 E. Hopkins Ave., tel. 970/920–2212. AE, D, DC, MC, V. No lunch.*

$$$$ MATSUHISA ASPEN. Aspen's newest sushi spot bears the name of New York's famous Nobu, but don't expect to see him in the kitchen. His recipes and techniques greet you at every turn, however. His jalapeño yellowtail is scrumptious, his anticuchu beef is delicious, his new-style sashimi indescribable, and his prices astronomical. You won't be disappointed in the food or the star-studded clientele, but only dot-com retirees should make it a regular haunt. *303 E. Main St., entrance on Monarch St., tel. 970/544–6628. AE, MC, V. No lunch.*

$$$–$$$$ TAKAH SUSHI. ★ This is the restaurant that started the sushi craze in Aspen, and the one that most locals call home (a certain local journalist actually gets his mail there). The atmosphere here is much more casual than Aspen's other two eat-in Japanese spots, but the food is just as good. The sushi chefs take a traditional approach to the art, while the kitchen adds touches of Pacific Rim flair. It is very hard to go wrong in your selection here. *420 E. Hyman Ave., tel. 970/925–8588. AE, D, DC, MC, V. No lunch.*

$$–$$$ SUSHI YA GO-GO. Aspen is undeniably a sushi town, and Sushi Ya Go-Go is how it gets its fix when it's too tired to get off its metaphorical couch. All of the classics are here, with plenty of

Markets

Though Aspen sits a fair distance away from just about anything, it's hardly cut off from the world. You'll be able to find all the basics if you happen to want to do a little entertaining at home. Prices may be slightly higher in Aspen, owing to freight costs, but you'll pay no more for a California avocado here than in St. Louis.

Aspen proper has two excellent supermarkets, Clark's and City Market. Although these aren't mega-markets, each should be able to provide for just about any reasonable need.

City Market (711 E. Cooper Dr.) is the larger of the two and carries just about every national brand. The produce selection is large and diverse and fresh, and locally baked bread is brought in daily. As befitting a high-profile resort town, there is also a good selection of "gourmet" items, and even an aisle of ethnic specialties ranging from Thai to Indian to kosher. City Market lacks a butcher counter, however.

At **Clark's** (300 Puppy Smith St.), there is an emphasis on local produce and products. Catering to health-conscious Aspenites, Clark's goes out of its way to stock organic and hormone-free items, and it features a large selection of vitamins, herbs, and vegetarian alternatives. Clark's also has manned deli and butcher stations.

In Snowmass, the **Village Market,** in the Snowmass Shopping Center, feels more like a small-town grocery store. It is not a small store, but selection is limited, and this grocery is best utilized for filling in gaps between your other excursions. The **Village Market,** on the mall, serves a similar purpose but at higher prices.

If you're in dire need of milk or Neosporin after midnight, your only course of action in the upper valley is the **Aspen Store** (435 E. Main St.), which stays open round the clock.

other Japanese favorites, all served without the surcharge for the groovy decor. There's also a small, informal bar for eat-in. 414 N. Mill St., tel. 970/544-0114. MC, V. No lunch.

Mediterranean

$$$ **MIRABELLA.** Many restaurants in Aspen claim Mediterranean ancestry, but only Mirabella stays true to its roots. Here you'll find authentic dishes from France, Spain, Italy, Greece, Turkey, and Lebanon—such as the Grillade de Viande, a specialty featuring lamb, chicken, and merguez sausage, accompanied by couscous and ratatouille—served in a room that evokes a Greek cottage. The colors of the room and the flavors of the food are bright, and the wine selection offers the best of the region. Mirabella also offers a private dining room downstairs. 216 S. Monarch St., tel. 970/920-2555. AE, DC, MC, V. No lunch.

Mexican

$$-$$$ **LA COCINA.** It may be Mexican, but no one can seem to explain the garlic bread that comes with every dish. You'll order by number here and receive portions that include some combination of beans, rice, chicken, tortilla, and chile verde. The atmosphere is casual and energetic, and the margaritas are the best in town. Best advice: ignore the gastronomic schizophrenia and have a good time. 308 E. Hopkins Ave., tel. 970/925-9714. MC, V. No lunch.

$$-$$$ **SU CASA.** Su Casa is Aspen's most authentic Mexican cuisine,
★ featuring recipes from the Pacific coast. The ceviche is excellent here, as are all the appetizers; entrées are also tasty, though most require some assembly. Any dish involving *carnitas* (fried pork) has to be good. Patio dining is available in the summer, and there's usually a crowd at the bar. Interestingly, Su Casa also serves one of town's best burgers. 315 E. Hyman Ave., tel. 970/920-1488. AE, MC, V. No lunch.

$$ CANTINA. Cantina offers cuisine of questionable authenticity, such as taco salad and chimichangas, but it offers it in an airy setting that defies the logic of Aspen real estate. The food is tasty if unimaginative, and the prickly pear margaritas are downright amazing. *411 E. Main St., tel. 970/925–3663. AE, MC, V.*

Pizza

$ NEW YORK PIZZA. Though most diners encounter this thin-crust pizza joint at two in the morning, it should not be overlooked for an affordable and crowd-pleasing meal. There are salads and sandwiches here as well, but the stars are the pies. Custom design your own, go for a specialty pie (the chicken pie is quite nice), or let everyone in the crew custom design a slice. NYP delivers, but sometimes slowly. *409 E. Hyman Ave., upstairs, tel. 970/920–3088.*

Seafood

$$$–$$$$ PACIFICA SEAFOOD BRASSERIE. One of Aspen's coolest-looking restaurants, Pacifica does a good job of making sure the cuisine matches the scene. Anyone wary of a seafood house so near the Continental Divide can sleep well knowing that the fish, clams, oysters, and crab are flown in fresh on a daily basis. The menu is designed by George Mahaffey, of the creative Conundrum, and features such treats as charred ahi tartare with foie gras, Dungeness crab cakes, and lamb and beef dishes for the fish-sensitive. *307 South Mill St., tel. 970/920–9775. AE, MC, V. No lunch.*

Steak

$$$ CHART HOUSE. Yes, we've got one, too. But interestingly enough, ours was the first, built way back in '61. Steaks and seafood are the obvious choices here (some pretty uncommon fishes grace the menu), but no one can resist the tempting salad bar. Corporate tried to eliminate it in 1998, but public outcry was

such that they soon brought it back, improved. The Chart House has a groovy, wide-open feel and knows better than to take itself too seriously. 219 E. Durant Ave., tel. 970/925-3525. AE, D, DC, MC, V. No lunch.

$$$ CRYSTAL PALACE. This dinner theater is better known for its satire than its steaks. The food here is good but not so good that you're distracted from the show. Prime rib, duckling, and shrimp also grace the menu. 300 E. Hyman Ave., tel. 970/920-9664. AE, MC, V. No lunch.

$$$ STEAK PIT. They make steak, and they make it well. The subterranean room is sleek and modern, but the portions are from a bygone era. The salad bar here equals its crosstown rival and has the added benefit of a variety of fresh-baked breads. You can actually watch your fillet sizzle in the open kitchen. The steak pit is also Aspen's source for king crab legs. Hopkins Ave. at Monarch St., tel. 970/925-3459. AE, DC, MC, V. No lunch.

$$-$$$ SKIERS CHALET STEAK HOUSE. "Nothing Fancy" could be the motto here. It's charming because it's so Old Aspen—no glitz, no glamour, just good honest food at only slightly inflated prices. The steaks are wonderfully prepared, though one suspects the lobster might have spent a little time in the freezer. Ask about the "Flob." 710 S. Aspen St., tel. 970/925-3381. MC, V. No lunch.

Swiss

$$$ GUIDO'S. Though some of Guido's cuisine derives from other Continental sources, the restaurant's alpine-lodge setting and its excellent fondue keep it anchored in the Swiss tradition. Wild game, lamb, and veal feature prominently on the menu. And when was the last time you had châteaubriand? (No, that's not a wine.) 430 S. Galena St., upstairs, tel. 970/925-7222. AE, D, MC, V. No lunch.

Thai

$$$ THAI TINI. Impossibly hip; surprisingly good. This remodeled Victorian has all the signs of a superficial restaurant: a martini list, hand-blown light fixtures, and a good-looking but confused staff. But the food actually scores points both in traditional dishes and new interpretations of the classics. Go here to watch, and watch the martinis. *316 E. Hopkins Ave., tel. 970/544-4664. AE, MC, V. No lunch.*

Vegetarian

$$-$$$ EXPLORE BISTRO. Aspen's only vegetarian venue sits upstairs from its largest bookstore and keeps the Victorian charm of the house it inhabits. The restaurant is small and cozy (tea fits in quite well here), and the menu is on the small side as well. You'll find both meatless and lacto-ovo options, and the vegan desserts are almost unbelievable. *221 E. Main St., tel. 970/925-5338. AE, MC, V.*

Vietnamese

$-$$$ VINH VINH. Light and wholesome are the watchwords here, as chef Vinh Hua takes on classic soups, volcano shrimp, and traditional clay-pot cooking. The room seems overly casual, as does the service, but Vinh Vinh is on the whole a good deal. *413 E. Main St., tel. 970/920-4373. AE, MC, V.*

SNOWMASS
American

$$-$$$ COWBOYS. If you can think of the slightly distressed room as "Western rustic," you'll probably enjoy a trip to Cowboys. They've carried a Western theme into the cuisine as well, with wild game, steaks, salmon, and the occasional trout, but like the room, the menu could use a little freshening up. *Snowmass Village Mall, next to the Silvertree Hotel, tel. 970/923-5249. AE, MC, V. No lunch.*

snowmass dining

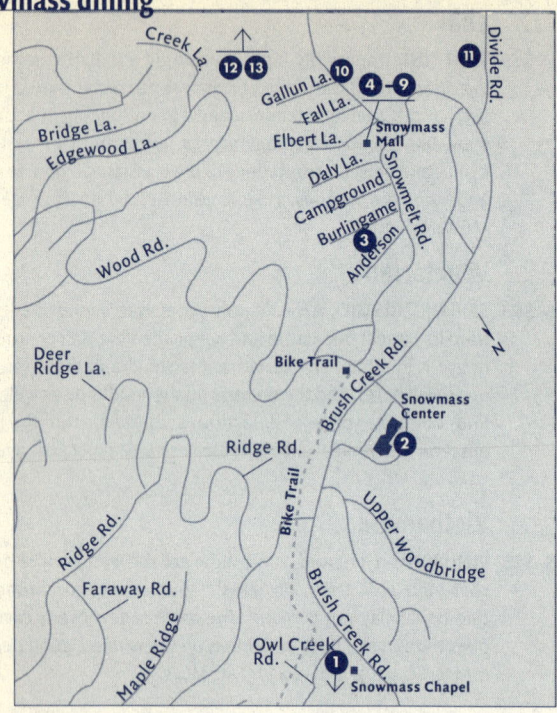

Butch's Lobster Bar, 10
Cirque Café, 9
Cowboys, 4
Finestra, 13
High Alpine, 12
Il Poggio, 5
Krabloonik, 11
Mountain Dragon, 6
Sage, 1
Stonebridge Restaurant, 3
Tower Restaurant, 7
Wildcat Café, 2
Zane's Tavern, 8

$$–$$$ STONEBRIDGE RESTAURANT. The Stonebridge sets an elegant tone with its Colorado cuisine, which is moderately priced. Nothing creative on the menu here; just good, solid food like Colorado beef, elk medallions, and chicken potpie. The wine list is not extravagant, but it is well priced. *Across from Lot 2, tel. 970/923–2420. AE, D, MC, V. No lunch.*

$$–$$$ TOWER RESTAURANT. This would be your run-of-the-mill tourist restaurant, as there is nothing inspired about the cuisine. However, the bartenders are magicians, and the occasional comedy show keeps everyone laughing. The food isn't light, but the atmosphere sure is. *Snowmass Village Mall, tel. 970/923–4650. AE, D, MC, V.*

American/Casual

$–$$ CIRQUE CAFE. This slopeside bar offers Snowmass's best deck, winter and summer. Food is standard pub fare: burgers and fries, hot wings, and lots of cold beer. For some reason, the chicken and chips (fried chicken and French fries) is uncommonly good. *Parking Lot 13, tel. 970/923–8685. AE, DC, MC, V.*

$–$$ WILDCAT CAFE. ★ Locals eat often at the Wildcat, and tourists with smarts will follow them there. The prices are lower than what you'll find in the mall, and the food, from breakfast through dinner, is tasty and unpretentious. If Snowmass had a truck stop, this would be it. *Snowmass Village Center, tel. 970/923–5990. MC, V.*

$–$$ ZANE'S TAVERN. This is a sports bar with loud rock-and-roll music and all the food that should accompany that mixture: burgers, cheese steaks, soups, salads, and pizzas. You will not come here for the food, but you might be surprised by it. *Snowmass Village Mall, upstairs, tel. 970/923–3515. DC, MC, V.*

Contemporary

$$$$ KRABLOONIK. ★ The food in this rustic slopeside lodge is memorable, and not only for the abundance of wild game on the menu. The preparation is creative, the staff knowledgable and polite, and the wine list extensive and interesting. The fact that diners can arrive by dogsled makes this one of the defining experiences of a trip to Aspen and Snowmass. *4250 Divide Rd., tel. 970/923-3953. AE, MC, V.*

$$$ HIGH ALPINE. Elegant surroundings and an astounding view characterize the first sit-down restaurant to grace the slopes of Aspen/Snowmass. The food is also excellent, drawing on cuisines from all over the world. Try the seafood puffs, seared sashimi salad, or grilled pheasant breast. The wine list has everything you might expect, plus a few surprises. A meal here makes you wonder why the gods like you so much. *Top of Alpine Springs chairlift., tel. 970/923-3311. AE, MC, V. Closed late Apr.–late Nov. No dinner.*

$$$ SAGE. Sage is a casual bistro with the usual suspects on the menu: pizzas, pastas, and hearty Colorado entrées, all with a creative twist that sometimes falls flat. This is a viable option if you're already in restaurant-deprived Snowmass, but not worth the trip from elsewhere. *0239 Snowmass Club Circle, tel. 970/923-0923. AE, MC, V. No lunch.*

Italian

$$–$$$ IL POGGIO. ★ Sure, it's just a little Italian place, but it may very well be the best casual restaurant in Snowmass. Here you'll find hearty pastas, hearth-baked pizzas, and classic Italian entrées, served in a fun and lively atmosphere. Il Poggio is smart enough not to take itself too seriously. *73 Elbert Lane, tel. 970/923-4292. AE, DC, MC, V. No lunch.*

$$ FINESTRA. The name means "window," and you'll know why after setting foot into this elegant on-mountain spot. The food,

Liquor Stores

As you might expect in towns with so many hot tubs, both Aspen and Snowmass have their fair share of liquor stores, and they are all fairly well stocked. Colorado has a taste for the microbrew and boasts dozens of breweries, and you'll find shelves and shelves of beers you may never see outside of the state. You'll also find plenty of imports, other states' microbrews, and case after case of domestics.

In the wine department, you'll find everything from wine-in-a-box to "we-got-the-only-case-in-the-state" French vintages. The staffs of every store in town go to frequent tastings in local restaurants, and therefore actually know what they're talking about. Some local liquor merchants moonlight by assembling cellars for the million-dollar homes that surround Aspen.

Liquor stores in Colorado close at 10 PM and are closed on Sundays. Beer can be purchased on Sundays in markets. Both Aspen and Snowmass have regulations against open containers of alcohol in public. They also have laws against public intoxication, though those are usually only enforced in conjunction with another offense.

Bringing your own wine to a restaurant is illegal in Colorado—not to mention bad for the restaurant's business. If, for some deeply meaningful reason (it's a very rare vintage; you made it in your bathtub), you feel you must bring your own, check with the restaurant manager first. If he casts a blind eye, compensation both to the restaurant and to your server will be expected.

In Aspen, check out **Aspen Wine and Spirit Co.** (300 Puppy Smith St., tel. 970/925–6600), **The Grog Shop** (710 E. Durant Ave., tel. 970/925–3000), **Of Grape and Grain** (319 E. Hopkins Ave., tel. 970/925–8600), or the small but well-stocked **Wine Cellar Liquors** (306 E. Main St., tel. 970/925–3273). In Snowmass, visit **Sundance Drug and Liquor** (Snowmass Shopping Center, tel. 970/923–5890) or **Village Liquors** (316 E. Hopkins Ave., tel. 970/923–4100).

hearty Northern Italian fare, is imaginative and tasty. The staff, however, makes it clear they'd rather be skiing. You'll have to ski to visit, but the ride down is an easy one. *Top of Sam's Knob chairlift, tel. 970/925–1220. AE, MC, V. Closed late Apr.–late Nov. No dinner.*

Pan-Asian

$$ MOUNTAIN DRAGON. Once upon a time, the Dragon was a traditional Mandarin and Szechuan restaurant. But recently it has taken turns for the Thai and Japanese. The restaurant seems a bit tired decor-wise, but offers fairly good value, and the best non-European food in Snowmass. Plus, it's the only place in Snowmass Village to get your sushi fix. *67 Elbert Lane, tel. 970/923–3576. AE, DC, MC, V. No lunch.*

Seafood

$$$ BUTCH'S LOBSTER BAR. Butch knows about lobster; he used to be a lobsterman off Cape Cod. He now offers lobster served half a dozen different ways, as well as crab legs, shrimp, and the occasional steak. While the atmosphere and the service are not fancy, the food is delicious. The wine list has dozens of excellent selections, but Butch recommends Champagne. *Parking Lot 13, tel. 970/923–4004. AE, MC, V. No lunch.*

ELSEWHERE
American/Casual

$$–$$$ WOODY CREEK TAVERN. For some, the Tavern defines the way Aspen could have been. It sits in a trailer park and features walls filled with newspaper clippings, as well as art and autographs by its famous guests. In heaven, the chicken enchiladas and fresh lime margaritas are catered by the Woody Creek Tavern. *0002 Woody Creek Plaza, 6 mi from Aspen via Hwy 82, tel. 970/923–4585.*

Austrian

$$$ CLOUD NINE CAFE. Though you'll need to ski (rather well) to make an appearance here, the view alone is worth several weeks of lessons. The food is superb as well, with two different entrées available each day. One is veggie, one is not, but both come from the Alpine tradition of Austrian chef Andreas Fischbacher. And don't forget to save room for the banana-caramel crepes. *Aspen Highlands, at the top of the Cloud Nine chairlift, tel. 970/544–3063. AE, MC, V. No dinner.*

Contemporary

$$$ PINE CREEK COOKHOUSE. This backcountry lodge offers delicious food, including trout, wild game, and succulent quail. And the trip makes it all worth it. Snuggled into the bosom of the Elk Range near the ghost town of Ashcroft, you'll have to cross-country ski or take the sleigh to arrive in winter. *11 mi from Aspen via Castle Creek Rd., tel. 970/925–1044. AE, MC, V.*

Shopping has become an important part of the Aspen experience. The streets are lined with tempting shops and galleries, offering everything from Southwestern jewelry to the latest designer creations. Bargains are rare, but it's still fun to explore the upscale shops.

In this Chapter

When and How 58 • DOWNTOWN ASPEN 58 • Antiques 58 • Art 58 • Books 63 • Crafts 63 • Clothes 63 • Fur 67 • Gifts 68 • Glass 69 • Home Furnishings 69 • Jewelry 70 • Leather 72 • Miscellaneous 73 • Musical Instruments 73 • Perfumes 74 • Shoes 74 • Sporting Goods 74 • Toys 75 • SNOWMASS VILLAGE MALL 76 • Books 76 • Clothes 76 • Gifts 76 • Jewelry 77 • Sporting Goods 77

By Cindy Hirschfeld

shopping

MORE THAN ANY OTHER MOUNTAIN RESORT in Colorado, Aspen is known for its shopping. And that reputation derives mainly from the proliferation of shops dealing in high-end merchandise. If you're looking for bargains, you'll be disappointed. If it's luxury goods you're after, however, there's no limit to what you can find. For a small town, Aspen offers an extraordinary variety of art, clothing, jewelry, and out-of-the-ordinary decorative objects.

That said, Aspen stores are in a constant state of flux. As the already sky-high rents continue to increase, the revolving door of merchants trying to make a go of it spins ever faster. And the growing number of chain stores (albeit generally pricier, less prolific chains) is lamented by many longtime locals. Nonetheless, whether you're a browser or an expert buyer, setting aside time to explore the shops can be rewarding, and the personalized service that many stores offer is not easily found elsewhere.

Shopping in Aspen is fairly centralized. Most browse-worthy stores are within a few blocks of one another in the downtown core, bounded by Main Street to the north, Durant Avenue to the south, Spring Street to the east, and Monarch Street to the west. Other clusters of stores are found at the pedestrian-only Cooper and Hyman Avenue Malls (which also have the highest concentration of T-shirt and souvenir shops), the Mill St. Plaza, the Ute City Banque building, and the Ajax Mountain Building.

In Snowmass, the shopping area is even more self-contained: the Snowmass Village Mall is an outdoor pedestrian plaza ringed by two levels of shops, open seven days a week. The variety of stores pales in comparison to Aspen, but you can certainly while away an hour or two browsing.

When and How

During the summer and winter, most stores and galleries in Aspen stay open until 8 or 9 PM. In the spring and fall off-seasons, many significantly cut back on hours, and some close altogether. Most stores are open on Sunday. Sales tax in Aspen is 8.2%.

Almost all stores in Snowmass close for several weeks during the spring (after ski season ends mid-April) and again in the fall (October to mid-November). The Snowmass sales tax is 9.8%.

DOWNTOWN ASPEN
Antiques

DANIELS ANTIQUES (431 E. Hyman Ave., tel. 970/544–4707) carries 19th-century furnishings and accessories from Britain.

OLD TOWNE ANTIQUES (601 E. Hopkins Ave., tel. 970/544–3364) has a plentiful inventory of high-end furniture, lighting, home accessories, and jewelry, specializing in 18th- and 19th-century French and other European styles.

Art

AFRICAN ODYSSEY (555 E. Durant Ave., tel. 970/544–5600) offers traditional art and artifacts from throughout the African continent. You'll find furniture made of cleverly reinvented old railroad ties, brightly colored ceramics from Zimbabwe known as Penzoware, and the expected rugs, masks, and intricately woven baskets.

ART EXPRESSIONS (450 S. Galena St., tel. 970/925–8625) has work by popular modern impressionist Leonard Wren, as well as selections from other contemporary artists.

ART SOURCE INTERNATIONAL (413 E. Hyman Ave., tel. 970/925–6856) specializes in vintage botanical prints, maps, and advertising posters. Some pieces of Western art (e.g., Albert Bierstadt and Thomas Moran) are also on hand.

ASPEN FINE ART GALLERY (410 E. Hyman Ave., tel. 970/920–0044) has a large selection of paintings and sculptures, from Russian impressionist Nikolai Timkov to California child prodigy Alexandra Nechita.

ASPEN GROVE FINE ARTS (525 E. Cooper Ave., tel. 970/925–5151) has traditional yet eclectic works. Among the featured painters are the late Earl Biss (a former Aspen resident), William Martin, and John Demott.

ASPEN MOUNTAIN GALLERY (303 E. Hopkins Ave., tel. 970/925–5083) shows Native American and Southwestern art.

BALDWIN GALLERY (209 S. Galena St., tel. 970/920–9797) is the most New York–like of Aspen's galleries, with its cool, minimalist interior and revolving exhibits by artists such as Jennifer Bartlett, Louise Nevelson, and Bruce Weber.

CHRISTOPHER CARDOZO GALLERY (424 E. Hyman Ave., tel. 970/925–4181) deals exclusively in photography, with an extensive selection of vintage Edward S. Curtis works, including goldtones, and the large-format Southwestern landscapes of Navajo photographer LeRoy DeJolie.

DAVID FLORIA GALLERY (312 S. Mill St., tel. 970/544–5705) features important contemporary artists such as Joe Andoe, Timothy Berry, James Surls, and William Wegman. The gallery also exhibits well-regarded local artists.

EDWARD CARTER GALLERY (525 Cooper Ave., tel. 970/544–9054) focuses on the ever-popular photographs of Ansel Adams and exhibits other photographers on a revolving basis.

E. S. LAWRENCE GALLERY (516 E. Hyman Ave., tel. 970/920–2922) offers paintings from a variety of contemporary artists

worldwide, including the photorealistic works of Croatian artist Zvonimir Mihanovic.

GALERIE DU BOIS (407 E. Hyman Ave., tel. 970/925–5525) has paintings that run the gamut from impressionism to contemporary realistic landscapes.

GALERIE MAXIMILLIAN (602 E. Cooper Ave., tel. 970/925–6100) is home to some true gems of 19th- and 20th-century fine works on paper, from artists such as Miró, Matisse, Chagall, Renoir, and Toulouse-Lautrec. Also on display are contemporary primitive and surrealist paintings and select works of sculpture.

GALERIE ZÜGER (555 E. Durant Ave., tel. 970/925–5299) has the giant, figurative paintings of Russian Anton Arkhipov as well as the neoexpressionist work of Peter Max and lucite-and-bronze sculptures from Frederick Hart (known for his work on the Vietnam war memorial).

HILL'S ASPEN GALLERY OF PHOTOGRAPHY (312 E. Hyman Ave., tel. 970/925–1836) is the place for large-scale scenic photos of the Aspen area and other natural landscapes. Many of the photographs are also available on note cards, including ones with vintage ski photos by longtime local photographer Margaret Durrance. One nifty feature is that you can view the entire collection via computer at the gallery.

HUNTSMAN GALLERY OF FINE ART (521 E. Hyman Ave., tel. 970/920–1910) is owned by Don Huntsman, a respected bronze sculptor who creates realistic human and animal representations. The gallery also carries works of all types and descriptions by more than 60 artists from around the world.

JAMES COLEMAN FINE ART GALLERY (411 E. Hyman Ave., tel. 970/925–5091) features the luminescent paintings of this former Disney animation artist as well as marine mammal paintings and sculptures from Wyland and a small selection of Italian glasswork.

Secondhand Shops

In Aspen, the aphorism that one person's trash is another's treasure couldn't be more true. The town's secondhand stores are a source of great finds. As with consignment shops anywhere, there's a lot to sift through before you spot the gems. The quality of goods, however, is generally quite high.

For clothing, visit **Susie's, Ltd.,** in a cozy Victorian (623 E. Hopkins Ave., tel. 970/920–2376); **Gracy's,** which has the largest selection (517 E. Hopkins, tel. 970/925–5131); or the **Thrift Shop** (422 E. Hopkins Ave., tel. 970/925–3121), which is run as a nonprofit. Furniture and housewares are available at **Aspen Home Consignment** (202 E. Main St., tel. 970/925–1870); Gracy's; and Susie's annex, in the alley behind the clothing outlet. For deals on sports gear, pay a visit to **Use It Again** (465 N. Mill St., tel. 970/925–2483).

JOEL SOROKA GALLERY (400 E. Hyman Ave., tel. 970/920–3152) may be small, but it has an array of fine-art photographs by both established masters and current photographers.

MAGIDSON FINE ART (525 E. Cooper Ave., tel. 970/920–1001) is known for its well-rounded collection of contemporary art, from names such as Picasso, Andy Warhol, and Annie Leibovitz.

MASTERPIECES RARE ART AND ANTIQUITIES (414 E. Hyman Ave., tel. 970/429–0326) specializes in the sort of artifacts that predate U.S. history: illuminated medieval manuscripts, Roman coin jewelry, rare books, antique maps, and early woodcuts.

MIRANDA GALLERIES (520 E. Hyman Ave., tel. 970/544–0345), a bright little spot east of the pedestrian mall, has originals and serigraphs from Spanish painter Royo and works by Latin American abstract expressionist Orlando. Sculptures include pieces by Tuan, an up-and-coming Vietnamese artist, and the geometric mahogany creations of French sculptor Pascal.

OMNIBUS GALLERY (422 E. Cooper Ave., tel. 970/925–5567) has an impressive collection of original vintage posters, including those for European resorts and sporting events, and the type of old-time advertisements that seem so refreshingly simple by today's standards.

PAM DRISCOL GALLERY (416 E. Cooper Ave., tel. 970/925–3881) is most notable for its extensive collection of realistic bronze sculptures and fountains; the gallery also exhibits paintings.

SUSAN DUVAL GALLERY (525 E. Cooper Ave., tel. 970/925–9044) offers a sophisticated array of contemporary glass art (Dale Chihuly, Dante Marioni, and William Morris) and paintings by artists such as Carol Anthony, Lamar Briggs, Scott Fraser, and Dan Namingha.

THOMAS INGERICK GALLERY (525 E. Cooper Ave., tel. 970/920–9236) has bronze sculptures from Native American sculptor Allan Houser, a contemporary of Georgia O'Keeffe. Also noteworthy are the modernist sculptures of pioneering glass artist Robert Willson and the color-washed works of abstract expressionist painter Peter Opheim.

TOKLAT GALLERY (11247 Castle Creek Rd., tel. 970/925–7345) is owned and operated by the Mace family, who first settled this part of the Castle Creek valley more than 50 years ago, so a visit here exposes you to both history and aesthetics. Most of the art in the rustic gallery—sculpture, painting, jewelry, rugs, and pottery—has a Native American bent. The nearby Pine Creek Cookhouse is a scenic spot for a post-browsing meal.

WIND RIVER GALLERY (505 E. Hyman Ave., tel. 970/925–3919) carries a comprehensive collection of Western American art, including bronze wildlife sculptures.

Books

ASPEN BOOKSTORE (665 Durant Ave., tel. 970/925–7427) may be small, but you'll find a carefully selected mix of publications and rental videos to keep you browsing.

EXPLORE BOOKSELLERS (211 E. Main St., tel. 970/925–5336), housed in a Victorian, would certainly win an award for most atmospheric bookstore. An incredible variety of publications is somehow packed into every nook and cranny. A vegetarian restaurant among the stacks lets you savor your newfound read over a meal or a cup of tea.

Crafts

HEATHER GALLERY (555 E. Durant Ave., tel. 970/925–6170) has an enchanting mix of jewelry, pottery, and objects for the home from local and other American artists. Look for brightly colored painted furniture, coat racks, and mirrors from Sticks; Janna Ugone's hand-painted lamp shades adorned with funky finials; and the popular pet clocks custom made by an Aspen local.

KOLOR WHEEL (720 E. Durant Ave., Suite E2, tel. 970/544–6191) is a paint-it-yourself pottery studio, with lots of mugs, bowls, vases, picture frames, and the like to buy and decorate as you please. It's a great outing for kids, too.

Clothes

MEN'S AND WOMEN'S

BANANA REPUBLIC (501 E. Cooper Ave., tel. 970/920–9626) sells the fashionable basics familiar to most U.S. shoppers. There always seems to be a good sale going on.

BOOGIE'S (534 E. Cooper Ave., tel. 970/925–6111), with its 1950s trappings and vintage vehicles on display, boasts Aspen's largest selection of designer men's and women's jeans, from vintage Levi's to Gianni Versace. There are also trendy shirts and sweaters, high-end kids' clothing, and an airbrush paint studio that produces customized T-shirts while you watch. And if it's your stomach and not your wallet that's feeling empty, walk on upstairs to the diner-style restaurant.

CASHMERE ASPEN (316 S. Hunter St., tel. 970/925–2747) stocks men's and women's items from its private-label Scottish brand as well as Loro Piana. A few leather and suede jackets as well as silk skirts, pants, and scarves round out the collection.

EDDIE BAUER (205 S. Mill St., tel. 970/920–9395) is one of the few places in Aspen for down-to-earth clothes at affordable prices.

FITIGUES (445 E. Hopkins Ave., tel. 970/920–2005) has the sweatshirt and thermal fabric casual clothes—for men, women, and children—that the chain has become known for.

GAP AND GAP KIDS (204 S. Galena St., tel. 970/920–9834) has a trendy assortment of the chain's styles. And if the Gap makes something in leather or suede, you'll be sure to find it here.

GORSUCH, LTD. (611 E. Durant Ave., tel. 970/920–9388), adjacent to the gondola, offers everything from men's and women's sportswear and skiwear to small home furnishings. You could browse all afternoon (especially if you're a sweater aficionado). The store specializes in the traditional European wear known as trachten but also carries clothing and shoes, from the classic to the hip, as well as Aspen-worthy ski outfits from Bogner, Postcard, Prada, Armani, and Descente.

GUCCI (203 S. Galena St., tel. 970/920–9150) is a multilevel pantheon of cool, the type of place from which you might feel like fleeing if you're not wearing black. If you stick around, you'll find men's and women's clothing; an extensive selection of shoes, bags, and watches; and a small group of home-furnishings accessories, such as glasses and bowls.

MANRICO CASHMERE (200 S. Mill St., tel. 970/920–3370) carries Italian-designed cashmere sweaters and coats under the store's own label. Styles, for men and women, tend toward the classic.

PEACHES EN REGALIA (520 E. Durant Ave., tel. 970/920–1280) is an established Aspen locale for men's and women's upscale attire, as well as shearling and leather jackets, with a European flair.

PITKIN COUNTY DRY GOODS (520 E. Cooper Ave., tel. 970/925–1681) has been selling men's and women's casual wear since 1969. Today's hip clothing selection includes Easel, French Connection, For Joseph, True Grit, and Three Dot, and jeans from Lucky to Levi's. There's also an extensive collection of leather coats and jackets. Accessories include Kate Spade bags and informal jewelry.

POLO RALPH LAUREN (520 E. Durant Ave., tel. 970/925–5147) sells men's and women's clothing from the Polo line—and, of course, RLX skiwear, the outfit of Aspen/Snowmass ski and snowboard instructors.

REGENT'S ROW (218 S. Mill St., tel. 970/925–1893) is a small, longtime Aspen boutique offering classic clothing for men and women, with many European brands.

WESTERN WEAR

CURIOUS GEORGE COLLECTIBLES (426 E. Hyman Ave., tel. 970/925–3315), a purveyor of vintage and contemporary Western goods, is an Aspen institution. Amidst the smell of leather from the legion of belts adorning the wall, you can browse through authentic Native American jewelry, antique firearms, a great array of sterling silver belt buckles, and Western garb.

FOOTLOOSE AND FANCY THINGS (240 S. Mill St., tel. 970/925–9155) has been plying Western wares in Aspen for more than two decades. In addition to Navajo jewelry, belts and silver buckles, and a variety of leather goods, the store is known for its custom-made moccasins, available in many styles.

KEMO SABE (434 E. Cooper Ave., tel. 970/925–7878) takes a humorous approach to retailing ("We're closed. Just slide the money under the door," reads a sign). It is the place for cowboy boots (Lucchese) and hats (Stetson and hard-to-find Charlie Tweddle). Also on hand are leather and shearling jackets, Pendleton blankets, animal heads, and Western memorabilia.

WOMEN'S

CHANEL (520 E. Durant Ave., tel. 970/544–0555) has the suits for which the French firm is renowned, as well as knitwear, bags, and cosmetics.

CHRISTIAN DIOR (201 S. Galena St., tel. 970/544–8200), which shares a store with Louis Vuitton, includes pieces from the French designer's line that appeal most to Aspen's hip clientele (e.g., body-conscious knitwear and fur-trimmed outfits), along with makeup, jewelry, sunglasses, and perfume.

DISTRACTIONS (465 E. Hopkins Ave., tel. 970/544–9946) is a sleek emporium for those drawn to such up-to-the-minute designers as Tracy Feith, Daryl K, TSE, Fake London, Gregory Parkinson, and Anna Sui. Shoes from Jimmy Choo, beaded bags from London designer Megan Park, and Kimme Winter's jewelry creations from vintage rosary beads are noteworthy accessories.

DKNY (103 S. Mill St., tel. 970/920–7772), a sister store to the only other independently owned DKNY store, in East Hampton, New York, has a small but comprehensive collection of Donna Karan's casual line, with merchandise that's always changing.

FENDI (208 S. Mill St., tel. 970/920–3100) carries women's couture clothing, furs, shoes, sunglasses, and perfume from the Italian designer known for his imaginative use of fabrics—and, of course, the Fendi baguette bag in multiple styles.

FREUDIAN SLIP (416 S. Hunter St., tel. 970/925–4427), true to its clever name, offers a comprehensive selection of lingerie and sleepwear, both practical and luxurious, from names such as Hanro, Donna Karan, Calvin Klein, and Olga.

GOLDIES AND THE KIDS (205 S. Mill St., tel. 970/925–1430) offers fanciful kids' wear and lots of crushed velvet, shimmery florals, and outfits in other sexy fabrics for mom.

HILDEGARD'S (228 S. Mill St., tel. 970/920–3239) caters to a sophisticated crowd, with clothing from Nicole Miller, Dolce and Gabbana, and Yeohlee; lots of high-quality knitwear; and designer evening wear suitable for any Aspen gala.

NUAGES (601 Cooper Ave., tel. 970/925–6569) has been keeping Aspen women (and visitors) stylish for years, with its small but chic selection of clothing and shoes. Regular lines include Prada, Jil Sander, and Alberta Ferretti.

OILILY (631 E. Durant Ave., tel. 970/925–3888), a branch of the Dutch chain, offers some of the most brightly patterned kids' clothes you'll ever see, in addition to fun and funky (and pricey) women's wear.

OLIVIA LEE (205 S. Mill St., tel. 970/544–9322) carries exquisite lingerie concoctions, including European luxury brand La Perla. A small line of clothing, including items from Tahari, is also available.

SCANDINAVIAN DESIGN (607 E. Cooper Ave., tel. 970/925–7299) carries colorfully patterned Scandinavian sweaters (including Dale of Norway) and an impressive selection of clogs.

Fur

AFFINITY (406 E. Hyman, tel. 970/920–2201) is one of only two specialty fur shops in Aspen (despite the perennial equation of Aspen with fur coats). Styles run toward the simple and classic, made primarily of mink, fox, coyote, or sheared beaver.

HILLIS (400 E. Hyman Ave., tel. 970/925–8298) has fur coats and jackets for men and women, in skins such as Italian shearlings, sheared beaver, Russian sable, and chinchilla.

Gifts

ASPEN TEDDY BEAR COMPANY (602 E. Hyman Ave., tel. 970/ 429–0689). You can't help but smile in this shop: there are shelves and shelves of bears of all shapes, sizes, and colors—and they're not just for kids. The one-of-a-kind bears, which can be quite pricey, are for true collectors of any age.

C. B. PAWS (420 E. Hyman Ave., tel. 970/925–5848) carries the latest in accessories for the pampered dog or cat.

COOKING SCHOOL OF ASPEN (414 E. Hyman Ave., tel. 970/ 920–1879), in addition to its classes, offers a large selection of cookbooks and an enticing array of gourmet condiments, oils, and kitchen accessories for foodies.

DEAR JOHN (205 S. Mill St., tel. 970/920–4400) has a tastefully edited selection of cards, stationery, and invitations, as well as ribbons and wrapping paper.

FUNKY MOUNTAIN THREADS (520 E. Durant Ave., tel. 970/ 925–4665) is the type of store you're more apt to find in Crested Butte or Telluride: Indian-print skirts and dresses, loads of silver jewelry, and offbeat picture frames, candles, and knickknacks.

LES CHEFS D'ASPEN (405 S. Hunter St., tel. 970/925–6217) is a colorful emporium of kitchenware, cookbooks, serving pieces, table linens, picture frames, and glassware.

PEN PERFECTO (645 E. Durant Ave., tel. 970/544–9777) specializes in writing instruments of all types as well as cigars and smoking accessories.

PORSCHE DESIGN (402 S. Galena St., tel. 970/920–2889) has novel, streamlined accessories and gear—watches, luggage, cookwear, the ultramodern bicycle—from the firm started by F. A. Porsche, of the German car family.

WALNUT HOUSE (303 S. Galena St., tel. 970/925–7973), affectionately known as the Nut House, carries unique frames and photo albums, in addition to cameras and film.

Glass

HIGHLINE GALLERY (213 S. Mill St., tel. 970/920–9098) features large-scale glass sculptures and other mixed-media work.

THE RACHAEL COLLECTION (433 E. Cooper Ave., tel. 970/920–1313) has exquisite glass art, ranging from large-scale sculptures to paperweights and wine glasses; the reverse-painted lamp shades from Ulli Darni are especially beautiful.

Home Furnishings

AMEN WARDY HOME (210 S. Galena St., tel. 970/920–7700) is a vast emporium of objects, from the sensible to the frou-frou. Nothing is in short supply: large-scale serving platters of ceramic or pewter, decorative glassware, dinnerware, candles of all shapes and fragrances, aromatherapy soaps and lotions, table linens in both fabric and high-quality paper, and specialty condiments.

THE ASPEN COLLECTION (205 S. Mill St., tel. 970/925–1368), housed in two locations in Mill St. Plaza, is a treasure trove of English and French country antique furniture, vintage European lighting, and unusual accessories. High-end upholstered furniture with designer fabrics is a new addition, and a stock of Kiehl's toiletries is a welcome holdover from a previous business.

CHEQUERS (520 E. Cooper Ave., tel. 970/925–7572) carries a nice selection of home accessories, including glass- and tableware, lamps, throws, and silk flowers. The look is a mix of French country, Tuscan villa, and Western mountain lodge.

ISBERIAN RUG COMPANY (520 E. Hyman Ave., tel. 970/925–8062) deals in ornate rugs of all kinds: Oriental, Navajo, kilim, and antique.

LIFEFORMS (614 E. Cooper Ave., tel. 970/920–3708) specializes in artistic wood furniture that mixes modern style with rustic forms. Bed frames, wine racks, and tables, for example, are created in woods such as juniper, bristlecone, birch bark, or salvaged barn siding. Many of the made-to-order pieces come out of the owner's studio in nearby Carbondale.

ZONA (107 S. Mill St., tel. 970/925–3763). Entering this store is akin to walking into a very upscale flea market, with an eclectic mix of home furnishings, jewelry, candles, body care items, linens, and books, all arranged in artfully created yet seemingly impromptu displays.

Jewelry

ROSS ANDREWS DESIGNER GOLDSMITH (520 E. Durant Ave., tel. 970/925–3909) has been operating in Aspen for close to two decades, offering a range of styles and custom designs (many in platinum) made on site. The shop also sells larger diamonds at wholesale prices.

THE ASPEN GOLDSMITH (205 S. Mill St., tel. 970/544–9410), Frank Heger, crafts classic, high-quality pieces out of 18-karat gold and platinum in his cozy on-site studio.

BLACK PEARL ASPEN (302 S. Galena, tel. 970/920–1511) does indeed specialize in jewelry creations featuring luminescent black pearls.

CHEPITA (525 E. Cooper Ave., tel. 970/925–2871) creatively mixes the fun and the beautiful in its selection of jewelry, watches, and decorative pieces. Humorous ceramic sculptures, wood carvings, ornate mirrors, and Mexican pewterware are also part of the mix.

GOLDEN BOUGH (433 E. Hyman Ave., tel. 970/925–2660) features the designs in 14-karat gold of owners Ingrid Antony and Susan Williams. Their singular collar necklaces can be customized with slide-on jeweled bands.

HWR JEWELRY (318 S. Galena St., tel. 970/925–4610) is one of only a few locations in the U.S. for Fred Leighton jewels. Much of

The Sky's the Limit

Money burning a hole in your pocket? A shopping spree through Aspen can help you get rid of it in a hurry.

First, make sure you're adequately hydrated (it's a dry climate, after all) by strapping on an ostrich water-bottle holder, sized to fit a liter of Evian, from **Lana Marks** ($1,490). Then pay homage to the Ute Indians who originally settled the valley with a visit to **Curious George Collectibles** to purchase Chief Ouray's Winchester rifle ($150,000). Need something for the game room? How about a custom-made pool table of Rocky Mountain juniper ($30,000 at **Lifeforms**) and a museum-quality Ansel Adams print of the Tetons and the Snake River to hang beside it ($180,000 at **Edward Carter Gallery**)? Of course, one shouldn't visit Aspen without acquiring jewelry of some sort. A pair of ruby-and-diamond earrings from **Christopher Walling** ($120,000) or an 18-karat gold, emerald, and pavé-diamond watch from **Bvlgari** ($214,000; 605 E. Cooper Ave., 970/925-6225) may fit the bill. And don't forget the pooch—surprise him with a handwoven leather dog bed from **Gucci** ($1,150) or maybe just a simple Gucci frisbee, in black, of course ($50). Is your spouse ready to divorce you right about now? Don an 18-karat gold ring embellished with "DIVORCED" just for the occasion, available at **Kieselstein-Cord** ($1,495). Stomach hurt after the spending spree? Lie back and relax with a cashmere-enveloped water bottle from **Malo** ($215; 520 E. Durant Ave., tel. 970/925-3111).

the other jewelry comes from Italy. You'll also find Patek Philippe and Gerald Genta watches for men and women.

A. HYKES STUDIO (205 S. Mill St., tel. 970/920–3364) is best known for the custom metal work of owner Allan Hykes, which includes intricate belt buckles and cigar accessories. Celebrity clients include Hank Williams, Jr., and Michael Jackson.

LANCIANI (402 S. Hunter St., tel. 970/544–6364) carries what it bills as "travel jewelry," from Italy—that is, pieces that look just like the expensive gems you bought but are now too afraid to wear.

MISSTYX (400 E. Hyman, tel. 970/544–3842) has oodles of hair accessories and affordable jewelry, in addition to fanciful hats and bags. A teenage girl could easily spend hours here.

CHRISTOPHER WALLING (431 E. Hopkins Ave., tel. 970/925–1930) carries the substantial creations of New York jewelry designer Walling—known for his work with 18-karat gold, pearls, and unusual flower-form pins—as well as the vintage-style work of Elizabeth Locke, which incorporates 19-karat gold and, often, 17th-century Venetian glass molds.

Leather

HENRY BEGUELIN (614B E. Cooper Ave., tel. 970/920–2925) is the first U.S. store of this Italian leather designer that handcrafts stylish shoes, jackets, bags, home accessories, and even furniture (the woven leather–topped tables are truly novel).

KIESELSTEIN-CORD OF ASPEN (635 E. Cooper Ave., tel. 970/544–5183), a branch for the New York jewelry and leather designer, seems more museum than store, with everything ensconced behind glass (perhaps the prices justify this). On display are formal purses, many with Kieselstein-Cord's trademark animal motif clasps; huge, sculpted belt buckles; and chunky jewelry.

LANA MARKS (211 S. Galena St., tel. 970/925–9333) showcases its beautiful albeit pricey purses throughout the gallerylike store. The South African–born designer is known for her use of exotic dyed skins, such as ostrich and alligator. Belts, small leather goods, and several items of classically styled women's clothing are also on view.

LOUIS VUITTON (201 S. Galena St., tel. 970/544–8200), which shares space with Christian Dior, carries luggage, purses, wallets, and other small leather goods, many adorned with the company's distinctive logo. There's even a Louis Vuitton dog carrier for the ultra-chic pooch.

Miscellaneous

ASPEN LUGGAGE COMPANY (529 E. Cooper Ave., tel. 970/925–9368) features its own line of rugged wheeled duffels, ski and golf bags, and carry-on luggage. You'll find standard brands here as well.

CARL'S PHARMACY (306 E Main St., tel. 970/925–3273) is Aspen's version of the general store—with a second story devoted to art supplies, kitchen items, sewing needs, housewares, and other small, practical goods—as well as a full pharmacy and the largest newsstand in town.

STARS MEMORABILIA (525 E. Cooper Ave., tel. 970/920–2920) stocks rare collectibles for avid sports fans, music lovers, movie aficionados, or history buffs, much of it autographed: baseball jerseys, guitars, album covers, film posters, historical documents, and photographs, to name a few.

Musical Instruments

GREAT DIVIDE MUSIC STORE (111 S. Monarch St., tel. 970/925–7492) specializes in stringed instruments, primarily guitars, though a few mandolins, violins, and others are snuck into the mix. Also worth a look are the CDs, which include bluegrass and folk as well as just about every local musician.

Perfumes

COS BAR (309 S. Galena St., tel. 970/925–6249) stocks designer scents as well as cosmetics and toiletries from companies such as Clinique, Bobbi Brown, Lancôme, and Bliss.

Shoes

BLOOMINGBIRDS (304 S. Galena St., tel. 970/925–2241) is the place for upscale fashionable shoes for women, from the likes of Manolo Blahnik and Robert Clergerie.

KENNETH COLE (101 S. Mill St., tel. 970/920–6875) has all the fabulous and funky styles (as well as leather goods and jackets) that this witty shoe designer is known for.

MEPHISTO (205 S. Mill St., tel. 970/925–8220) carries the French company's feet-friendly, well-constructed walking shoes.

OZZIES SHOES (312 S. Hunter St., tel. 970/925–6270) has a well-rounded selection of functional and fun styles for men, women, and children, including hiking boots and athletic shoes.

Sporting Goods

ASPEN SPORTS (408 E. Cooper Ave., tel. 970/925–6331) carries sports gear as well as lots of casual sportswear for men and women at its largest location on the Cooper Avenue mall. The second level is devoted exclusively to ski and snowboard attire from Aspen's own Obermeyer.

HAMILTON SPORTS (520 E. Durant Ave., tel. 970/925–1200), owned by world-champion speed skier Jeff Hamilton, has a selection of hip ski and snowboard wear from up-and-coming lines like Kaotic, Ten 80, Ripcurl, and Eider. In the summer, the store carries surf and beach wear as well as hiking accessories.

MCDONOUGH'S (419 E. Cooper Ave., tel. 970/925–7576) specializes in high-end skiwear for men and women, including the largest selection of Bogner in Aspen.

PERFORMANCE SKI (408 S. Hunter St., tel. 970/925–8657) is where the style-setters flock to get outfitted in Prada and Postcard before hitting Bonnie's on Aspen Mountain for lunch.

POMEROY SPORTS (614 E. Durant Ave., tel. 970/925–7875) carries men's and women's casual clothing along with ski and hiking gear.

STEFAN KAELIN FOR WOMEN (447 E. Cooper Ave., tel. 970/925–2989) is one of very few ski shops in the country that cater solely to women (in summer, the focus switches to tennis and golf). The shop stocks two levels of primarily high-end women's sports clothing as well as skis and boots specifically designed for women. Another Stefan Kaelin outlet, with men's and unisex gear, is at 516 Durant Avenue.

SUREFOOT (520 E. Durant Ave., tel. 970/925–9235) is a ski-boot specialist, offering custom footbeds and solutions to fit problems, in addition to a large selection of boots.

UTE MOUNTAINEER (308 S. Mill St., tel. 970/920–2094) has everything for the outdoor enthusiast: men's and women's clothing from companies such as Marmot, Mountain Hardwear, Patagonia, Cloudveil, and Sierra Designs; sleeping bags, packs, and tents; hiking boots; telemark skiing equipment; guidebooks and maps—and friendly advice.

Toys

GERANIUMS 'N SUNSHINE (208 E. Main St., tel. 970/925–6641), housed in a cheerfully painted Victorian, is a bit removed from the main shopping district, but worth the trip if you have kids. You'll find a multitude of upscale children's clothing, pre-Nintendo-era toys, and hand-painted furniture. For adults, there are brightly colored gift items, casual jewelry (some of it made locally), and primitive-style furniture.

SHORT SPORT (613 E. Cooper Ave., tel. 970/920–3195) has all manner of games, toys, and stuffed animals for young visitors.

In winter, Aspen's largest selection of kids' skiwear fills about half of the store; in summer, bathing suits and kids' active clothing—and even more toys—fill the space.

SNOWMASS VILLAGE MALL
Books

SNOWMASS PHOTOS AND BOOKS (tel. 970/923-5898), under the Silvertree Hotel, stocks regional guidebooks, best-sellers, and an extensive selection of souvenir picture frames.

Clothes

COLLECTIONS (tel. 970/923-2134) is a snug, two-level shop with women's Western garb on the first floor and home furnishings with a Western bent on the second.

LOCAL COLOR (tel. 970/923-6058), a sister store to Local Traffic, carries casual, nontrendy women's sportswear and jewelry. There's a small kids' section, too.

LOCAL TRAFFIC (tel. 970/923-4983) is known for its high-end women's Western clothing and accessories, lots of leather and suede, and Southwestern jewelry. The Milligan sweaters, intricately patterned chenille pullovers made by rural women in New Mexico, are always striking.

STEIN ERIKSEN (tel. 970/923-3665) is the Snowmass venue for men's and women's designer skiwear from Bogner, Postcard, and Versace, along with sophisticated casual clothing and small home accessories.

Gifts

SNOWPAWS (tel. 970/923-7755) has a great selection of unique gift items for cats and dogs, including collars, leashes, treats, and toys. Owners can enjoy housewares, books, and fun accessories related to their four-legged friends.

STEPHEN'S (tel. 970/922–0047) carries fur, leathers, and shearlings in winter; in summer, the store undergoes a bit of a transformation, increasing its stock of Southwestern and Native American goods, including drums, totem poles, and carved animal furnishings.

Jewelry

BRIGHT AND SHINY THINGS (tel. 970/923–4666) lives up to its name, with lots of informal jewelry, primarily in silver.

ELIZABETH RYAN (tel. 970/923–1777) sells classic women's jewelry as well as paperweights, glassware, Swarovski crystal figurines, and small Waterford crystal boxes.

Sporting Goods

ASPEN SPORTS (tel. 970/923–6111). *See* Aspen store description, *above.*

CHRISTY SPORTS (tel. 970/923–2717) offers moderately priced skiwear in addition to sporting goods.

D&E SNOWBOARD SHOP (tel. 970/923–2337).

GENE TAYLOR'S SPORTING GOODS (tel. 970/923–4336) carries sports gear as well as unique ski hats handloomed on site in the winter by Detha Mika; she also does custom designs.

SHORT SPORT (tel. 970/923–5010). *See* Aspen store description, *above.*

Aspen was a languishing silver-mining town until the startling discovery that the real riches were not buried within the mountains but lying on their surface. The first ski run was cut on Aspen Mountain in the late 1930s, and word spread quickly. Today, Aspen and Snowmass are regarded as world-class ski resorts—and for good reason.

In this Chapter

THE SLOPES 81 • Aspen Mountain 81 • Aspen Highlands 87 • Buttermilk Mountain 92 • Snowmass 100 • AMATEUR AND PROFESSIONAL COMPETITIONS 105 • SKI EQUIPMENT AND SERVICES 107

By Gavin Ehringer

downhill skiing

ASPEN. THE WORD ALONE CONJURES UP MYRIAD IMAGES. Movie stars and supermodels. Cobblestone walkways lined with gingerbread brick buildings. Ballet, theater, and classical music concerts. Women in fur coats escorted by men with cell phones glued to their ears. Wealth and privilege. But at the heart of Aspen, there are the mountains and the skiing. Aspen's ski slopes are as much the embodiment of the "Aspen Idea" as the Wheeler Opera House, the Aspen Institute, and the Summer Music Festival.

It is the interplay of body, mind, and soul that visionaries like Walter Paepcke and Freidl Pfeifer were after when, back in the 1940s, they set about building Aspen up from a decrepit mining town to a world-renowned center of culture, intellect, and of course, great skiing. And that's what sets Aspen apart from the other ski resorts of Colorado—the entire Aspen experience. Some ski resorts have great mountains, others have great towns. Aspen has both.

Four different mountains comprise Aspen. All are managed by the Aspen Skiing Company, and one lift ticket gives access to all. Nonetheless, you'll find that each of Aspen's mountains has its own distinct personality and purpose.

ASPEN MOUNTAIN. Rising up from the very heart of downtown, Aspen Mountain is known for its steep terrain, its torturous bumps, and its historical claim to being Colorado's first true resort skiing destination. The mountain, which is

the only Colorado ski area off-limits to snowboarders, has the clubby pretentiousness of an exclusive private golf club—and its visitors seem to prefer it that way.

ASPEN HIGHLANDS. The renegade. The untamed wild child. A place where hardcore skiers can test their mettle against some of the most challenging in-bounds, off-piste extreme skiing in the state. A place of unsurpassed views and uncrowded runs.

SNOWMASS. Big, bold, and modern, with an emphasis on comfort and convenience. A sprawling mountain with a suburban flavor and a reputation for gentle rolling boulevards of groomed perfection. But with enough spirit (and terrain) to test the limits of even the boldest skier or snowboarder.

BUTTERMILK. The teaching mountain. The area that fills a fond place in the hearts of first-time skiers and snowboarders long after they've graduated to other peaks.

Aspen once bragged that its lift passes were the most expensive in the U.S.; today, the resort downplays that somewhat dubious distinction. Still, skiing here remains expensive, with a top day rate of $65. However, almost nobody pays full price. For details on costs of passes, and just about anything else, contact the **Aspen Skiing Company.** As a rule, kids under six ski free, as do seniors 70 and over. Reduced rates are available for children 7–12, teens 13–17, and seniors 65–69. Adults 18–64 can purchase advance tickets, with prices as low as $52 per day based on a 6-day pass. Off-season prices (Nov., Apr.) may be lower. Lift tickets are valid at Aspen Mountain, Aspen Highlands, Buttermilk Mountain, and Snowmass. For advance ticket sales, call 877–AT–ASPEN. *Aspen Skiing Co., Box 1248, Aspen, CO 81612, tel. 970/925–1220 or 800/525–6200. $65 for 1-day pass. Nov. 20–April 23, Mon.–Sun. 9 am–4 pm. AE, MC, V. www.skiaspen.com*

THE SLOPES
Aspen Mountain

Base Elevation: 7,945 ft
Summit Elevation: 11,212 ft
Vertical Drop: 3,267 ft
Skiable Terrain: 675 acres
Number of Trails: 76
Longest Run: 3 mi
Lifts and Capacity: 1 gondola, 1 high-speed quad, 2 quads, 1 high-speed double, 3 doubles; 10,775 skiers per hour
Average Annual Snowfall: 300 inches
Number of Skiing Days 1999–2000: 139
Snowmaking: 210 acres
Terrain Mix: Novice 0%, Intermediate 35%, Expert 65%
Snowboarding: no

Two things initially surprise first-time visitors to Aspen Mountain: the first is its size, just 675 acres—less than one-quarter the acreage of nearby Snowmass; the second is the absence of any novice runs. Those curiosities aside, this is a magnificent, rippling mountain whose peaks thrust high above its namesake town. Steep chutes, mogul-rich pitches, and gladed ridges are tucked in the folds of its granite apron.

What you see from the base area is only the tip of this multifaceted mountain, but the hidden treasures are relatively easy to discover. From the top you can reach any of the three main ridges that comprise the mountain's skiing network. To your left as you look down (the west) is Ruthie's Ridge, the site of most of the straight-ahead giant-slalom cruising runs; from Ruthie's you can also reach the area known as the Dumps, a series of double–black-diamond gladed chutes. On the far west extreme of Ruthie's is Aztec, site of one of the toughest World Cup downhill courses in the world.

The middle ridge is actually a separate peak called Bell Mountain, and its three sides—Face, Ridge, and Back—offer a series of snow-packed mogul pitches and some outstanding tree skiing. The uppermost part of the mountain, on the eastern fringe, is Gentleman's Ridge, with both the easiest intermediate runs and the tough, mean, and unrelenting far-eastern pitches of Walsh's Gulch.

In between Gentleman's Ridge and Bell Mountain Ridge are Spar and Copper gulches, which funnel skier traffic to the gondola base. Spar has the steepest sides as it cuts a distinct V-shaped groove through the heart of the mountain, but it's also well groomed and begs to be skied fast. Copper is wider and gentler, with a ripple of moguls just smooth and round enough to provide exhilaration without acceleration.

Getting up the mountain is a snap, as the entire town serves as a base area. On Durant Avenue in the center of town is the Silver Queen gondola, a six-passenger bullet that shoots to the summit in just 15 minutes. Although this is the fastest way to be transported up the mountain, it's also the most crowded; during weekends and holidays savvy skiers head over to the slower but less busy Lift 1A, a few blocks west of the gondola, between S. Monarch and Aspen streets. Lift 1A begins a two-lift ride that lets you off at either the lower mountain, Ruthie's Ridge and the Dumps, or at the summit runs. The three-leg journey all the way to the top (1A to Ruthie's Lift, then a short run down to the bottom of Ajax Express) takes about 25 minutes.

Aspen Mountain's simple layout and lift system make it easy to reach all sectors. There are no terminally tedious traverses, few flat spots, no endless cat tracks—just an honest, straightforward ski area best characterized by the 3-mi descent down 3,300 vertical ft from the summit to the base area at the bottom of the gondola.

NOVICES

There are no novice trails on Aspen Mountain. Even the most modest intermediate runs—of which there are precious few—are beyond the capability of beginners and even wannabe intermediates. Beginners and borderline intermediates should head either for Snowmass, or better still to Buttermilk's superb novice terrain.

INTERMEDIATES

If you can't handle bumps or are unable to link together strong, precise turns on unforgiving terrain, you may be overestimating your ability to handle—and, more important, to enjoy—Aspen Mountain. For the steady, strong intermediate skier, however, Aspen Mountain has a tremendous mix of steep giant-slalom cruising and even steeper bump skiing.

The Silver Queen gondola is the fastest route to the summit, where most of the tamest intermediate runs are found. You can stick to the upper part of the mountain by riding Lift 3, the high-speed quad, which serves the runs to the left (looking down); or Lift 7, which gives access to the runs off Gent's Ridge to the right. Keep in mind that this moderate terrain can be the most crowded part of the mountain. From the summit try 1&2 Leaf, a wide, well-groomed trail that's one of the easiest on the mountain. Next to that is Copper Cutoff, which is slightly steeper but still consistently maintained.

Another good, well-groomed cruiser is Dipsy Doodle, which cuts under Lift 3 and winds across to Bonnie's Restaurant. Stay to the right on the upper part of the run if you don't like bumps. Buckhorn is still another good cruiser, although it becomes heavily traveled and as a result develops icy and bare spots. Silver Bell and Silver Dip are a pair of smooth trails that feed you back to the bottom of Lift 3; after skiing on either you can try Blondies, a slightly steeper and shorter run that sometimes develops small moguls.

When the crowds start to build on the upper mountain, head for Bell Mountain—the middle peak—which tends to be much less crowded than the runs served by the gondola. If you're heading over from the summit, take 1&2 Leaf, staying to the right of the gondola, then follow one of the traverses that go to either side of Bell. You can also get to Bell Mountain runs from the base area by taking Lift 4, skiing across Little Nell to the bottom of Lift 5, and then cruising down Deer Park.

If you want a little challenge, try the Face of Bell, which is not a single run but a broad area of glade skiing that holds the snow well. It occasionally develops a good crop of moguls that tend to be well rounded and fairly easy to pick through. You can spend several hours exploring the Face, taking different routes through the trees and riding Lifts 3 and 6 for shorter runs or Lift 5 for longer runs. Although the Face is considered an expert area, a strong intermediate can handle most of the terrain—and avoid the rest. It's a good place to head after you've warmed up on some of the more traditional blue runs.

Spar Gulch is a good warm-up run if you start the day on Bell, but as it's the main thoroughfare down the mountain, it gets crowded, especially in the afternoon. You can pick up the tempo on Spar by skiing up and down the Face.

Another good way to avoid the crowds is to start your day on Lift 1A, at the west end of town. This takes you halfway up the western ridge, Aztec, and from there you can ski down to Lift 8, which takes you to the top of the area known as Ruthie's. Ruthie's Run is a fantastic high-speed cruiser that forms part of the World Cup downhill course. For the full measure of this run, take Ruthie's, which is fairly flat; veer left on Summer Road to the top of Aztec, which is steep but smooth; and then pick up Spring Pitch to Strawpile to 5th Avenue, heading back to the bottom of Lift 1A. Keep in mind that while Ruthie's side of the mountain is less crowded than other areas, it's best to ski it in the morning before the sun turns the snow heavy and the moguls develop.

Don't overlook the lower part of the mountain—to the west side—served by Lift 1A. Magnifico Cutoff/Lower Magnifico is a smooth, groomed cruiser; or try Strawpile, a wide giant-slalom cruiser with good pitch. You can add some zest to Strawpile by cutting right just below Ruthie's restaurant and hammering down the small, well-rounded moguls on Corkscrew.

EXPERTS

In the morning before the snow gets junky, head up Lift 1A (at the west end of town), then shoot up Lift 8 to the area known as the Dumps (from the gondola you can reach the Dumps by skiing down Buckhorn to Ruthie's Run and staying left all the way over to the top of Lift 6). Immediately to the left of Lift 6 is Bear Paw Glade, a steep section with monster moguls and deep snow that will really wake up your knees. When you reach the end of Bear Paw, keep right to reach Lift 6 again. If you stay left, you'll shoot into Spar Gulch for a faster and longer run down to the bottom of Lift 5. Zaugg Dump, Perry's Prowl, and Last Dollar are other bump runs in the Dumps; all tend to have good snow, fat but well-shaped moguls, and not much skier traffic. These trails are for those who can launch a turn anytime on any bump. All these short, steep bumpers are reached from International, which is a fairly tame, wide boulevard from which most experts cut away as soon as possible. However, if you stick it out past Last Dollar to Silver Queen, you'll be rewarded: this is an outrageous deep-powder power run that begins with a mogul field and then plunges down toward the Elevator Shaft, a precipitous pitch that's one of the steepest on the mountain. From the Elevator you can go down one of two steep, narrow, and mogul-packed runs: either cut right down Niagara over to Lift 5 or go left via Tower Ten Road to Franklin Dump.

In late morning take Lift 5 to the Face of Bell Mountain, where you can dance in the glades; or from the top of Lift 5, follow the Ridge of Bell to Shoulder for the longest ride on Bell Mountain. Just before Tower 19 cut left onto the Shoulder of Bell—a steeper, more heavily moguled run than the Face. The Ridge and the Shoulder usually have the best mogul runs on the mountain, and you'd better be prepared to handle the terrain because everyone in the gondola gets a "bump's-eye" view of your talent, especially when you're on the Ridge. Both the Shoulder and the Ridge feed back down to the bottom of Lift 5, but skier traffic can become heavy at lunchtime and at the end of the day, especially through the Grand Junction area. You can avoid the crowds by keeping right (looking down) through the trees.

If you have a hankering for super-steep and deep trails, head for the Walsh's Gulch area, on the east side of the mountain. Be warned, though, that this is tough, ungroomed terrain, so don't overestimate your ability. Take the gondola to the summit and ski across 1&2 Leaf to North Star for a good, steep bump run. Take the same route to a trio of runs that drop like elevator shafts down toward the Roaring Fork River. These three runs were opened in 1985, along with a number of unnamed, unpatrolled, and officially unrecommended alternatives. Before that they were the private preserve of the daring. Sadly, during the 1970s three local skiers were killed as they attempted to take on the 500 vertical ft of the most sustained steeps and avalanche-prone runs on Aspen Mountain.

These days, active patrolling and steady traffic reduce the avalanche danger, but they're still the sort of runs that can beat you to death with their relentless 35- to 40-degree pitch and primo moguls. The first run you'll encounter is Walsh's, where—unless there was a good dump the night before—the first 100 yards or so is too steep to hold a lot of snow. Going into Walsh's straight over the top can be disastrous, so if there isn't much snow, it's best to cut left by the trees for a few turns and head back to the main chute to Hyrup's. This run merges into Walsh's halfway down, then into Kristi. Both are as mean and unrelenting as Walsh's, with the same penalty for the adrenaline-challenged: whichever route you choose, there's only one way back to the

Gent's Ridge chair, and that's via Lud's Lane—a terminally tedious flat (even a bit uphill) that requires a lot of momentum to overcome.

Aspen Highlands

Base Elevation: 8,040 ft
Summit Elevation: 11,675 ft
Vertical Drop: 3,635 ft
Skiable Terrain: 680 acres
Number of Trails: 70
Longest Run: 3.5 mi
Lifts and Capacity: 3 high-speed quads, 1 triple; 5,400 skiers per hour
Average Annual Snowfall: 300 inches
Number of Skiing Days 1999–2000: 111
Snowmaking: 110 acres
Terrain Mix: Novice 20%, Intermediate 33%, Expert 47%
Snowboarding: yes

With its steep, backcountry terrain, its inspiring views of the Maroon Bells, and its isolated location 3 mi outside the town of Aspen, Highlands long ago established itself as the locals' preferred ski area. Less crowded than either Snowmass or Aspen Mountain, Aspen Highlands tends to be shunned by tourists, who seem to prefer the ample amenities of Aspen Mountain or the groomed highways of Snowmass.

Once viewed as the maverick ski area, Aspen Highlands came under the direction of the Aspen Skiing Company in 1993. Almost immediately, the resort began undergoing a transformation. Three new high-speed quad lifts have replaced the aging two-seat chairs of old, and a new base area, Highlands Village, featuring a pedestrian mall with shops, restaurants, condominiums, and residential homes, is already under way. The design motif of this developing base area recalls the National Park architecture constructed in the Depression era, relying heavily upon massive

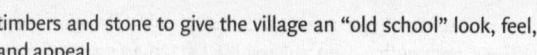

timbers and stone to give the village an "old school" look, feel, and appeal.

Such changes are likely to bolster the allure of Aspen Highlands and forever damage the area's reputation as a "best-kept secret" among the Aspen ski areas. No matter. The essential experience of Aspen Highlands—great skiing and unsurpassed scenery—will not be diminished.

Aspen Highlands is laid out in a narrow vertical line along the ridge of Loge Peak, an 11,675-ft mountain that stands as a sentinel to the exquisite Maroon Valley. Heavily laden with black and double–black-diamond experts runs, which make up about half of the trails here, Highlands is most enjoyable to the skier or snowboarder who is comfortable with steep runs, tricky double-fall lines, and moguls.

The vast majority of easy runs are clustered west of the main Exhibition quad chair, where grooming equipment transforms the gentle valleys into broad boulevards suitable for rank beginners. Intermediates have a plethora of choices underneath the Cloud Nine chairlift, a mid-mountain lift featuring an intimate cabin dining experience at the Cloud Nine Bistro, located just below the top lift shack. Experts, however, have the run of the high-alpine Loge lift, which accesses the Highland Bowl and the recently opened "Y Zones," a section of steep chutes characterized by massive moguls, double-fall line steeps, and pine-covered glades. Don't venture out onto these trails unless you have solid skills on wild and ungroomed terrain, or pay the penalty trying to gingerly pick your way down some of the most difficult and challenging terrain to be found inbounds anywhere in Colorado.

NOVICES

Your best strategy is to stick with the runs below the Exhibition lift, as there are no beginner-friendly trails farther up the mountain. From the top of Exhibition, you can take any of the trails that stretch like fingers extending out below the cafeteria-style restaurant located just west of the lift shack. Exhibition is an especially wide and easy run that takes you down Prospector Gulch, whose banked sides are especially favored by snowboarders. Down mountain, the runs funnel into a short intermediate run called Golden Barrel, where you may encounter some mild moguls. When you reach Park Avenue, a cat road, don't make the mistake of continuing straight down Lower Stein, a tilted mogul field that is designated "experts only."

Instead, make a sharp right on Park Avenue and stay high on the cat road as it winds its way back to the base via the Smuggler Trail. Other suggested runs in the Prospector Gulch area include Red Onion, Apple Strudel, Prospector, and Riverside Drive. When you get bored with these easy groomers, you can step up to the challenge of the Golden Horn intermediate trail, a broad expanse of snow directly below the resort's spine. From the Exhibition chair, head skier's right down Prospector. Follow the T Lazy 7 trail (be sure to maintain your speed, as this area is quite flat), until the terrain opens up to become Golden Horn. Don't take any of the chutes to your left as you wind through the woods on T Lazy 7, as all of these runs are steep, ungroomed, and difficult.

INTERMEDIATES

If the lift line at Exhibition is crowded first thing in the morning, skip the crowd and hop aboard the Thunderbowl lift for the first warm-up of the day. This lift will deposit you right at the top of Golden Horn, a wide and easy groomer that takes you down to Thunderbowl. Once your blood is flowing, you can ride the Exhibition quad, skirt the restaurant at skier's right, and drop down a short section of Apple Strudel to catch a ride on the Cloud Nine lift. From here, your choices are myriad. Upper Robinsons, located on the ski area boundary closest to the Maroon Creek Valley, is an obvious choice for powder hounds, as it tends to be one of the last runs skied. Similarly, the run adjacent to it, Pyramid Park, is another good bet for facials.

If you'd like to take a full-mountain cruise to the Highlands base, follow any of the runs near the Cloud Nine lift—Gunbarrel, Scarlett's Run, Heather Bedlam, and Dean's are all popular choices. These will funnel you into the area above the Exhibition lift and down Prospector Gulch, the easiest (and most crowded) area at Highlands. After making some turns on either Red Onion or Exhibition, cross the tree bands at the foot of Prospector Gulch and head skiers' left to take a stroll down Memory Lane, a short but fun groomer that leads to the Park Avenue cat road. Stay on Park Ave. as it meanders underneath the Exhibition and Thunderbowl lifts into Upper Jerome, a slow-skiing area that's broad, easy, and sometimes a little bumpy. Later in the day, you may want to take the Loge Peak lift to the top to take in the view. Take the Broadway Trail underneath the lift, dropping off the ridgeline on either Hayden, Meadows, or Kandahar to return to the Loge Peak Trail. Don't even think of running any of the double–black-diamond terrain in the Highland Bowl Y Zones, however tempting they may look.

EXPERTS

Early in the day, the best strategy for skiing Highlands is to use the morning sun to your advantage. That means avoiding the shaded areas on the mountain's north-facing slopes in favor of the sunny runs near the Loge Peak summit. Before plunging into the chutes, all of which are accessible from the Loge Peak chair, take some turns from the summit on Broadway, following Hayden or Meadows back down to the base of the Loge Peak lift. While you cruise Broadway, take the opportunity to scope the double-black expert runs to your right. The first three runs—Hyde Park, Mushroom, and Lucky Find—are narrow chutes with plenty of trees and moguls. Temerity, on the outer fringes, is strictly a tree run, best tackled later in the day after the more obvious slopes have been chewed up. Above Temerity are the Y Zones and the B Zones, recently opened "backcountry" areas with some of the steepest inbounds skiing anywhere. It's a 20-

to 30-minute hike along the ridge, but well worth the effort if you want to experience some untrammeled bowl skiing.

If you are not comfortable with extreme tree skiing, pass these first few trails off of Broadway for either Kessler's Bowl or Garmisch, which are less constricted. Kessler's can be a little disconcerting—it has a wicked double-fall line that inclines you toward a stand of trees. Not a nice place to take a tumble.

All of the trails here deposit you onto the Grand Traverse, an uncomfortably long pathway that skirts an aspen grove and pine forest before depositing you onto Andrew's, the access trail that leads you to the base of the Loge Peak lift.

If there's been a recent snow storm, you might wish to bypass the lift and continue down the mountain to connect with the T Lazy 7 trail, which accesses the steep and short runs that branch off from Golden Horn. All of these runs—Sherwood Forest, Bob's Glade, Upper Stein, Lower Golden Horn, Audacious, and Epicure—tend to be great powder stashes. Once the powder is skied off, these shorties become bone-jarring bump runs, enjoyable only to those who like mogul skiing.

SNOWBOARDERS

Given Aspen Mountain's "no snowboarders" policy, a large proportion of the "big mountain" boarders come to Highlands. The result is an atmosphere that is more funky and boarder-friendly than any of the other Aspen peaks. Beginners should stick with the easy runs located underneath the Exhibition quad, and pay attention to the black diamond "experts" signs all over the mountain—a wrong turn can get you into some hairy situations. For nice, easy groomers, try Prospector, Exhibition, Red Onion, and (lower on the mountain) Nugget. All of the trails funneling down to Prospector Gulch area are wide and smooth, and they have the added bonus of being rimmed gullies that allow for mellow surfing on the banked walls.

Intermediates can pass on the lower mountain and head up the Cloud Nine lift to board the many blue-square runs located below the Olympic Bowl. A terrain park, "Spin Cycle," is also located just beneath the Cloud Nine lift and features an excellent halfpipe once a sufficient snow pack has developed.

After sampling the intermediate runs on Cloud Nine, pass the Merry-Go-Round Restaurant at the top of Exhibition and take a long cruiser back to the base, or cut some turns on Prospector. By staying high on Prospector, you can follow the cat road that runs along the ridgeline to Golden Horn, the wide-open cruiser that deposits you into Thunderbowl, and from there you can continue down to the Highlands Village base.

Finally, here's a top-to-bottom romp suggested by Aspen's director of snowboarding, Kevin Byford: starting from the top of the Loge Peak lift, head down Broadway to Hayden Meadows, then catch Prospector Gulch to Golden Barrel along Park Avenue and into Jerome Bowl. The entire trip will yield about 20 minutes of uninterrupted blue cruisin'.

Buttermilk Mountain

Base Elevation: 7,870 ft
Summit Elevation: 9,900 ft
Vertical Drop: 2,030 ft
Skiable Terrain: 420 acres
Number of Trails: 48
Longest Run: 3 mi
Lifts and Capacity: 1 high-speed quad; 5 doubles; 1 handle tow; 7,500 skiers per hour
Average Annual Snowfall: 200 inches
Number of Skiing Days 1999–2000: 111
Snowmaking: 108 acres/27%
Terrain Mix: Novice 35%, Intermediate 39%, Expert 26%
Snowboarding: yes

A logger who was fond of buttermilk is said to have inspired the name for Aspen's "teaching mountain." Like its namesake beverage, Buttermilk goes down smoothly.

Conceived by pioneering Aspen skier Freidl Pfeifer as a learning center that would accommodate skiers not yet skilled enough for unforgiving Aspen Mountain, Buttermilk opened in 1958 with a single rope tow lift and a warming hut. More than four decades later, the ski area has expanded considerably, but its basic purpose remains intact. Six chairlifts (including a high-speed quad), a surface lift, and a "magic carpet" lift for children serve the area's 420 acres of ballroom-smooth terrain, 75 percent of which is groomed on any given night. Functional rather than opulent, the 1960s-era base compound includes a cafeteria-style restaurant, retail shops, a rental equipment store, and a resort conference center.

Due to its "buttermilktoast" reputation, locals tend to bypass this ski area on their way to big-shouldered Snowmass, or stay closer to town and ski the mogul-studded Aspen Mountain or the wild and barely tamed Aspen Highlands. But a core contingent of skiers and boarders have discovered that Buttermilk provides an uncrowded and blissful cruiser's paradise.

Sure, Buttermilk attracts more than its share of neophytes, tiny tots, Midwesterners in Kansas City Chiefs jackets, and old-timers with blown-out knees. But it also lures a group of hardcore former world champion surfers like Joey Cabell, Mickey Munoz, and Gerry "Mr. Pipeline" Lopez. These surfers-cum-snowboarders have been among the more than 100 participants in the annual Pure Carve Expression Session, an event sponsored by a local snowboard shop that specializes in racing/carving snowboards. By laying down six-inch-deep trenches on Buttermilk's corduroy, these riders demonstrate the potential of this often-derided "beginners" area. Also among the carving enthusiasts is Martina Navratilova, who joins friends on an almost weekly basis to crank turns on the gentle piste.

Extreme Terrain

While Aspen can lay claim to many superlatives, it is neither the steepest nor the deepest extreme skiing in Colorado. Nevertheless, Aspen offers true experts plenty of heart-pounding opportunities to test their abilities.

Those who prefer the open glacier skiing of Europe will feel most at home at Snowmass. The Cirque Headwall, Gowdy's, and AMF (locals say it stands for "Adios, My Friend") offer terrain that can usually be found only on backcountry heliskiing adventures. Gowdy's, a gully that traps snow during storms, is a particular favorite of snowboarders.

Loge Peak at Aspen Highlands, somewhat lower (11,675 ft) and more protected than the Cirque, offers more consistent conditions. On the negative side, the runs of Highland Bowl are shorter, the hike in longer, and long traverses out of the area are the rule. Those who hunger for untracked steeps will nonetheless head directly to Loge Peak's summit and make the 30-minute hike to the Highland Bowl. Here, one can drop the rabid runs of the B Zones, until recently an off-limits series of ungroomed steeps that give pause to all but the boldest extreme skiers. On Fridays, the Ski & Snowboard Schools of Aspen offer free guided tours of the B Zones, Y Zones, and Highland Bowl. Those unfamiliar with the terrain are advised to attend.

Aspen Mountain abounds with steep, bumpy experts' slopes, particularly Kristi's, Hyrups, and Walsh's, near the 11,212-ft summit. Sustained 40-degree slopes make these the most challenging runs in the Aspen ski areas. Those who like to dodge trees in addition to negotiating slopes that even a Humvee can't climb will find satisfaction on the Shoulder of Bell. If solitude is what you seek, sign up at the Aspen Mountain base concierge desk for "First Tracks," in which eight early birds board the gondola at 8 AM. The program is free to anyone with a lift pass—but only if you get there first.

To get a sense of Buttermilk's layout, it helps to think of the resort as having three distinct parts: Main Buttermilk, Buttermilk West, and Tiehack. Standing at the base area adjacent to the Summit Express quad chair, you can look directly to either side of the lift and see most of Main Buttermilk. Made up almost entirely of intermediate (blue) runs, Main Buttermilk also features the winding Homestead Road Trail, a green beginner's trail that makes it easy for novices to get back to the base.

At about the two o'clock position, you can gaze upward and make out the West Summit, Buttermilk's highest point at 9,900 ft. Below West Summit, which is served by the Buttermilk West chair, lie the eight named trails that comprise Buttermilk West. Nearly all of these trails are freeway-wide beginner runs or easy intermediate runs, with the exception of the gladed Little Teaser Trail. What is unique about this arrangement is that Buttermilk is one of the few ski areas in North America where even the novice can enjoy the view from the highest point. And what a view it is—from the top, you can gaze down on the Maroon Valley, Pyramid Peak, and the often-photographed Maroon Bells.

On the eastern side of the mountain is Tiehack, whose moderately steep slopes afford skiers an excellent view of Aspen Highlands and its high point, 11,675-ft Loge Peak. Although designated an "advanced" skiers area, Tiehack's short pitches and impeccable grooming make it manageable for most intermediates. Be forewarned, though: conquering Tiehack's black-diamond runs doesn't adequately prepare you for the expert-only runs at Aspen Highlands, Snowmass, and Aspen Mountain, which tend to be ungroomed and bump-ridden or very steep. Keep in mind, there is no standard rating system for ski area slopes, and trail designations vary from one area to another. Tiehack's most challenging slopes would in all likelihood rate only as intermediate slopes on the other peaks.

That said, let's take a quick look around the base area. If you drove into the parking lot, you probably noticed very few cars. Don't be misled—you won't have the mountain all to yourself. Most people ride the excellent (and free) shuttle buses, which depart approximately every 15 minutes from Snowmass or Aspen between the hours of 8 AM and 4:30 PM. Look for the bus marquee that reads "Buttermilk."

Bus passengers disembark in front of Bumps, the main lodge area that houses a cafeteria-style restaurant, lockers, and retail shops. Directly across from Bumps is Pro Mountain Sports, the only rental facility at Buttermilk. Whether you are renting here or at one of the shops in Aspen or Snowmass, take this tip: try to stop in on the afternoon of your arrival, rather than in the morning when shop techs are busier than bees in a field of clover. The techs will have more time to fit you properly, you'll get a better selection of equipment, and your skis or snowboard will be ready and waiting when the lifts open the next morning. And, if you want to ski at another mountain later in the week, the rental shop's ski valet will deliver the skis to your next destination so you won't have to schlep your equipment yourself.

Pro Mountain Sports (with shops at the base areas of Aspen Highlands, Buttermilk, and the Two Creeks base at Snowmass) participates with the Ski & Snowboard Schools of Aspen to offer a special program called Beginner Magic. If you've never skied, this package of equipment, lift passes, and group instruction comes highly recommended. Single- and multiple-day packages are available. Buttermilk also offers the Powder Pandas program for kids 3 to 6, and age-group classes for school-aged children and teens. For information, check with Ski & Snowboard Schools of Aspen (tel. 970/923–1227).

BEGINNERS

Given Buttermilk's reputation as a teaching mountain, you owe it to yourself to take a lesson. Skiers and ski journalists routinely rank the Ski & Snowboard Schools of Aspen among the best in North America. The instructors at Buttermilk are hand-picked for their ability, patience, and courteousness. Classes meet in the area adjacent to the Summit Express quad lift.

Most novices begin at the lift-served ski-school hill just east of the Inn at Aspen Conference Center. Small children learn on Panda Peak, where a "magic carpet" helps get them up the gentle slope. (Tip: If you have kids but prefer to ski at Aspen Mountain, a purple bus will pick them up at Aspen's Gondola Plaza and bring them to Buttermilk. Inquire with the ski school for information.) From the learning areas, students graduate to the Summit Express, which carries passengers to the East Summit. Unless you want to descend to the base via the Homestead Road cat trail, head skier's left (that is, facing down the hill) toward Westward Ho, a wide, gentle highway that takes you to the bottom of West Buttermilk. Plan on spending at least half the day exploring the trails serviced by the Buttermilk West lift—Red Rover, Larkspur, Tom's Thumb—and the intermediate Camp Bird and Teaser. All of the runs are wide cruisers, with Camp Bird and Teaser earning their more difficult ratings due to short, moderately steep drops near the tops of the runs.

Once you've gained confidence skiing West Buttermilk, you can disembark from the lift and head skier's right down the short Tom's Thumb Trail. Catch Freidl's, which intersects with the intermediate Lover's Lane trail just west of the Savio Lift. This long, easy cruiser takes a sweeping right-hand dog leg through a stand of pine trees before intersecting Government, which ends at the Main Buttermilk base.

INTERMEDIATES
Buttermilk is a cruising and carving paradise, so brush up on your turning skills and be prepared to really set those boards on edge. Most first-timers stick close to the Summit Express lift, getting to know the wide expanses of the Lover's Lane,

Columbine, and Baby Doe trails. But in the early morning, when the ski schools are going out, the base area can become crowded, and the chairlift operators make frequent stops to untangle beginning skiers who have failed to load or unload properly. To avoid snafus, head east from the Cliff House restaurant at the East Summit and follow the short Savio Trail to where it connects with the Buckskin Trail. You can cut turns on this trail all the way to the base, or veer skier's right midway down the trail and explore the lower half of Sterner's, which features some natural jumps and catwalks.

Once at the base of Tiehack, you'll be riding the Lower Tiehack lift across relatively flat terrain to get to the Upper Tiehack lift, which takes you back to the Summit. To avoid having to ride both lifts again, take Ptarmigan on your next run and stay to the far right of the trail to connect with lower Sterner. As the trees on your right give way to open trail, you can spot the Upper Tiehack lift.

When the crowds thin around lunchtime, it's time to move to Main Buttermilk and explore the runs there. Lover's Lane, on the ski area boundary left of the chair, includes the Jacob's Ladder "teaching park," an intermediate snowpark that's much less intimidating than the Drop Zone terrain park located on the Spruce trail. Aspiring Jonny Moselys can gain some valuable skills here without paying heavily for mistakes.

EXPERTS

Before you start peering over at Aspen Highlands (just across the valley and visible from the top of the Summit Express lift) and wondering what you are doing at Buttermilk, take a deep breath and set your mind on improving your skiing form. There's no better place than Tiehack when you want to concentrate on your skiing rather than on the next series of bumps or trees ahead. So relax, go with the flow, and drop down Ptarmigan Trail for a quick warm-up run. Stay to the right or you'll miss the turnoff for Sterner's, which will take you to the Upper Tiehack chair.

Given Buttermilk's all-mountain grooming, you're unlikely to find many powder stashes here, but your best bets are Tiehack Trail and Racer's Edge, which define the eastern boundary of the resort. If, however, you like using trees as slalom poles and have grown weary of the groomed trails, either drop down Tiehack Parkway and ski the Ptarmigan Glade or continue down the trail just a few hundred feet to Timber Doodle Glade.

Once you've exhausted the possibilities of Tiehack, you may want to cross back over to Main Buttermilk and launch a few airs in the snowboard halfpipe. Just be sure to wait your turn at the top, shout "dropping in," when you go, and don't crowd any riders who are farther down the pipeline. Break any of these rules, and suffer the derision of the snowboarders, who practically live on this section of Buttermilk.

SNOWBOARDERS

Buttermilk's Drop Zone snowboard park has been hailed by snowboard magazines as one of the best in the country. Add to that Buttermilk's unparalleled cruising terrain and events such as the Pure Carve Expression Session and the annual Aspen Boarderfest (the entire mountain is turned over to boarders-only), and Buttermilk has found a place of respect in the snowboarding community. All ability levels can find something to like at Buttermilk, although all-mountain freeriders and those who enjoy backcountry terrain would do best to skip the trip. Aspen Highlands and Snowmass better fit the description of big, "all-mountain" mountains.

But beginners, freestylers, halfpipe pilots, and carvers can find much to love here. Novice riders should start with a group class and instructor from Ski & Snowboard Schools of Aspen. After learning the basics on the easy ski-school hill, you'll graduate to riding on the trails of Buttermilk West. Once you've mastered stopping and linked turns, you'll be ready for the easy runs on Main Buttermilk, such as Columbine, Spruce, and Lover's Lane.

Expect to ride for three to five days before moving up to the blue intermediate runs, however.

Intermediate riders can perfect their turns on the Tiehack side, emphasizing the Buckskin run, or try Teaser on the West Buttermilk side. These groomed cruisers are perfect for hard-boot carving boards or just laying down lines with your all-mountain stick. If you like bumps (very few boarders do), you won't find many here. But the mini-moguls that form on Javelin, Tiehack Trail, and Sterner will help intermediates find their groove. For introductory-level glade riding, try the well-spaced trees on Timber Doodle Glade, also located on the Tiehack side.

Expert boarders can either head straight for the Drop Zone terrain park and halfpipe on Spruce Trail in Main Buttermilk, or if there's been a fresh snowfall, point your board toward the Tiehack side and hunt for powder on Tiehack Parkway, Javelin, Sterner, and Racer's Edge. Check the grooming report, noting the trails that haven't been pawed by the snow cats. Carvers will usually find the nicest corduroy on Ptarmigan, Teaser, Lover's Lane, and Buckskin Trails.

Snowmass

Base Elevation: 8,104 ft
Summit Elevation: 12,510 ft
Vertical Drop: 4,406 ft
Skiable Terrain: 3,010 acres
Longest Run: 5.05 mi
Lifts and Capacity: 7 high-speed quads; 8 fixed-grip doubles; 5 surface lifts; 24,321 skiers per hour
Average Annual Snowfall: 300 inches
Number of Skiing Days 1999–2000: 139
Snowmaking: 140 acres
Terrain Mix: Novice 7%, Intermediate 55%, Expert 38%
Snowboarding: yes

Locals refer to it as "Snowmassive," an apt description of this sprawling 3,010-acre ski area. Although Snowmass is known for its long, groomed cruising runs, it's a little-known secret that the mountain offers some of Colorado's best advanced skiing, too. From bowl skiing below The Cirque's 12,510-ft summit to the massive bumps on Sam's Knob to the aspen and fir tree glades of Hanging Valley Wall, Snowmass is a veritable superstore when it comes to terrain features. Other than Vail, no other Colorado resort offers up the variety of Snowmass.

Unlike Vail, which seems to have been planned with all the forethought of the California state freeway system, Snowmass has a logical layout. There are six distinct sectors, each of which could constitute a modest ski area in its own right: Elk Camp, High Alpine/Alpine Springs, the Big Burn, Sam's Knob, Two Creeks, and Campground. With the exception of the last two, all funnel into the Snowmass Village base area.

Snowmass is laid out east-to-west along a ridge, with valleys separating the resort's six distinct sections. Beginning on the easternmost edge of the resort and low on the mountain is Two Creeks, a new expansion area made up entirely of easy intermediate cruisers. Nestled within the aspen groves just below the ski area boundary is a community of vacation condos and homes. Although most of these trails are merely a means to provide home owners and vacationers the benefit of ski-in, ski-out accommodations, there is one trail worthy of inspection: Longshot, an intermediate run that originates in the Elk Camp area and winds more than 3,200 ft through spacious glades of fir trees before ending at the Two Creeks base.

Elk Camp itself is notable for its assortment of above-treeline cruising runs, which are among the easiest and most enjoyable anywhere on the mountain. Due to its exposure, the area tends to be cold and the visibility low during snowstorms; it is best avoided on cold, cloudy days. West of Elk Camp is High Alpine, where the majority of advanced and expert slopes are concentrated. Higher up along the ridge is The Cirque, a recently opened area accessible either by hiking or via a Pomastyle surface lift. This treeless area is a favorite of backcountry "extreme skiers" tempted by dizzyingly steep runs on the largely untracked face. Only the bold and skillful should venture out onto The Cirque Headwall; intermediates can descend on the relatively manageable Rocky Mountain High (named, of course, to honor Aspen's long-time resident troubadour, John Denver).

Comprising the central area of Snowmass is the Big Burn, whose broad intermediate slopes are quite popular, particularly on sunny days. When the winds whip up or the snow falls, however, skiers are advised to abandon the Big Burn and head down to Sam's Knob, whose lower elevation and dense tree cover offer better protection from the elements. Sam's Knob is located above the main base area; from the summit, one can access Campground, on the westernmost boundary of Snowmass. Here, advanced skiers can enjoy relative seclusion, as very few snowriders venture this far from the beaten path. There are no beginner or intermediate trails in Campground.

Each of the individual Snowmass areas is easily reached from the central base village. Early morning traffic tends to spread out quickly; the only notable traffic jam usually occurs at the Burlingame lift, which takes you up to the Sam's Knob lift. From the top of Sam's Knob you can ski down to the Big Burn lift or head down into the Campground area. To avoid this crush, you can go to the Alpine Springs or Naked Lady lifts (via the Wood Run chair from the lower village area) or take the Funnel chair up to the Elk Camp lift or Two Creeks area.

For snowboarders, Snowmass has a comprehensive boarding program that is among the best in the country. A special terrain map points out the numerous snowboard-friendly trails and terrain parks while steering riders away from flat spots. Air junkies will want to visit Trenchtown, a new terrain park in the Coney Glade area that has two lift-accessed halfpipes, video evaluation, piped-in music, and a furnished yurt hangout.

BEGINNERS

True novices can head over to Assay Hill, a teaching area located just east of the Snowmass Center. If you are staying in Snowmass Village, just follow the trail over a stone footbridge until you spot the Assay Hill chair. Otherwise, walk out from the mall onto Fanny Hill, a gentle groomed run where most of the ski-school instruction takes place. A main thoroughfare, Fanny Hill can become quite crowded by midday. Since this area serves as a central meeting place, you may have to contend with overzealous snowriders who fail to heed the "slow skiing" signs, so be advised to keep your eyes open for speedsters.

Having mastered these beginner slopes, head up the Coney Glade lift to the steeper but still easy Max Park run, which curves around a pine forest before joining Lunchline. This meandering trail will lead you to Scooper and Dawdler, and eventually back to the Fanny Hill lift and Snowmass Village.

INTERMEDIATES

When you're ready to move up to gentle intermediates, your best bet is to head for the Elk Camp area on the eastern side of the resort. The mostly blue runs in this area are wide and well groomed and provide an excellent place to work on turns and enjoy gentle cruising. The cut of the runs is graceful and gradual, and if you continue past the bottom of the Elk Camp lift you can enjoy a long top-to-bottom intermediate cruise of more than 2 mi on smooth Adam's Avenue. If the weather isn't suitable for the exposed Elk Camp, head for the top of Big Burn but keep in mind that the easiest runs from the top are those to the left (looking down); the runs get more difficult as you go to the right. The easiest way from the top is via Sneaky's (to the far left, looking down) or Mick's Gully, which, although it has a slight gully shape, doesn't have the steepness or walls usually found in similar gully runs. It has a steady, easy pitch, and like Sneaky's, brings you back to the beginner's run, Max Park.

EXPERTS

The vast majority of expert terrain can be found far from the madding crowds who cluster around the Snowmass Village base. That means catching several chairlifts before actually getting to where you'd most like to ski. To jump-start your day, skip the Fanny Hill quad lift (the most obvious ride from Snowmass Village), and instead head for the Wood Run chair. After riding this short lift, head off skier's right to the Alpine Springs quad. From the top of this lift, follow the intermediate Turkey Trot trail right to the High Alpine lift.

There are any number of ways to ski High Alpine, the most obvious being to stick close to the chairlift and bash the bumps on Showcase, Reidar's, and the Edge, then catch the chair back to the top. Going farther afield begins to present logistical problems, as there is no single chair back to the top. Any of the trails on Hanging Valley Wall will require that you drop down to the intermediate Turkey Trot run, then circle back on Adam's Avenue to the Naked Lady lift. From the top of Naked Lady, ski off down Turkey Trot to once again pick up High Alpine.

For those who'd rather avoid the chairlift shuffle, continue down Turkey Trot past Gwyn's High Alpine Restaurant to the Sheer Bliss lift. This will deposit you in The Cirque. A short hike along up the ridge is well worth the effort, as the bowl area here is beautiful to behold—right out of the pages of *Powder* magazine. If hiking isn't in your plans, however, you can simply drop off the ridge into Gowdy's, KT Gully, or Garrett Gulch.

SNOWBOARDERS

The folks at Aspen Skiing Company go out of their way to coddle snowboarders at Snowmass. That's resulted in a lot of unique snowboarding terrain features and amenities unknown to other resorts. Every lift, for example, has its own tool table for fine-tuning snowboard bindings. Beginners would be advised to start at Buttermilk Mountain rather than learning to snowboard at Snowmass; fewer people and plenty of mellow beginner runs make the learning process there smoother. That said, Snowmass also has excellent instructors and plenty of novice trails.

Many classes begin on Assay Hill, a mellow beginner run just below the main Snowmass Center. Most beginners progress quickly to the Fanny Hill, Burlingame, and Coney Glade chairs, which access big, freeway-width runs ideal for learning to link turns. Intermediates find Snowmass ideal, particularly those who enjoy long, steady all-mountain cruisers.

From Elk Camp, intermediates can try Bull Run to Funnel to Fanny Hill. From High Alpine, take the black-diamond run Edge (a little steep and untamed, but manageable for strong intermediates) to the mellower Naked Lady, then follow that down to the Alpine Springs chair. From the Big Burn, take Mick's to Max Park to Lower Bonzai down to Fanny Hill. And from Sam's Knob, take a ride down Sunnyside to Ute Chute to Lunchline to Scooper and into Fanny Hill.

Experts may become addicted to Trenchtown, the new terrain park and halfpipe area in the Coney Glade area. However, it's worthwhile to do some backcountry roots riding in The Cirque, the massive bowl area in the Big Burn. It's a hike to get there, but The Cirque offers narrow chutes, bomb drops, and powder stashes that justify the extra effort. For dawn patrollers, the best place to find early morning, fresh powder is Sam's Knob, but hit it early—it gets trampled out by midday, when it's best to turn your attention to the trees in Sneaky's or over in the Big Burn.

AMATEUR AND PROFESSIONAL COMPETITIONS

Aspen hosts a long list of professional and amateur competitions including several annual events unique to this mountain town. Among the most famous is the Gulfstream 24 Hours of Aspen charity race, deemed the world's most grueling ski race. Held in December, the race involves 12 teams that ski round the clock down Aspen Mountain at speeds of up to 90 mi per hour. The only break the ski racers get is during the 14-minute gondola rides between runs.

On the opposite extreme is the annual Aspen Boarderfest, which gives never-evers a chance to try snowboarding on the gentle slopes of Buttermilk Mountain. Held in December, Boarderfest includes free demo boards, instruction, and a local boardercross competition. More formalized amateur snowboard competitions take place at Aspen Highlands and Snowmass, where United States Amateur Snowboard Association events are held sporadically throughout the ski season. Professional snowboarders take to the air during the Kick Aspen Big Air event held in January on Aspen—a rare chance to see boarders hucking aerials on the (usually) verboten slopes.

One other popular snowboard event is the Pure Carve Expression Sessions, which attracts hard-core surfing champions and carving board enthusiasts to the slopes of Aspen Highlands, Snowmass, and Buttermilk each January.

Ski racers can take part in the Aspen Town Race series, held at Aspen Highlands. The series includes advanced and recreational division Giant Slalom Races. Those who prefer freestyle competition can compete in (or just watch) Freestyle Fridays, a rather zany and informal event held January through March near the Merry-Go-Round Restaurant at Aspen Highlands.

Another popular participation event is the annual Mardi Gras "Mother of All Ascension Snowshoe Race," held each March at Snowmass. Snowshoers depart from the base area on a grueling climb up the slopes of Snowmass. For those who want to stargaze, Aspen hosts the Spirit of Skiing Pro/Celebrity race in January.

Late in the season, telemarkers get their chance to shine in the America's Uphill Race held on Aspen Mountain. Held in March, the event tests the endurance of skinny-ski enthusiasts as they slog their way up Aspen—with no assistance from the ski lifts. Also in March is the Rocky Mountain Masters Super G Downhill Race at Aspen Highlands.

Finishing the competitive season are the Snowmass Spring Ski & Snowboard Jam, a raucous party and competition involving professional and amateur snowboarders, and the Elk Mountain Grand Traverse, a tough cross-country event in which skiers race over the pass separating Aspen and Crested Butte. Information on any of the ski-racing events can be obtained by calling the **Aspen Skiing Company** (tel. 970/925–1220).

SKI EQUIPMENT AND SERVICES

The following listings cover Aspen Mountain, Aspen Highlands, Buttermilk, and Snowmass.

ASPEN SPORTS (408 E. Cooper Ave., Aspen, tel. 970/925–6332; 303 E. Durant, Aspen, tel. 970/925–6332; Snowmass Village Mall, Snowmass, tel. 970/923–6111; Snowmass Center, Snowmass, tel. 970/923–3566). Ski and snowboard rentals, sales, ski repair, custom boot fitting, gear and clothing for biking, camping, fly-fishing, workout.

BREEZE SKI RENTALS (555 E. Durant Ave., Aspen, tel. 970/925–1360; Snowmass Village Mall, Snowmass, tel. 970/923–3443). Performance ski and snowboard equipment, clothing, accessories, tune-up and repair.

CHRISTY SPORTS (50 Village Square, Snowmass Village, tel. 970/925–2717). Ski demos, ski sales, rentals, repair, clothing, and accessories.

GENE TAYLOR'S SPORTS (Snowmass Village Mall, Snowmass, tel. 970/923–4336). Ski and snowboard rentals. Demo equipment, clothing, accessories, skis, snowboards.

D&E SNOWBOARD & SKI RENTAL SHOP (Snowmass Village Mall, Snowmass, tel. 970/925–2337). Tuning, repair, rentals. Snowboard shop. Snowboard clothing and accessories.

GORSUCH LTD. (611 E. Durant Ave., Aspen, tel. 970/920–9388). Equipment rental, designer ski wear, resort fashions.

Freestyle Fridays

An old western saying holds that some cowboys work far from the road, and others work close to the highway. In ski country, there are those who ski far from the lifts, and those who ski close to them. Freestylers, who tend to be exhibitionists by nature, fall in the latter category. That's why Freestyle Fridays, a zany, fun, and often thrilling competition featuring Jonny Mosely wannabes, are a hit at Aspen Highlands. Held throughout February and March at Aspen Highlands, Freestyle Fridays attract Aspen's best bump-and-jump freestylers throwing their most daring tricks for the appreciative spectators gathered on the sundeck of the mid-mountain Merry-Go-Round restaurant. Open to anyone who is fearless or foolish enough to throw down in front of their friends, Freestyle Fridays provides a fitting stage for skiing exhibitionists.

HAMILTON SPORTS (Gondola Square, Aspen, tel. 970/925–1200). Demos, rentals, overnight ski storage, ski tuning, clothing, accessories.

HIGH SOCIETY (555 E. Durant Ave., Aspen, tel. 970/925–7889). Exclusive dealer of High Society skiwear and Stockli skis.

INCLINE SKI SHOP (555 E. Durant Ave., Aspen, tel. 970/925–7748). Ski rental equipment.

MCDONOUGH'S (419 E. Cooper Ave., Aspen, tel. 970/925–7748). Aspen's largest Bogner skiwear dealer; U.S. and European ski clothing.

PERFORMANCE SKI (408 S. Hunter St., Aspen, tel. 970/925–9657). Ski and snowboard equipment. Postcard, Armani, Chiemsee ski wear.

POMEROY SPORTS (614 E. Durant Ave., Aspen, tel. 970/925–7875). Skiing and biking repairs, sales, rentals.

PRO MOUNTAIN SPORTS (base of Buttermilk Mountain, Aspen, tel. 970/920–0980; base of Aspen Highlands, Aspen, tel. 970/544–3013; Two Creeks Lodge at Snowmass, tel. 970/923–8740). Owned by Aspen Skiing Co. Full-service equipment rental, clothing, accessories. Ski and snowboard tuning.

SKI SERVICE CENTER/BOARD WERKS (609 Rio Grande Place, Aspen, tel. 970/925–4469). Hand-tuning, repairs.

SNOWMASS SPORTS (Silvertree Plaza, Snowmass Village, tel. 970/923–3567). Ski rental and demos, ski sales, tuning.

SPORTSTALKER (428 E. Hyman Ave., Aspen, tel. 970/925–9237). Ski equipment, demos, accessories.

STAPLETON SPORTS (430 S. Spring St., Aspen, tel. 970/925–9169). Owned by former World Cup racer David Stapleton; rentals, demos, ski sales, repairs and tune-ups, clothing.

STEFAN KAELIN SKI & SPORTING EQUIPMENT (447 E. Cooper Ave., Aspen, tel. 970/925–2989). Parabolic skis, carving boards a specialty. Clothing, accessories.

SUIT YOURSELF, LLC (Aspen. tel. 970/920–0296). Mobile clothing, rental service for skiing and snowboarding. Mobile service in the Aspen and Snowmass area.

SUREFOOT (520 E. Durant Ave., Aspen, tel. 970/925–9235). Custom boot fitting and sales.

USE-IT-AGAIN (465 N. Mill St., Aspen, tel. 970/925–2483). Used ski and snowboard equipment sales.

UTE MOUNTAINEER (308 S. Mill St., Aspen. tel. 970/925–2849). Cross-country skis, telemark equipment, hut tours, telemark skiing. Rental equipment. Technical climbing equipment and mountain gear.

Aspen and Snowmass are famous for downhill skiing, but don't miss out on the other options, such as the superb cross-country skiing, snowshoeing, or dog sledding. When the snow melts, hiking, mountain biking, river rafting, and horseback riding are just a few of the ways to enjoy Aspen's natural beauty.

In this Chapter

THE MOUNTAINS 111 • WINTER SPORTS 113 • Cross-Country Skiing 113 • Dog Sledding 114 • Ice Climbing 114 • Ice Skating 114 • Sledding 115 • Sleigh Rides 115 • Snowmobiling 115 • Snowshoeing 116 • SUMMER AND YEAR-ROUND SPORTS 117 • Ballooning 117 • Bicycling 117 • Fishing 118 • Fitness Clubs 119 • Golf 120 • Hang Gliding/Paragliding 121 • Hiking 121 • Horseback Riding 123 • Mountain Biking 124 • Mountain Climbing 125 • Off-Road Driving 125 • Rafting, Kayaking, Canoeing 126

By Gavin Ehringer

other sports

ASPEN IS A HAVEN for active, adventurous souls. Whether snowshoeing up Ajax Mountain on a winter's morning or mountain biking along the Roaring Fork River in summer, Aspenites and visitors alike stay in near-constant motion. In summer they're out mountain biking along the Roaring Fork River, hiking, horseback riding, and fly-fishing for trout in any number of local streams. So whether your idea of a vacation includes scaling a 14,000-ft-high peak or just working on your golf handicap with a cocktail glass sweating in your cart, you'll not lack for recreational opportunities here.

THE MOUNTAINS

The Colorado Rockies provide some of the finest mountain scenery in the world, easily rivaling the Swiss Alps and the South American Andes. It's hard not to be moved and even awed by their raw, preternatural beauty, especially in Aspen. Situated as it is at the head of the 50-mi-long Roaring Fork River Valley, Aspen is a polished jewel nestled in an ornate setting of mountain ranges. To the north and west are the Elk Mountains wherein lie Aspen's famous ski areas as well as the Maroon Bells. To the east lies the Sawatch Range, a sawtoothed stand of glacial peaks that contains 15 of Colorado's 54 "Fourteeners"—mountains that rise more than 14,000 ft above sea level. Among these is nearby Mt. Elbert (14,433 ft), the highest peak in Colorado. In summer, bicyclists often brave automobile-choked Highway 82, riding to the top of 12,095-ft-high Independence Pass to get a view of this massive monolith.

That should be a tip-off to one truism about adventuring in Aspen—almost anything worth doing outdoors requires physical exertion, sometimes in copious quantities. Being in good shape makes it easier to enjoy the broad range of activities here, so if you've been lounging on the couch throughout much of the winter, you may want to start exercising weeks or even months in advance of your vacation. While the up-and-down nature of outdoor travel here is itself physically taxing, the lack of oxygen at high altitude (Colorado's air is about one-quarter less oxygen-dense than the air at sea level) means that even a gentle hike through the woods or a cross-country ski trip around the golf course can set most "flatlanders" to huffing and wheezing. Locals have an acquired advantage: living at altitude makes their blood more efficient at processing oxygen.

Therefore, give yourself a day or two to acclimate, go easy on the booze, and don't try and do too much when you first arrive. Listen to your body—a persistent headache, nausea, malaise, loss of appetite or restless sleep may be symptoms of altitude sickness. Anyone who exhibits such symptoms should rest and not venture to higher altitudes. If symptoms worsen and you experience confusion, loss of coordination, vomiting, or difficulty breathing, descend immediately to a lower elevation and seek medical help.

Don't let the beauty of the hills mask their dangers: mountain travel can be treacherous and even life-threatening at any time of year. Mountain weather is extremely unpredictable, and many are the hikers, golfers, and mountain bikers who have been overwhelmed by mid-afternoon summer thundershowers bearing golf ball–size hailstones and temperature drops of 20 degrees or more in an hour's time. Each winter, backcountry snowmobilers, skiers, and snowshoers are trapped in avalanches—Colorado leads all states in avalanche fatalities and injuries. Unless you are an experienced winter mountain traveler, it's advisable to hire a guide.

WINTER SPORTS
Cross-Country Skiing

It's hard to imagine a more serene way to see Colorado in wintertime than gliding on a pair of skinny skis, the sun glinting off freshly fallen powder snow. Aspen offers numerous cross-country skiing possibilities. Foremost among them are the Snowmass Club Cross Country Center and Aspen Cross Country Center. With a combined 40 mi of pathways, these two areas comprise the largest system of free, groomed Nordic trails in North America. At the **Snowmass Club Cross Country Center** (239 Snowmass Club Circle, just east of the Snowmass ski area base, tel. 970/923–3148), guests may rent or purchase equipment, take lessons, or register for scenic tours. The **Aspen Cross Country Center** (308 S. Mill St., tel. 970/544–9296) offers lessons, rentals, tours, and a retail store.

An option favored by wilderness devotees and gourmands is the trip up to the **Ashcroft Ski Touring Center & Pine Creek Cookhouse** (11399 Castle Creek Rd., Ashcroft tel. 970/925–1971 touring center; 970/925–1044 restaurant). Once a prosperous mining camp, Ashcroft fell on hard times before being revived as a cross-country ski center in 1971. Surrounded by 14,000-ft peaks, the center features 22 mi of groomed and maintained trails running through a wilderness of pine, fir, and aspen. Instruction programs for all age and ability levels, plus rental equipment, are available.

For the ultimate winter challenge, **Aspen Expeditions** (426 E. Spring St., tel. 970/925–7625) teaches courses in ski mountaineering, expedition training, winter camping, and avalanche forecasting. If you're interested in a multiday hut trip via the 10th Mountain Hut System (a premier winter touring system) or a guided "off-piste" snowboarding or alpine skiing trip from Aspen Highlands or Snowmass, the company can design group or individual trips to suit your ambitions.

Dog Sledding

A unique and much-talked-about experience in Aspen is the dog-powered sledding adventure organized by **Krabloonik Kennels** (4250 Divide Rd., Snowmass, tel. 970/923–3953). A team of loving and incredibly strong huskies takes you on a two-hour tour of the Snowmass–Maroon Bells wilderness. Each year, these same dogs compete in Alaska's famed Iditarod Dog Sled Race, a grueling 1,049-mi trek from Anchorage to Nome. You won't have to endure such hardships: the journey includes a four-course lunch and stops for scenic photos.

Ice Climbing

If you're truly adventurous, you may want to enlist the experienced alpine guides at the Rocky Mountain Climbing School to lead you up some of North America's best waterfall and alpine ice routes. Whether you are a beginner, an experienced intermediate, or an expert climber looking to advance your skills, the guides help to provide a safe and enjoyable climbing experience. Adventurers can also book trips to climb one of the Elk Mountain Range's 14,000-ft peaks, take a conditioning "hike" up 12,000-ft Mount Sopris, or take on the challenge of a more technical ascent of Capitol Peak, Pyramid Peak, or the Maroon Bells. **Aspen Expeditions/Rocky Mountain Climbing School** (426 S. Spring St., tel. 970/925–7625).

Ice Skating

Kids love ice skating, and there's no better excuse for romantic couples to spend an afternoon holding hands. You can skate indoors year-round at the **Aspen Ice Garden** (233 W. Hyman, tel. 970/925–5141). Hours vary due to hockey and figure-skating schedules; call in advance for the public skating schedule. **Aspen's Silver Circle Ice Rink** (433 E. Durant, tel. 970/925–1940), a small outdoor rink, rents skates and is open from 10 AM to 10 PM during ski season.

Sledding

Ride a classic wooden toboggan at the **Snowmass Cross-Country Ski Center** (239 Snowmass Club Circle, just east of the Snowmass ski area base, tel. 970/923-3148). The padded and fenced sledding hill at the center provides a safe, controlled sledding environment, and best of all—it's free! (Tip: If you don't have the dough to rent a toboggan, bring your own flexy flyer, plastic saucer, or a cookie sheet). Open daily, 9-4:30.

Sleigh Rides

If you've always wanted to dash through the snow in a one-horse open sleigh, the **T Lazy 7 Ranch** (3129 Maroon Creek Rd., tel. 970/925-4614) offers 90-minute tours to the Maroon Bells. Horse and buggy rides are also available in downtown Aspen— look for the draft horses and carriages at the east end of the Cooper Street Mall, near the Popcorn Wagon.

Snowmobiling

Smug cross-country skiers, snowshoers, and other self-propelled backcountry users may scoff at these noisy, polluting machines—until they've ridden one. It's hard not to be seduced by the thrilling speed and ground-covering capability of snowmobiles, and, to their credit, snowmobile companies are making quieter, less-polluting machines than in years past.

To appease both serenity seekers and thrill seekers, all but a few of the trails in the Aspen area and the surrounding White River National Forest are off-limits to snowmobiles with the exception of what is perhaps the most spectacular winter pathway of all: the road leading to the Maroon Bells. Daily tours to the Bells are offered at the **T Lazy 7 Ranch** (3129 Maroon Creek Rd., Aspen, tel. 970/925-4614). If you're staying in Snowmass Village, you need only stroll over to the **Snowmass Stables** (1020 Brush

Creek Rd., tel. 970/923–3075) to rent machines for a self-guided tour of the area.

Farther down the Roaring Fork Valley, snowmobiling abounds. In Woody Creek, **Western Adventures** (0555 Allen Way, Woody Creek,, tel. 970/923–3337) offers two- and three-hour guided tours through the White River National Forest, or you can rent machines for self-guided excursions. **Rocky Mountain Sports** (tel. 970/945–8885), adjacent to the Sunlight Mountain Resort ski area, has guided snowmobile tours on what is claimed to be the biggest groomed trail system in Colorado.

Snowshoeing

Snowshoeing has become the preferred winter exercise of Aspen's chic young women. Early in the morning, you'll spot these women (and a few men) stepping their way up Ajax, Snowmass, and Buttermilk. Guests can snowshoe up any of the four Aspen area mountains and get a free lift ride back down—it's much easier to climb in snowshoes than to descend. Route and time restrictions exist, so before you go, be sure to check with the **Aspen Skiing Co.** (tel. 800/525–6200 or 970/925–1220).

The **Aspen Center Environmental Studies** (Hallam Lake Wildlife Sanctuary, 100 Puppy Smith St., Aspen, tel. 970/925–5756) offers daily snowshoe tours atop Aspen Mountain and at Two Creeks at Snowmass. The two-hour tours familiarize guests with local flora and fauna as well as mountain ecosystems. The snowshoeing here is not strenuous and is suitable for people of almost any fitness level.

If you'd just like to rent snowshoes and tour on your own, get your gear at **Gorsuch Ltd.** (Aspen Gondola Plaza, tel. 970/925–3203). At **Ute Mountaineer** (308 S. Mills St., Aspen, tel. 970/925–2849), you can rent snowshoes, pick up maps, and get advice from the staff on the safest and most scenic routes.

SUMMER AND YEAR-ROUND SPORTS
Ballooning

Floating in a hot-air balloon 11,000-plus ft above the Roaring Fork Valley will add a whole new perspective to your visit. There is absolutely no more tranquil way to view the glacier-covered peaks of the Elk Range and the gingerbread Victorian mining town. Trips start at sunrise, when the air is cool and calm, so be sure to dress warmly. Your voyage ends with the traditional popping of champagne corks and a toast.

Two balloon companies operate in the Roaring Fork Valley: **Above it All Balloon** (tel. 970/379–3591), based in Basalt, offers family adventures or romantic escapes. **Unicorn Balloon** (tel. 970/925–5752) will videotape your adventure. Takeoff and landing sites depend on wind conditions. You can arrange with either company to be picked up and returned to your hotel.

Bicycling

Road bikers will find excellent rides around Aspen. First, there's **Maroon Creek Road,** a 20-mi stretch with an elevation gain of 1,700 ft. This is a popular biking route because traffic is sparse and the views of Maroon Bells are spectacular. From Highway 82 in Aspen, go west to Maroon Creek Road. You can park at the ski resort parking lot or bring your bike up on the Roaring Fork Transit bus.

Another popular ride is **Castle Creek Road,** which takes you to Ashcroft, an abandoned mining town. This trip is a little bit more difficult, since the altitude gain is just over 2,100 ft. The road is narrow and can have heavy traffic in summer, so it's best to get an early start. From Highway 82 in Aspen, go west to Castle Creek Road.

You can rent bikes from a number of companies. **The Hub of Aspen** (315 E. Hyman, tel. 970/925–7970), located directly

across the street from the Wheeler Opera House, offers bike rentals plus something more: mountain biking lessons through the Aspen Cycling School. Other rental shops include: **Ajax Bike and Sports** (635 Hyman Ave., Aspen, tel. 970/925–7662; 419 Main St., Carbondale, tel. 970/963–0128); **Aspen Velo Bicycles** (465 N. Mill St., Aspen, tel. 970/925–1495); **Breeze Ski Rentals/Aspen Bike Rentals** (635 E. Hyman, Aspen, tel. 970/925–1360); **Aspen Sports** (408 E. Cooper St., Aspen, tel. 970/925–6331). In Snowmass, contact: **Aspen Sports** (Snowmass Village Mall, Snowmass, tel. 970/923–6111); **Christy Sports** (50 Village Sq., Snowmass, tel. 970/923–2717); or **Gene Taylor Sports** (Snowmass Village Mall, Snowmass, tel. 970/923–4336).

If you prefer to sign up for a bicycle tour, the following outfits operate in the Roaring Fork River Valley. **Five Star Bicycle Tours** (tel. 970/544–4700); **Aspen Bike Tours** (tel. 970/920–4059); **Blazing Pedals Bike Tours** (tel. 970/923–4544); or **Timberline Bicycle Tours** (tel. 970/920–3217).

Fishing

Aspen is an angler's dream come true. In fact, fly-fishing has even become a popular winter pastime in Colorado. A surplus of sunny days and much less crowded streams than in the summer make angling in Aspen's frigid waters enjoyable.

The Aspen Ranger District of the White River National Forest offers some of the finest lake and stream trout habitat in the Rockies. Portions of the Roaring Fork River are designated for fly-fishing only, while nearby Frying Pan River offers challenging—and less crowded—waters. Several smaller streams (Lincoln Creek, Hunter Creek, Castle Creek, Maroon Creek, and Snowmass Creek) offer up their secrets to the most diligent fly fisherman, but don't ask a local outdoorsman where you might find a good pool—chances are, he'll just lie.

Fishing licenses are required for anyone 16 or older, and you must abide by daily bag requirements. Nonresidents can purchase annual licenses from the Colorado Department of Fish & Wildlife at a cost of $40.25; five-day and single-day licenses are also available. For information on fishing licenses, rules, and requirements, contact the **Colorado Department of Fish & Wildlife** (806 W. Hallam St., Denver, tel. 303/289–0232).

For guided trips and equipment, contact: **Aspen Outfitting Co.** (315 E. Dean St., in the lobby of the St. Regis Hotel, tel. 970/925–3406); **Aspen Sports** (303 E. Durant Ave., tel. 970/925–6332; **Aspen Trout Guides** (Stefan Kaelin Pro Shop at 516 E. Durant St., Aspen, tel. 970/925–1050); **Oxbow Outfitting Co.** (Little Nell Hotel, 675 E. Durant St., tel. 970/925–1505); and **The Outfitters** (Snowmass Village Mall, Snowmass, tel. 970/923–5959).

Fitness Clubs

Aspen's rich and famous keep their bodies beautiful at the **Aspen Club & Spa** (1450 Crystal Lake Rd., tel. 970/925–8900), a 77,000-square-ft facility that includes a full-service spa, health and fitness center, sports medicine institute, and the Center for Well-Being, a holistic health center addressing new-age therapies (acupuncture, meditation, yoga) as well as nutrition, reflexology and body work, and orthotics.

Just east of downtown, the facility is very chi-chi, with polished mirrors and carpeted locker rooms with saunas, whirlpools, and steam baths. While you work out, you can gaze out at the Elk Mountains or simply gaze at all the beautiful people as they sweat through their workouts in designer gear.

For those who prefer a more down-to-earth gym, try the **Aspen Athletic Club** (720 E. Hyman St., tel. 970/925–2531), which features the standard free weights, weight machines, indoor pool, cardiovascular machines, and aerobics classes.

Those interested in physical wellness may want to check out **Bikram's Yoga College of India** (465 N. Mill St., tel. 970/925-7276), where hatha yoga classes are held. The **Aspen Wellness Group** (449 E. Hopkins Ave., tel. 970/925-5070), is a holistic health clinic featuring nutritional counseling, acupuncture, massage, skin care, and chiropractic services.

Golf

Golfers will find an added bonus on high-altitude mountain courses: golf balls carry farther in the thin air and are less inclined to slice or hook. However, don't expect to see your scores drop miraculously, as these courses do not tend to reward the long ball, due to their tight designs and the occasional steep rises and falls necessitated by mountain topography.

The municipal golf course, called simply **The Aspen Golf Course** (39551 Hwy. 82, tel. 970/925-2145), is an 18-hole championship layout located just outside of town on Hwy. 82, the main thoroughfare. Tee times are apportioned on a first-come, first-served basis and must be made within 24 hours. Check in at the pro shop for rental clubs, golf carts, lessons, and practice balls. Greens fee: $45, $65–$85, depending on time of day.

The Snowmass Lodge & Club (Highline Rd., Snowmass, tel. 970/923-3148) is an 18-hole championship public course with driving range, equipment rentals, a pro shop, and snack bar. Greens fee: $98, golf cart included.

Take a 30-minute drive downvalley to Carbondale to play the **River Valley Ranch Golf Course** (303 River Valley Ranch Dr., Carbondale, tel. 970/963-0132). This 18-hole championship course affords excellent views of Mount Sopris and winds over and around the Crystal River, providing plenty of interesting water hazards. The pro shop offers rental clubs, carts, and lessons. Greens fee: $90, $105 with golf cart.

ONE LAST TRAVEL TIP:

Pack an easy way to reach the world.

Wherever you travel, the MCI WorldCom Card℠ is the easiest way to stay in touch. You can use it to call to and from more than 125 countries worldwide. And you can earn bonus miles every time you use your card. So go ahead, travel the world. MCI WorldCom℠ makes it even more rewarding. For additional access codes, visit **www.wcom.com/worldphone**.

MCI WORLDCOM.

EASY TO CALL WORLDWIDE

1. Just dial the WorldPhone® access number of the country you're calling from.
2. Dial or give the operator your MCI WorldCom Card number.
3. Dial or give the number you're calling.

Belgium ◆	0800-10012
Czech Republic ◆	00-42-000112
Denmark ◆	8001-0022
France ◆	0-800-99-0019
Germany	0800-888-8000
Hungary ◆	06▼-800-01411
Ireland	1-800-55-1001
Italy ◆	172-1022
Mexico	01-800-021-8000
Netherlands ◆	0800-022-91-22
Spain	900-99-0014
Switzerland ◆	0800-89-0222
United Kingdom	0800-89-0222
United States	1-800-888-8000

◆ Public phones may require deposit of coin or phone card for dial tone.   ▼ Wait for second dial tone.

EARN FREQUENT FLIER MILES

American Airlines AAdvantage      Delta Air Lines SkyMiles

    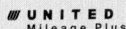   

Limit of one bonus program per customer. All airline program rules and conditions apply. © 2000 WorldCom, Inc. All Rights Reserved. The names, logos, and taglines identifying WorldCom's products and services are proprietary marks of WorldCom, Inc. or its subsidiaries. All third party marks are the proprietary marks of their respective owners.

© 2000 Visa U.S.A. Inc.

Paris, France.

Paris, Texas.

When it Comes to Getting Cash at an ATM, Same Thing.

Whether you're in Yosemite or Yemen, using your Visa® card or ATM card with the PLUS symbol is the easiest and most convenient way to get cash. Even if your bank is in Minneapolis and you're in Miami, Visa/PLUS ATMs make getting cash so easy, you'll feel right at home. After all, Visa/PLUS ATMs are open 24 hours a day, 7 days a week, rain or shine. And if you need help finding one of Visa's 627,000 ATMs in 127 countries worldwide, visit **visa.com/pd/atm**. We'll make finding an ATM as easy as finding the Eiffel Tower, the Pyramids or even the Grand Canyon.

It's Everywhere You Want To Be®

Hang Gliding/Paragliding

Step into the sky and soar with a certified U.S. Hang Gliding Association tandem pilot. With its strong thermals and exquisite scenery, Aspen is the perfect place to try paragliding, a hybrid sport that has grown out of advances in hang glider and parachuting design. You and your flight instructor take a running leap off a mountain peak, and within seconds, you are soaring over the Roaring Fork River. And, if you decide you want to make this once-in-a-lifetime thrill something you can do every weekend, **Aspen Paragliding** (426 S. Spring St., tel. 970/925-7625) offers equipment along with private and group courses leading to USHGA certification.

Hiking

Hiking is by far the single most popular summertime activity in Aspen. Of course, it requires very little in the way of specialized equipment and can be tailored to suit any fitness level. You can, for instance, take a leisurely stroll along the almost flat Rio Grande Trail that parallels the Roaring Fork River, or push yourself hard to reach American or Cathedral Lake.

At a slow pace, one sees not only the majestic grandeur of the mountain peaks but also the subtle beauty of the plants and animals. Each turn of the trail can bring a new perspective, and the occasional breathtaking spectacle of a waterfall, a doe with a newborn by her side, or an eagle taking flight.

There are numerous trails to hike: for complete information on trail conditions and advised routes, contact the **White River Forest Service** (806 W. Hallam St., tel. 970/925-3445). Here are three recommended hikes based on difficulty (easy, moderate, and difficult), close proximity to Aspen, and accessibility throughout most of the summer season.

Weller Lake Trail #1989. An easy stroll amid pines and aspens leading to a subalpine lake. Just over ½ mi in length, the trail is

easy to follow and can be covered in two hours' time. The snow pack melts off early here, allowing hikers to make the trek in late June all the way until the first snowfall in the fall. Access: take Highway 82 east out of Aspen, driving approximately 9 mi to the Weller Campground. Turn into a small parking lot just beyond the entrance to find the trailhead.

Crater Lake Trail #1975. This moderate hike over rocky trails, just under 2 mi in length, can be accomplished in two hours, round-trip. The Crater Lake Trail is popular as a starting point for extended forays into the Maroon Bells wilderness. The trail passes through groves of aspen and around intriguing rock formations, ending at a high mountain lake. Begin at Maroon Lake parking lot, head to your right to follow the Maroon Snowmass Trail. After traversing a meadow, you will come to a Forest Service signpost. From there, the trail climbs on rocky paths past aspens. After cresting a rise, you descend to the lake. To make a loop trip, head back to the rise, then watch for the signpost for the Maroon Creek Scenic trail. After a short, steep descent, the trail levels off somewhat. Two bridges allow you to cross over Maroon Creek, which feeds into Maroon Lake at the end farthest from the parking lot. A trail alongside the lake returns you to your starting point.

Cathedral Lake Trail #1984. Hikers and fishermen rave about the views of the Elk Mountain Range as seen from Cathedral Lake, but you'll have to work hard to earn them on this difficult, demanding trail. Just over 3 mi in length, the trail ascends through forest, alpine meadows, and loose rock called "scree" before reaching the pristine alpine lake. Plan on spending the better part of the day hiking, take plenty of extra food, clothing, and water, and be sure to get an early start if you hope to make it back to the car by sunset.

The trail climbs through an aspen forest before entering the Maroon-Snowmass Wilderness. Following a steeper second ascent, the trail follows Pine Creek, which is contained by a very narrow and, some might say, gloomy canyon. Near the top of the canyon, the trail levels off briefly, then takes a steep ascent through spruce forests and loose rock, followed by a series of tight switchbacks. When the trail forks (and it will, several times), always take the left fork. Cross Pine Creek, choosing the easiest route; you'll discover the lake just beyond the meadow on the right-hand side of the creek. Access: Drive ½ mi west of Aspen on Hwy. 82. Turn left at Maroon Creek Rd., then take an immediate left onto Castle Creek Rd. Drive 12 mi up Castle Creek Rd., turning left shortly past Ashcroft onto a gravel road. Continue ½ mi to the trailhead.

Horseback Riding

Aspen: where the Old West collides with the nouveau riche. While most of the cowboys that made this valley colorful have long since sold their saddles and moved to less expensive ranges, a few remain. Many of those that do earn a living running guest ranches or operating dude strings, so finding an outfitter here is quite easy.

Before you go, inquire into the nature of these guided trips. If you hope to canter or even gallop a little, you may be disappointed, as many outfitters prefer a gentle, controlled ride. This may be perfect for you, however, if you simply want to get out into the countryside and see a little scenery. **Snowmass Stables** is a licensed Colorado outfitter offering trail rides, hunting pack trips, and winter sleigh rides. Call ahead to reserve a saddle (1020 Brush Creek Rd., Snowmass, tel. 970/923–3075). **Capitol Peak Outfitters** (0554 Valley Rd., tel. 970/923–0211) offers rides by the hour, half- and full-day wilderness excursions, trips to the Maroon Bells and several high-alpine lakes, and overnight wilderness trips. **Snowmass Falls Outfitters** (11500 Snowmass Creek Rd., tel. 970/923–6343) has overnight pack trips, day rides, fishing trips, and big-game hunts. If pushing cattle around the rangeland strikes your fancy, pull your Stetson down low on your head and mosey down to Carbondale and

book a trip with **Rocky Mountain Cattle Moo-vers** (579 Main St., Carbondale, tel. 970/963–9666). Finally, the **T Lazy 7 Ranch** (3129 Maroon Creek Rd., tel. 970/925–4614) features day trips and overnight camping trips in the Maroon Bells wilderness.

Mountain Biking

Mountain biking was practically invented in Colorado (although Californians might claim otherwise). Regardless of where it began, there is no dispute that the state, with its hundreds of miles of single-track trails, forest-service roads, and paved bike paths, lends itself to the sport. Whether you are looking for a leisurely ride down a tree-lined pathway or a serious white-knuckle descent along the edge of a 1,000-ft-high cliff, you'll find it here.

Any of the local bike shops can supply you with trails and routes, but here are a few blue-ribbon favorites to begin with.

Rio Grande Trail. A flat, easy ride popular with cyclists, joggers, and dog walkers alike. The trail meanders along beside the Roaring Fork River for just over 4 mi. The first 2 mi from town are paved, then the trail switches to a broad dirt pathway that was formerly a railroad bed. Plan on a minimum of three hours to make the 8-mi-long ride. An excellent place for experienced cyclists to acclimate to high altitude.

To access the paved portion, take Main Street in Aspen. Turn north onto Mill Street and left at the four-way stop onto Puppy Smith Road.

Smuggler Mountain/Hunter Creek. Smuggler Road is a strenuous ride but one that doesn't require much technical riding skill. If you want to make a short, two-hour ride of it, simply follow this well-maintained four-wheel-drive road around to the back of Smuggler Mountain, where you will find a short, steep pathway on the right. The path leads to a platform affording a spectacular view of Aspen.

If you wish to continue, and have the skills to negotiate some steep single-track trails, continue onward to the place where the trail forks. Take the left fork and stay on the main trail for 2 mi until you come to a gate. Go around the gate and continue up hill. After approximately 1½ mi, you will come to an old bridge. Cross the bridge and turn left, following the trail along the west side of the river, crossing back over the stream via the Tenth Mountain Bridge. From there, a single-track trail continues steeply through the trees and crosses Benedict Bridge. Keep going straight, and you'll reach the paved road of Hunter Creek. Follow this to the intersection of Red Mountain Road, hang a left, and follow Red Mountain Road back to Aspen.

For a list of local companies that rent mountain bikes, *see* Bicycling, *above*.

Mountain Climbing

It is hard to describe the feeling of accomplishment that comes with reaching the summit of a high peak and looking out over a vast landscape of mountains far below. Aspen attracts a great number of climbing adventurers, and many of them pay for their beans and bread by leading tourists up the peaks. Unless you've had serious backcountry training and experience, it's best to climb with a certified mountain guide. You should start a strenuous exercise program long in advance of your trip to prepare for the demands of climbing at altitude.

For more information on rock climbing and mountaineering, contact **Aspen Alpine Guides** (Box 659, Aspen 81611, tel. 970/925–6618) or **Aspen Expeditions/Rocky Mountain Climbing School** (426 Spring St., tel. 970/925–7710).

Off-Road Driving

There are several four-wheel-drive "jeep" roads near Aspen. The following three are suggested:

Lincoln Creek Road to Ruby. Drive east up Independence Pass on Hwy. 82 approximately 11 mi to Lincoln Creek Road. Turn right and drive 6 mi to Grizzly Creek Reservoir.

Lenado to Kobey Park. Lenado is a semi–ghost town that was once a center of logging activity in the Roaring Fork region. Drive west on Hwy. 82 from Aspen. Take the Woody Creek turnoff on the right-hand side. At the bottom of the hill, cross the bridge and turn left ¼ mi beyond the Woody Creek Tavern. Make a sharp right onto Woody Creek Road and drive 10 mi to Lenado. Continue on Lumber Road #405 to the top of the mountain and Kobey Park. This old logging area has many spur roads winding through it, all of which are suitable for exploring. Here you can find outstanding views of the Sawatch Range and the Williams and Elk mountains. It is especially popular in fall, when the aspen leaves are in high color. Be cautious in early summer, as the roads can be muddy and nearly impossible, even with a capable four-wheel-drive vehicle.

Capitol Creek Road. Drive 14 mi west on Hwy. 82 to Old Snowmass, and turn left at the Conoco gas station. Continue 2 mi to a "T". Go right and proceed 5 mi until the pavement ends. Follow the road approximately 3 mi to the Capitol Creek trailhead.

Four companies offer four-wheel-drive "jeep" tours: **Aspen Adventure** (311 Aspen St., tel. 970/925–4386); **Alpine Safaris** (534 Spruce St., tel. 970/925–6643); **Aspen Redhead Tours** (Box 1886, tel. 970/925–6643); and **Blazing Trails Backcountry Excursions** (Mill St. & Hyman Ave., tel. 970/923–4544).

Rafting, Kayaking, Canoeing

Aspen doesn't offer much thrilling whitewater rafting, but nearby Glenwood Springs (located along the banks of the mighty Colorado) does. Whitewater season begins in late May and runs through October on the Colorado and the Roaring Fork. For

Preparing for Mountain Adventures

Whatever the season, you should always be prepared when venturing into the mountains: at a minimum, summertime adventurers should carry extra food and water, waterproof rain gear, and clothing sufficient to weather an emergency overnight stay in the woods. Other potentially life-saving gear includes a topographic map and compass, a first-aid kit, signaling devices such as a mirror and a whistle, a lighter, sunglasses, and sunscreen.

Even if your ramblings take you no farther than the ski slopes or the golf course, it's a good idea to bring along water, a sun hat, and plenty of sunscreen. Dehydration is a real hazard at higher altitudes, and in the thin air, severe sunburns can occur even on cloudy days.

One final caution: don't count on your cellular phone in the mountains, where peaks often cause signal interference. For further information on safe mountain travel, contact **Mountain Rescue Aspen** (630 West Main St., Aspen, 81611).

guided raft trips, contact **Aspen Adventure** (311 Aspen St., tel. 970/925–4386), **Blazing Paddles Raft Trips** (407 E. Hyman Ave., tel. 970/923–4544 or 800/282–7238), or **Colorado Riff-Raft** (555 E. Durant Ave., tel. 970/925–5405 or 800/759–3939).

If you'd rather captain your own ship, you can get kayaking instruction with American Canoeing Association–certified instructors at the **Aspen Kayak School** (315 Oak Lane, tel. 970/925–6248).

For the past 50 years, Aspen has been a cultural mecca. Locals and visitors can sample opera and ballet performances, outstanding music festivals, and an intriguing and well-documented mining history.

In this Chapter

WHAT TO SEE 129 • Aspen 129 • Snowmass 142

By Cindy Hirschfeld

here and there

IN ADDITION TO HISTORIC REMINDERS of Aspen's mining past, the Aspen/Snowmass area offers a compelling combination of towering 14,000-plus-ft peaks, renowned showcases of art and music, and organizations like the intellectually provocative Aspen Institute. The best way to explore Aspen is on foot, meandering among the many Victorian-era buildings of downtown or marveling at the meticulously restored Victorian houses, or the newer luxury homes of the residential West End. If you'd prefer to leave the walking to someone else, horse-carriage tours leave regularly from the eastern end of the Cooper Avenue pedestrian mall in summer and winter. Despite the accusations of overwhelming glitz that are often tossed Aspen's way, you'll discover that beneath its polished facade, Aspen is still a living, breathing town, with plenty of genuine charm. To reach the outlying ghost towns, as well as some of the Snowmass sights, a car is helpful, though there are several sightseeing tour companies that will drive you around on guided forays (look for the information flyers at one of Aspen's three visitor centers).

WHAT TO SEE
Aspen

ASHCROFT GHOST TOWN. Located in a wildflower-strewn meadow in Castle Creek Valley, Ashcroft was established by silver prospectors in the summer of 1880. During its heyday, the mining town was home to as many as 2,500 residents, as well as up to 20

saloons, two newspapers, and a dance hall. By 1887, however, many of its citizens, drawn by Aspen's richer mines and new railroad service, had moved away, taking their cabins with them.

Today several buildings remain, including the Hotel View and the Blue Mirror Saloon, which were somewhat rehabilitated in the 1970s. Several other remaining cabins provide a picture of a mining town that, unlike Aspen, did not make it past the stage of cabins and smaller wooden buildings.

The Ashcroft site later played a role in the establishment of skiing in Aspen. The Highland-Bavarian Lodge was built in 1936 while a group of "powder prospectors" explored the surrounding area, including Mount Hayden, as the site for Aspen's first ski area. World War II delayed the plans, however, and after the war's end, focus shifted to the more centrally located Aspen Mountain.

The former town site is now managed by the Aspen Historical Society, and an information booth is staffed daily from 10–4, mid-June to Labor Day. For more insight into the natural history of the area, join the free one-hour walk guided by naturalists from the Aspen Center for Environmental Studies, Mondays, Wednesdays, and Fridays at 10 AM. Note that dogs are not allowed in the ghost town. *10 mi from Aspen up Castle Creek Rd., tel. 970/925–3721. $3. Year-round.*

ASPEN ART MUSEUM. This museum is a small treasure, with two gallery spaces that house an ongoing series of revolving exhibits, almost all produced by the museum itself. The museum's emphasis is on American contemporary art and, in accord with the rest of the town's sophisticated cultural scene, the shows feature thought-provoking collections of world-class art. Each October the work of local artists is shown at the Roaring Fork Open/Annual.

Located in a parklike setting on the Roaring Fork River, the museum was established in 1979. It's housed in a building of some interest in and of itself: one of the first hydroelectric plants west of the Mississippi. Free lectures, featuring prominent artists and museum directors, are scheduled regularly. *590 N. Mill St., tel. 970/925–8050. $3, free Sat. and Thurs. after 6. Tues.–Sat. 10–6; Thurs. 10–7; Sun. noon–6.*

ASPEN HISTORICAL SOCIETY. Two regularly scheduled guided walking tours are organized by the historical society in the summer: one through Aspen's West End and the other through downtown. Both give insight into some of Aspen's more notable Victorian-era buildings and those from the early 20th century. Highlights include the Italianate-style Community Church, built of local sandstone; the classically Victorian Sardy House, now a hotel; the Wheeler Opera House; and the historic Hotel Jerome. The tours last about an hour. Downtown tours meet at the Wheeler Opera House; West End tours begin at the Wheeler-Stallard House, in front of the Historical Society offices.

If you prefer to wander at your leisure, look for a new brochure from the Historical Society at hotels in Aspen. It details a self-guided walking tour and gives the history of various significant sites and buildings around town. *620 W. Bleeker St., tel. 970/925–3721. $10. Mon., Wed., Fri., 9:30.*

ASPEN MEADOWS. The symbolic heart of modern Aspen, Aspen Meadows is where Walter Paepcke's vision of the "Aspen Idea"—nurturing body, mind, and spirit—was conceived and implemented. Located on 40 acres adjacent to the Roaring Fork River, in the West End, the Meadows encompasses the Aspen Institute, the Aspen Center for Physics, and the Benedict Music Tent and Harris Hall, the two principal venues of the Aspen Music Festival. The annual June International Design Conference in Aspen is also held at the Meadows.

A stroll through the Meadows' bucolic grounds is a pleasant way to while away an hour or so. Pick up a map at the Bandar bin Sultan Reception Center on Meadows Road. Views of the ski

aspen exploring

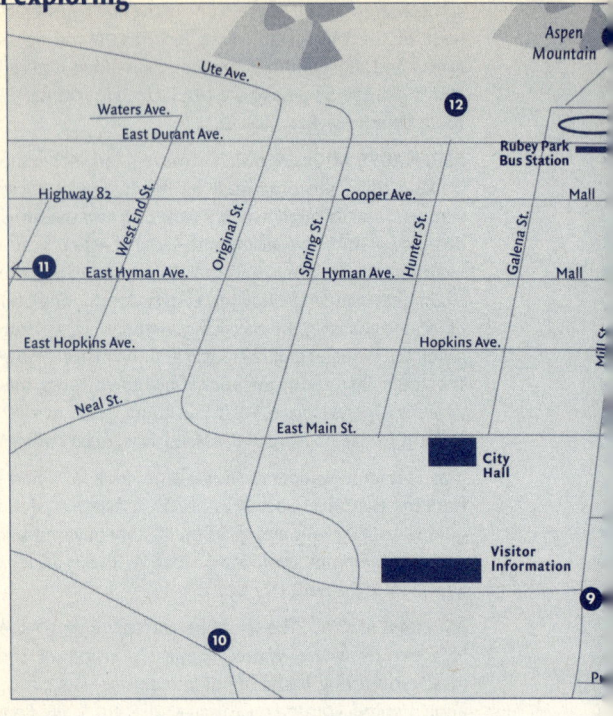

Ashcroft Ghost Town, 1
Aspen Art Museum, 9
Aspen Historical Society, 5
Aspen Meadows, 4
Basalt, 3
Benedict Music Tent, 7
Compromise Mine, 13
Gondola, 12
Hallam Lake Nature Preserve, 8
Hotel Jerome, 15
Independence Ghost Town, 11
Maroon Bells, 2
Smuggler Mine, 10
Wheeler Opera House, 14
Wheeler-Stallard House, 6

133

Aspen Mountain • 13
Snark St.
Silver Circle Ice Rink
East Dean St.
Juan St.
Durant Ave.
Koch Park
Mall
Wagner Park
Cooper Ave.
Mall
Hyman Ave.
Aspen Ice Garden ■
• 14
Mill St.
Monarch St.
Aspen St.
Garmisch St.
First St.
Second St.
❸–❼ →
❶❷ ↗
• 15
Main St./Highway 82
West Main St.
Bleeker St.
Hallam St.
• 9
• 8
Puppy Smith St.

areas and other peaks in the Elk Range are more dramatic than those from downtown Aspen. The distinctive architecture of the Aspen Institute's buildings reflects the design aesthetic of Austrian Bauhaus architect Herbert Bayer, who came to Aspen in 1946 at Walter Paepcke's behest. Streamlined, geometric facades, white walls accented by primary colors, and integration of natural light are all trademarks of the Bauhaus school, which held that art and design are inseparable.

Other features of note include the earthworks (in Anderson Park), a series of moundlike sculptures created by Bayer and inspired by the mountains surrounding Aspen. Bayer also designed the marble garden with 19 pieces from the quarry in the nearby town of Marble; the garden is across from the reception center, between the Crown and Wachner guest buildings. A geodesic dome constructed by Buckminster Fuller—now obsolete but once covering a swimming pool—sits between the tennis courts and the Arco and Crown guest buildings.

On the Meadows' east side, three gardens—Japanese, wildflower, and the "music garden"—are quiet places for contemplation. The Adelson Gallery, in the Paepcke Memorial building, hosts art exhibits and is open weekdays, 9–4. *845 Meadows Rd., tel. 970/925-4240.*

BENEDICT MUSIC TENT. Set on the Aspen Meadows campus, the music tent debuted in summer 2000. Designed by Aspen architect Harry Teague, the tent is the third, and most sophisticated, outdoor site for the Aspen Music Festival's annual summer concert series.

The original tent, designed by Eero Saarinen, was erected in 1949 and was the music festival venue until 1964. It was then replaced by another tent, conceived by Bauhaus architect Herbert Bayer, that seated 1,700 and had a sliding canvas ceiling. After some debate (the inevitable response to change in Aspen), the newest tent was commissioned to provide enhanced acoustics, an improved stage layout, and more backstage space.

The current tent seats 2,050 and cost $11 million to construct. A system of steel cables designed to withstand heavy snow loads supports the Teflon-coated fiberglass outer fabric; the tent no longer has to be disassembled each winter. A 100-ft acoustic disk reflects sound to both performers and audience. Canvas suspended "kites" and specially painted canvas also assist with the carefully engineered acoustics.

The music festival offers tours of the music tent and of adjacent Harris Concert Hall (named the state's best performance venue by the *Denver Post*) on Mondays. During the summer performance season, free "tours to the tent" depart from the Hotel Jerome. These guided walking tours of approximately an hour amble through part of Aspen's historic West End, focusing on notable homes and past residents as well as the history of the music festival, before culminating at the tent in time for the day's performance. You can also tour the music school campus off Castle Creek Road (Tuesdays, 11 and 1). Take the free shuttle from downtown Aspen, as parking at the campus is limited. *Aspen Meadows campus, tel. 970/925–3254 ext. 122.*

HALLAM LAKE NATURE PRESERVE. A 25-acre oasis adjacent to downtown Aspen, the nature preserve serves as home to the Aspen Center for Environmental Studies (ACES). A self-guided tour, doable year-round, takes you through the preserve; pick up an interpretive brochure, which corresponds to numbered trail markers, in the ACES main building. You could walk through the preserve in as little as 15 minutes but would be well advised to linger, watching the waterfowl on the lake or biding time in one of the observation platforms along the trail. Free sunset beaver walks in summer (7:30) with an ACES naturalist provide a slightly different perspective of the lake. The preserve also contains a cutthroat trout restoration program, organic garden, domestic animal area, and bird-of-prey house.

Basalt

Just 18 mi west of Aspen on Hwy. 82, the town of Basalt is emerging as a charming destination of its own. The two-block-long main street, Midland Avenue, houses a diverse selection of shops and restaurants. Stop by the Basalt Gallery (200 Basalt Center Circle), which showcases Aspen area artists. Just northeast of downtown is the start of the scenic Frying Pan River valley. About a ½-hr drive farther up Frying Pan Road is Ruedi Reservoir, with campsites, beaches, picnic areas, and boat launches (a fee is charged at each). The paved road continues past Ruedi, eventually passing by the settlement of Norrie and a few mi later becoming Forest Service Road 505 (unpaved and, in winter, unplowed). The road comes to a dead end at the Frying Pan Lakes trailhead after about 6 mi. You'll need a car to reach the reservoir, although public buses run regularly to the town from Aspen and Snowmass Village (about a 30-minute ride).

Before its incarnation as a nature preserve, Hallam Lake was once an amusement park in Aspen's mining era. ACES, and the preserve, were established in 1968 by Elizabeth Paepcke, who with her husband, Walter, was instrumental in creating modern-day Aspen. Today ACES offers a comprehensive educational program, including guided nature walks in the Aspen area, naturalist field school courses, snowshoe tours, and a full slate of children's activities. On Wednesday evenings from January to April, the center hosts Potbelly Perspectives ($3), a series of talks and slide shows primarily by Aspen-area residents who have traveled the world. Naturalist Nights ($5) run on Thursdays from January through March and include a short film or slide show on a specific theme, a snowshoe walk through the preserve, and hot drinks and desserts around the potbelly stove. 100 Puppy Smith St., tel. 970/925–5756. $2 suggested. Dec.–Apr., weekdays 9–5; May–Nov., Mon.–Sat. 9–5.

HOTEL JEROME. One of Aspen's best-known historic buildings, the Hotel Jerome dates from 1889. It's gone through several refurbishments since then and is now an elegant example of Victorian grandeur. An exhibit of photographs adjacent to the hotel lobby provides a fascinating glimpse into Aspen's past. (☞ Where to Stay) 330 E. Main St., tel. 970/920–1000.

NEED A BREAK? Pick up some sustenance from the **Main Street Bakery and Café** (201 E. Main St., tel. 970/925–6446), which has a selection of decadent cakes and pastries as well as coffee drinks.

INDEPENDENCE GHOST TOWN. A once-thriving gold-mining community of approximately 1,500 perched 10,900 ft below the Continental Divide, Independence is believed to have been Aspen's first mining camp. The name supposedly was bestowed because prospectors found a nearby gold lode on July 4, 1879, though the town was called by at least six other names. At one point, Independence had more than 40 businesses, three post offices, a stamp mill, and a sawmill. By 1888 there were only about 100 residents, the rest gone to seek more fortune in Aspen. In 1899, during a fierce snow storm that cut off supplies, these diehards evacuated—by crafting skis from the boards of their homes. Today just a few rustic buildings remain. Aspen can trace its ski history, in part, to these rugged pioneers of Independence.

The ghost town is maintained by the Aspen Historical Society, but there are no interpreters on site. You're free to wander among the ruins as long as you leave things in their current state. A brief brochure and map in a dispenser near the parking area can give you some insight about the layout. 13½ mi up Hwy. 82 from Aspen, tel. 970/925–3721. $3 suggested. Late May until first heavy snow after Oct. 1.

MINE TOURS. Aspen was established during the mining boom of the late 19th century and though the town's mining heritage exists mainly in tribute, two silver mines are still open, offering a glimpse of Aspen's hard rock (that's pre–Hard Rock Café) past.

Smuggler Mine. At the base of Smuggler Mountain on the outskirts of Aspen, the mine is still being worked and rehabilitated, though as more avocation than business. Once one of the world's richest silver mines, it began production in 1880 and was in full-time operation until 1918. In 1894, the largest silver nugget in the world (1,840 pounds) was pulled from the mine. Underground walking tours of two levels of the mine are available year-round on request and last between an hour and an hour and a half. The tour focuses on the mine's history, the technical aspects of mining, and the tools and equipment used throughout the years. *Tel. 970/925–2049. $20, year-round.*

Compromise Mine. Sitting within Aspen Mountain, its main entrance at the bottom of the Silver Queen run, Compromise Mine started up in the early 1880s and operated full-time until 1893. It, too, is being rehabilitated and explored in the hope that silver may again one day become a viable commodity. The name derives from a legal settlement among competing mine operators, who each asserted ownership of the highly productive ore veins that ran through five originally separate mining claims. Two-hour tours include a ride into the mine on narrow-gauge rail cars to view the stopes, or underground chambers created by removing ore. Tours take place during the summer. Reservations are necessary, and children under five are not allowed. *Tel. 970/925–2049. $30. July–Aug., tours leave Sat. at 11, 1 and 3.*

MAROON BELLS. Two 14,000-plus-ft rock peaks that dominate the end of the Maroon Creek Valley, Maroon Bells is one of the most-visited attractions in the Aspen area—and with good reason. The reddish mountains jut strikingly above the classically U-shaped glacial valley, which began its formation 300 million years ago. On calm days, the reflection of the Bells in Maroon Lake makes for the quintessential Colorado photograph.

As this is such a popular site, don't expect an experience of mountain solitude. If you want to avoid the heaviest summertime crowds, go in the early morning or late afternoon. From Maroon Lake, you can set out for a short stroll along the lake or one of several longer hikes. Be prepared for mountain weather, i.e., potentially cold temperatures and afternoon thunderstorms in summer. Naturalists from the Aspen Center for Environmental Studies offer free 45-minute nature walks daily in summer, on the hour, from 10 to 2—a great way to learn more about the wildlife, plants, and geology of the area.

The best—and often only—way to reach the Bells is via bus, from the Rubey Park transit center in downtown Aspen. From 8:30 to 5, mid-June through Labor Day, Maroon Creek Road is closed to vehicle traffic (other than buses and overnight campers with permits) past the T Lazy 7 Ranch. Weekends in September also have the same restrictions. Buses leave Aspen at least every half hour from 9 to 4:30 and return from the Bells with the same frequency, from 9:30 to 5. On the ride up, the driver provides running commentary on local history, geology of the valley, and its wildlife inhabitants. If you do take your own vehicle to the Bells (before 8:30 AM or after 5 PM), you must purchase a 5-day pass for $10. Bicyclists, who can ride up to the Bells at any time, still get free access.

In winter Maroon Creek Road is unplowed beyond the T Lazy 7, and you can access the Bells only by snowmobile or cross-country skis. The road usually opens in mid-May; it closes following the first significant snowstorm after October 1. *End of Maroon Creek Rd., tel. 970/925-3445 Aspen Ranger District; 970/925-8484 for bus info.*

SILVER QUEEN GONDOLA. The 18-minute ride on Aspen Mountain's gondola is the easiest way to get a breathtaking—literally, as you'll be at 11,212 ft—view of town, the surrounding Elk mountains, and the Continental Divide, just to the east. Once at the top, there are several things you can do in addition to gawking at the view: the Sundeck restaurant, renovated and expanded in 1999, is open for lunch; the world's highest Frisbee golf course puts a new spin on a classic; and free 45-minute walks guided by naturalists from the Aspen Center for Environmental Studies leave on the hour from 11–3 daily. A network of hiking trails and dirt roads leads south on Richmond Ridge as well as down the mountain. The Aspen Skiing Company hosts twilight barbecue dinners on Tuesdays during July and August.

In addition to individual tickets, family passes—$30 for an adult and two children, $40 for two adults and a child—are also available. *Aspen Mountain, tel. 970/925-1220. $19. Early June, weekends 10–4; mid-June–Labor Day, daily 10–4; Labor Day–late Sept., weekends, 10–4.*

NEED A BREAK? On a warm day, head over to **Boogie's Diner** (534 E. Cooper Ave., tel. 970/925–6610) for one of their killer milkshakes.

ULTIMATE TAXI. The notorious taxi lives up to its name—you'd be hard-pressed to find a cab ride to equal it. Picture a 1978 yellow Checker cab that practically pulses as it slowly cruises the streets of Aspen. Now envision a disco/laser-light show/entertainment act/photography and Web studio inside. The combination is what owner and driver Jon Barnes terms "the funnest ride in the history of public transportation."

If you use the Ultimate Taxi to actually get from one place to another, however, you'll miss the point. The half-hour rides are designed as a theatrical event (kids, especially, will be enthralled). The cab, which seats four to six people, is replete with neon lights,

The Aspen Institute

In 1949 Chicago industrialist Paepcke organized the 200th birthday celebration of German poet/philosopher Johann Wolfgang von Goethe. He invited leading intellectuals and artists from around the world, in the hopes of forging a humanistic-based unity in the aftermath of World War II. More than 2,000 visitors attended, including philosopher Albert Schweitzer, playwright Thornton Wilder, philosopher José Ortega y Gasset, pianist Arthur Rubinstein, and architect Eero Saarinen. Out of this one-time event evolved the Aspen Institute, a non-profit organization that sponsors seminars and policy programs for leaders in politics, business, and the humanities. The institute's first seminar was held in 1950 and, under the direction of University of Chicago president Robert Hutchins and professor Mortimer Adler, was modeled after the university's "Great Books" seminars. Today the institute has offices in five countries, with headquarters in Washington, D.C. The original Aspen campus continues to attract a who's who of politics, as well as other luminaries.

---

a veritable galaxy of glow-in-the-dark stars, laser lights, strobes, 3-D effects, even a fog machine. There's also wireless Internet access and a camera that regularly snaps your picture and downloads it to the Web, meaning that you can watch yourself riding in the cab with just a few seconds' delay. And when you think there can't be any more, Barnes fires up the kicking sound system and sings and plays along on an electronic keyboard, sax, and drum kit—all while negotiating the car through downtown Aspen. Five batteries in the trunk power the whole kit and caboodle. *Tel. 970/927–9239. $125. www.ultimatetaxi.com*

WHEELER OPERA HOUSE. One of Aspen's finest restored buildings from the Victorian era, the opera house was built in

1889 by mining tycoon Jerome B. Wheeler. Constructed of 900,000 native Peachblow sandstone bricks, the graceful exterior is a hallmark of downtown Aspen.

Even after the town's fortunes went bust in 1893, the year silver was demonetized, the Wheeler continued to host shows. In 1912, two fires of mysterious origin razed the theater's interior and it was boarded up, though the building's street level was still used as commercial space. In 1947 Walter Paepcke leased the theater, and it was restored by Bauhaus architect Herbert Bayer, once again becoming a popular entertainment spot. The Wheeler has been refurbished several times since then, and now that it is restored to its Victorian opulence, there's no better place to watch the incredible variety of concerts, movies, plays, ballets, and other performances that are regularly scheduled. Guided tours are available on request. *320 E. Hyman Ave., tel. 970/920-5770.*

WHEELER-STALLARD HOUSE. Now a museum, this imposing house was built in the West End by Aspen businessman Jerome Wheeler in 1888, though he never actually lived there. In 1905 Edgar and Mary Ella Stallard took up residence here, buying the property in 1917 and occupying the house for a total of 40 years.

The Aspen Historical Society purchased the Wheeler-Stallard House in 1968 and operated it as a museum with a self-guided tour. The architecture is an excellent example of the Victorian Queen Anne style, due to the steep roofs, bay windows, fish-scale shingles, and deep porch. The museum has undergone some renovations and reopening is planned for winter 2000-01. Interactive exhibits and programs will cover aspects of local and regional history. *620 W. Bleeker St., tel. 970/925-3721. Call for price. Call for hours.*

Snowmass

ANDERSON RANCH ARTS CENTER. This ranch is an inspiring example of Aspen area historic buildings that have been transformed and given new life. Now a thriving artists' community, the site traces its roots to an early 20th-century cattle-and-sheep ranch. In 1966 a group of local artists began to use the barns as studios. Since then, the ranch has grown, garnering a national reputation for both the art that is produced there, by resident and visiting artists, and for its summer workshops, in fields such as ceramics, photography, printmaking, painting, and sculpture.

Visitors can walk through the ranch's campuslike setting anytime. A brochure outlining a self-guided tour is available at the Dows Barn, which houses the administrative offices. The architecture is an intriguing mix of rustic and contemporary. The most interesting time to visit is from October to April, when workshops are not in session and visitors are welcome in the studios. The annual art auction in August is a well-attended event and an opportunity to purchase artwork by ranch artists and others. There's also a small gallery in the Dows Barn that exhibits ceramics, photographs, prints, and other work from visiting artists and ranch faculty. *5263 Owl Creek Rd., tel. 970/923–3181. Free. Galleries open Mon.–Fri. 9–5.*

CHAIRLIFT RIDES. Two of the ski lifts at the Snowmass ski area—the Burlingame and Sam's Knob lifts—take foot passengers partway up the mountain in summer. The experience is on a slightly smaller scale than that of taking the gondola up Aspen Mountain but is quite scenic nonetheless. Learn more about the abundant wildflowers and summer wildlife by taking a free naturalist-guided walk put on by the Aspen Center for Environmental Studies; a group meets daily at 1 at the Snowmass Village Mall information booth and then takes the chairlift up the mountain. *Snowmass Ski Area, tel. 970/925–1220. $10. Mid-June–Labor Day, daily 9:30–4.*

NEED A BREAK? After your chairlift ride, head down the Snowmass Village Mall to **Cafe Ink** (45 Snowmass Durant Ave., tel. 970/923–7828) and get a frozen black and white blended—it's like a mocha Slurpee.

snowmass exploring

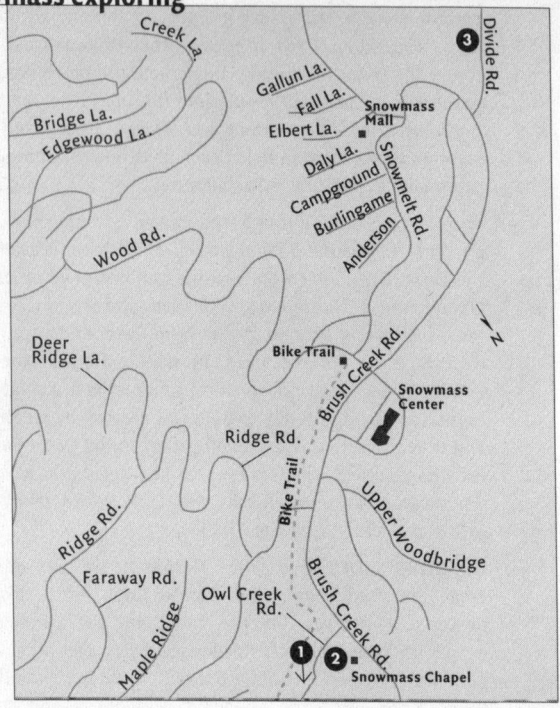

Anderson Ranch Arts Center, 2

Harry Vold Rodeo Company, 1

Krabloonik Restaurant and Kennel, 3

HARRY VOLD RODEO COMPANY. Weekly amateur rodeo competitions take place in Snowmass Village. Competitions and a barbecue take place at 5 PM every Wednesday and Saturday in the summer at the Snowmass Rodeo Arena (100 Elbert La., tel. 970/923-4433, call for prices).

KRABLOONIK RESTAURANT AND KENNEL. There's nothing like 250 sturdy, howling Alaskan huskies to evoke a response from a dog lover. Located above Snowmass Village, Krabloonik (the name comes from a native Alaskan term for "big eyebrows") has twice-daily tours of its sled-dog kennel. The guided tours, which last about an hour, include a brief video about dog sledding and cover the major aspects of the operation, including the canines' diet and training and sled-building techniques. And, yes, you can interact with the dogs, who can raise quite a racket at mealtime.

The kennel is owned by Dan MacEachen, a seven-time Iditarod competitor who worked for local dog-sledding pioneer Stuart Mace in the 1960s. In 1974 MacEachen took over the dogs and moved them from the Castle Creek valley to the Snowmass location. In 1981 the Krabloonik restaurant opened adjacent to the kennels. In winter the dogs keep busy with sled tours; summer is their time for rest and relaxation. 4250 Divide Rd., tel. 970/923-4342. $5. Late June–Labor Day, Mon., Wed.–Sun. 11 and 2:30.

In winter the fun starts early with a bustling après-ski scene, and extends into the night and throughout the year with live jazz, country-and-western dancing, and bars and lounges galore.

In this Chapter

How and Where 148 • Sources 148 • ASPEN 149 • Bars and Lounges 149 • Dance and Music Clubs 155 • Nightclubs 156 • SNOWMASS 157 • Bars and Lounges 157

By David Gibson

nightlife

ASPEN IS A PARTY TOWN. From its high-society galas to its dive bars, Aspen is proud of the fact that the fun doesn't stop when the lifts close. To that end, there are more bars per capita in Aspen than in any town you're likely to visit.

Nightlife in Aspen is first and foremost about socializing. Most locals meet at parties or bars, and cliques form around particular watering-hole loyalties. Aspenites, as well as the typical tourists, bar-hop, taking one or two drinks at each establishment before moving on. Accordingly, certain bars have become late-night places, and certain others don't see a soul after 11 PM. A quick glance through a window can instantly tell you what sort of bar you're about to walk into.

Secondly, nightlife in Aspen is about getting drunk; it's an odd situation where days are largely defined by physical activity, but perhaps it's a holdover from Wild West attitudes. Aspen recognizes that tourists play a little harder on vacation and has responded to that wish. You'll notice that almost every bar has a preponderance of shot glasses, and the bartenders are more than happy to fill those at any time (Tuaca and Grand Marnier are local favorites). Martinis are gargantuan, drinks are stiff, and the bartenders are on the whole unjudgmental. Cops are sympathetic (unless, of course, you attempt to get behind the wheel, in which case they are unyielding), and the city provides a free bus service so no one has to worry about having one too many.

Keep in mind, however, that alcohol can have very adverse effects at altitude. Those little cards in your hotel room speak the truth; it's a good idea to lay off the sauce your first few days up here. Otherwise, your Aspen vacation may consist of a week in the hospital recovering from pulmonary edema.

How and Where

Aspen has a variety of nightlife venues. Those that contain restaurants usually open at dinnertime, though often earlier in the winter for après ski, and close shortly after the last table has left the restaurant.

Venues that do not serve food usually have a 9 PM opening, and these venues stay open until 2 AM. By that time, every glass, even if it only contains water, must be out of the customers' hands and behind the bar. Last call is rarely given after 1:30, and a busy bar might give it even earlier. Aspen has no after-hours clubs, though an occasional rave (dry, of course, or selling $5 fruit juices) has been put on.

Most nightspots are fairly casual, though hotel bars and private clubs may enforce dress codes; if in doubt, call first, or better yet, just dress nicely.

A quick tip on tipping: most bars and clubs allow their bartenders to give away a portion of their drinks each night. Tipping well will usually ensure that you get one of the free ones, and then everyone leaves the bar happy.

Sources

Although you may hear about upcoming events on the radio, by far the best sources for finding out about live bands or special events are Aspen's two free daily papers. The *Aspen Times* has daily listings, as well as a weekend section that features calendars, reviews of upcoming events, and artist profiles. The *Aspen Daily News* also has daily listings, as well as a section entitled "Time Out," which gives a calendar, previews, and reviews. Both papers produce special sections during special events such as Comedy Fest and Gay Ski Week.

ASPEN
Bars and Lounges

ACME RESTAURANT AND BAR. In spite of an awkward layout and a dungeonlike location, Acme has become one of the more popular nighttime hangouts for locals and tourists alike. The bar features a variety of domestic and imported beers, as well as a healthy selection of microbrews and a full bar with moderate prices. Karaoke every Wednesday night usually brings in the crowds, especially in summer, when students from the Aspen Music School turn Acme into town's best variety show. Occasional live music features local talent. *320 S. Mill St., downstairs, tel. 970/925-3775.*

ASPEN BILLIARDS. This is not your average pool hall. The tables here are in excellent shape, and the room is elegantly outfitted in antique prints, beautiful wood, and beautiful people. Tables are rented at an hourly rate, with service provided by a roaming cocktail waitress. Smoking is not allowed in the room itself, though smokers can venture next door to the Cigar Bar. Players who like "to make it interesting" should beware of sharks. *315 E. Hyman Ave., tel. 970/920-6707.*

ASPEN CLUB LODGE. This quiet bar, complete with roaring fireplace, is a perfect spot to relax in the early evening and is most often inhabited by tourists and a few die-hard regulars. You will not find a large assortment of high-end liquors here, so stick to the basics. The ACL (an unfortunate skiing acronym) is one of the town's busiest bars during sporting events, owing to a multitude of television sets. *Spring St. at Durant Ave., tel. 970/925-6760.*

AJAX TAVERN. Calling nine stools tucked into a narrow walkway a "bar" may be stretching it a bit, but Ajax offers a wonderful

selection of wines by the glass, great martinis, and some rather amusing bar patter from bartenders who would rather talk to you than make drinks for the restaurant. Beware of venturing in during prime dining hours, when the bar will be crowded with diners waiting for seats; a better bet is for an early nightcap, or a civilized drink to start the evening. Smoking is not allowed. 685 E. Durant Ave., tel. 970/920-9333.

BENTLEY'S AT THE WHEELER. Bentley's is one of Aspen's most popular bars, with location being its prime advantage: it occupies a corner of the historic Wheeler Opera House, and the people-watching through its high windows is excellent. The clientele consists primarily of local twenty-somethings smoking and drinking Bud, with the occasional tourist thrown in early in the evening. You may find the service to be inattentive, even surly, but locals consider that part of the charm. 328 E. Hyman Ave., tel. 970/920-2240.

CACHE CACHE. This elegant little bar serves as the waiting area for the immensely popular bistro of the same name. It is usually filled with diners taking advantage of Aspen's best bar menu. Wine, beer, and spirit selections are excellent here, and the service is casual but superb. This is a great smoke-free environment for a relaxed glass of wine, but don't miss the food. 205 S. Mill St., downstairs, tel. 970/925-3835.

CAMPO DE FIORI. The name of this bar means "Field of Flowers," and that's exactly the impression you get looking at the crowd that calls this bar home. There's tons of energy among the beautiful twenty-somethings who crowd in here practically every night of the week, and the wine selection and generous martinis make Campo a great spot for anyone. Food is also served at the bar and the bar tables, allowing you to turn Campo into an evening unto itself. 205 S. Mill St., downstairs, tel. 970/920-7717.

CANTINA. Chips, salsa, and killer margaritas define this watering hole, which is one of Aspen's most popular meeting places. Cantina features a great happy hour, as well as some of the best-looking waitresses north of the Rio Grande. Its Main Street patio is a popular destination on warm afternoons. *Corner of Mill and Main Sts., tel. 970/925-3663.*

CIGAR BAR. This elegantly furnished room began life as a well-ventilated cigar room serving elegant wines and liquors, and remains so through the early evening. As the night crowd settles in, however, the Cigar Bar becomes a haven for cigarette smokers exiled from the adjoining Eric's Bar, Aspen Billiards, and Su Casa, and often becomes unbearably smoky. The crowd begins the night as older and touristy, but becomes young and local as the night wears on. *205 S. Mill St., downstairs, tel. 970/920-7717.*

COOPER STREET BAR AND RESTAURANT. Practically every Aspen local spent his first year at the tables of Cooper Street. The reasons will be evident immediately: cheap pitchers of bad beer, cheap bar food, and plenty of pinball. Today, the crowd still consists of lift ops and waitresses, who gather in what could only be called a dive to spend not very much of their hard-earned cash. Video games, pool, and shuffleboard also play a big role in Cooper Street's popularity. This bar will make you forget you're in Aspen, which isn't always a bad thing. *508 E. Cooper Ave., tel. 970/925-7758.*

ERIC'S BAR. This is Aspen's hottest nightspot for the twenty-something crowd, with sleek, modern decor, big comfy sofas, and a great selection of microbrewed beers and reasonably priced drinks. It is also Aspen's largest no-smoking bar. Eric's greatest attraction is its proximity to (and shared liquor license with) Aspen Billiards, Su Casa, and the Cigar Bar, which combine to make the largest and most diverse nightlife venue in Aspen, though you'll have to find someplace else to go dancing. *408 E. Hyman Ave., tel. 970/920-6707.*

HOTEL JEROME BAR. Aspen's famous J-Bar has been the centerpiece of town's drinking life since miners dropped in for a

The Art of Après

It's been a hard day on the hill, and you're looking for a little relaxation before dinner. Lucky for you, Aspen is an après paradise. But beware: there are a few rules every aprèsnaut should follow.

Limit your intake. You're at altitude, and you've been engaging in strenuous activity all day. A 3½-ounce martini is going to hit you like a nine-pound hammer.

Watch the boots. Baryshnikov himself couldn't look graceful in ski boots. Consider changing into a pair of hiking boots or tennis shoes before trying to squeeze between bar stools.

Don't change clothes. It's après ski, so you'd better look like you've been skiing. Walk in in street clothes and you'll just look like a social parasite.

Leave early. You'll have time for a soak and a nap, and you'll avoid the knowing stares of diners as they take over the restaurant.

---

quick rye whiskey. Today the bar caters to tourists and locals alike with inexpensive drinks, a small but delicious bar menu, and a lively atmosphere. Monday Night Football parties here are among the best on earth. *330 E. Main St., tel. 970/920–1000.*

JIMMY'S AMERICAN RESTAURANT AND BAR. Two words: tequila and mescal. Though this beautiful bar is rarely mobbed, any fan of the two preceding words should venture to Jimmy's. Jimmy Yeager has assembled the finest collection of these two Mexican liquors known to man, and he's more than happy to regale any interested party with an educational tasting accompanied by tales of his adventures south o' the border. His margaritas are the culmination of the art. *205 S. Mill St., upstairs, tel. 970/925–6020.*

L'HOSTARIA. Quiet and elegant, the bar at L'Hostaria is the perfect place for an intimate drink or a sampling from their wonderful bar menu. There's also a carpaccio bar here, which offers thinly sliced delicacies of cured meat and fish. *620 E. Hyman Ave., tel. 970/920–9022.*

LIBRARY BAR AT THE HOTEL JEROME. This quiet and rarely busy room is filled with all the Victorian charm you'd expect from the Hotel Jerome. This is a great nightcap venue for a port or single-malt Scotch but also serves appetizers, entrées, and desserts. *330 E. Main St., tel. 970/920–1000.*

LITTLE ANNIE'S EATING HOUSE. This often smoky bar serves up drinks in a casual atmosphere inhabited primarily by locals. Draft beer is the usual order here, and it's usually ordered over the din of the Grateful Dead or the Allman Brothers Band by flannel shirt–wearing refugees from the University of Georgia. Fun and lively, those long out of the college bar scene may find it a bit much to deal with. *517 E. Hyman Ave., tel. 970/925–1098.*

LITTLE NELL. The bar at the Little Nell has, from its genesis, been the most popular tourist bar in town, though many older and wealthier locals call it home as well. Après ski is a mob scene here, with doormen stationed during high season to control the crowds. Light jazz is performed nightly during the winter, and a neighboring lounge with a fireplace and sofas offers a peaceful oasis in the evenings. *205 S. Mill St., downstairs, tel. 970/920–7717.*

MCSTORLIE'S. This eclectic space does a fair job of imitating an Irish or English pub, though its clientele seems to come primarily from Australia and New Zealand. You'll find a great selection of draft beer here, as well as some interesting foreign whiskeys and rums. This is not a place to start trouble; Aspen's rugby team is in frequent attendance. *205 S. Mill St., downstairs, tel. 970/920–7717.*

MEZZALUNA. This horseshoe bar sits in the middle of Aspen's most popular restaurants and is always packed with some of

Aspen's most beautiful and well-heeled personages. There's a very nice selection of wines by the glass, as well as the famous Mezzatini. This is not the place to go for an intimate glass of wine or a secret tryst. 205 S. Mill St., *downstairs, tel. 970/920–7717.*

OLIVES. Buried deep in the St. Regis Hotel, the large and airy bar of Olives restaurant offers plenty of seating with stools, tables, chairs, and sofas. The wine selection is outstanding and the bar menu is fantastic, though neither is inexpensive. This elegant bar could stand on its own but receives bonus points for serving a beautiful restaurant as well. *315 E. Dean St., tel. 970/920–7356.*

O'LEARY'S. Don't be fooled into thinking that this is a friendly Irish pub. In fact, this is the only Aspen bar to celebrate "Grumpy Hour." The booze and beer is cheap and plentiful, however, and you'll be able to glimpse a side of Aspen you won't see anywhere else. Do not mention to the regulars that you're staying at the Little Nell. *205 S. Mill St., downstairs, tel. 970/920–7717.*

RED ONION. The Onion has been around for more than a century, and looks it. Its decaying charm is the favored spot of many Aspen locals, from twenty-somethings to seventy-somethings, but it also offers a welcoming hand to tourists. There is a whole lot of drinking going on here, so don't expect your barstool neighbor to carry on a very coherent conversation after 11 or so (PM, that is, but not after 11 beers either). *205 S. Mill St., downstairs, tel. 970/920–7717.*

SU CASA. This Mexican bar offers a great happy hour and wonderful margaritas (try the "half and half" of strawberry and regular), as well as a tasty bar menu. This is the least-crowded bar in the Eric's/Su Casa/Cigar Bar/Aspen Billiards complex, and it is a bit sterile until it fills up after dinner. *315 E. Hyman Ave., tel. 970/920–1488.*

UTE CITY BAR AND GRILL. Ute City had its heyday in the late 1980s but will always remain popular, thanks to its old-time decor and fantastic location. There is frequently live music here of the Eagles cover band variety, and the clientele leans to the older (but still partying) tourist. *501 E. Hyman Ave., tel. 970/920–4699.*

WHISKEY ROCKS. The folks who brought you the world-famous Whiskey Bar and Sky Bar now bring you Aspen's most expensive bar. This is the place to go if you're hoping to spot a celebrity, and the overstaffed bar makes sure all of your needs are met, unless you have a need for value. *315 Dean St., tel. 970/920–3300.*

Dance and Music Clubs

COUNTRY-AND-WESTERN

SHOOTERS SALOON AND DANCE HALL. Aspen's only Country-and-Western bar packs in the Texans, but welcomes city slickers as well. Shooters offers live C/W music, as well as boot-scootin' lessons on Thursdays, but has been known to house the occasional after-hours rave. *Corner of Galena St. and Hyman Ave., tel. 970/925–4567.*

JAZZ

SYZYGY. Aspen's only true jazz club offers some astoundingly good jazz every night starting at 10 PM. Steve Peer heads up the house band, and many other musicians drop by to sit in. Cozy booths and a great wine list make this the place for a relaxing, romantic evening. *520 E. Hyman Ave., tel. 970/925–3700.*

ROCK

DOUBLE DIAMOND. This smoky and slightly shabby club is Aspen's premier venue for live music, and it attracts nationally famous acts, as well as local bands, reunion tours, and the occasional has-been. You have a better chance of catching an up-and-coming star here than anywhere else in the Rockies. Live music is featured every night of the week during high season, and less frequently as town empties out. Many nationally known acts sell out well before the show, so be sure to call in advance for ticket information. *450 S. Galena St., tel. 970/920–6905.*

HOWLING WOLF. The Wolf features live bands that run the gamut from folk to rock, with a big emphasis on the "World Roots" genre. You'll be able to catch some top-notch reggae and jazz here. The staff, unfortunately, seems more intent on watching the show than getting you your next beer, so avoid the place if you're thirsty. *424 E. Cooper St., tel. 970/920–7771.*

Nightclubs

CARIBOU CLUB. They won't let you in off the street, but if you happen to wrangle an invitation, you'll be treated to the posh luxury of the premier private club in the Rockies. Overstuffed sofas and mounted animal heads surround members with overstuffed wallets and taxidermic facial structures. The bar stocks almost every liquor known to man, and the wine list is unparalleled. If you want to see Aspen at its most Aspen-y, beg, borrow, or bribe your way in. *411 E. Hopkins Ave., downstairs, tel. 970/920–2929.*

CLUB CHELSEA. This subterranean space tries to be all things to all people, incorporating a dance floor, a cigar room, light fare at the bar, and a plush lounge. It is, however, too small a space to do everything well, and should stick to what it does best: big drinks in the elegantly relaxed front lounge. Here you'll often catch live jazz or blues performed by some rather talented musicians. Chelsea never seemed to catch on with the locals, but the (primarily older) tourist crowd has made it a popular destination. *415 E. Hyman Ave., tel. 970/920–0066.*

FOUR TWO SIX. Aspen's sleekest private club features a cocktail lounge and a dance floor but won't let you in unless you're a member or with one. The crowd here is diverse, leaning toward Aspen's young go-getters, trust funders, and Gucci-clad party girls. Aspen's best dance music makes it worth the attempt to wrangle your way in. *426 E. Hyman Ave., tel. 970/544–9444.*

SNOWMASS
Bars and Lounges

COWBOYS. This happening bar with a Western motif offers live music most nights during the season, as well as some nice happy hour specials. Like anywhere in Snowmass, you'll find mostly tourists here. *Next to the Silvertree Hotel, tel. 970/923–5249.*

LA PIÑATA. Locals crowd into this Alpine/Mexican bar for delicious margaritas and the fact that the tourists have trouble finding it. Happy hour and après specials, and the occasional free buffet, make this a fun spot. *Daly La., across from parking lot 6, tel. 970/923–2153.*

MOUNTAIN DRAGON. Complimentary appetizers make the happy hour here, and the Dragon has been known to host some good local bands. The decor is haphazard and aging, but the crowd is usually young and vibrant. *67 Elbert La., tel. 970/923–3576.*

TOWER BAR. This clean and sophisticated bar offers a little something extra: magic shows, performed by the bartenders throughout the night. Yes, they'll still have time to make your drinks. If you find yourself stuck in Snowmass after nine and are looking for some excitement, this may be the only place to find it. The Tower is a welcome change from the average fern bar. *Snowmass Village Mall, tel. 970/923–4650.*

ZANE'S TAVERN. This is a sports bar like any other sports bar, with cheap booze and pub-style eats accompanying the darts, billiards, foosball, and requisite blaring jukebox. Zane's is the spot for the younger crowd, or the older-but-acts-younger crowd. *328 E. Hyman Ave., tel. 970/920–2240.*

The sleepy ex-mining town of Aspen began to attract the world's attention fifty years ago, not only as a burgeoning ski resort but also as a haven for culture and ideas. Today, Aspenites and visitors are still reaping the benefits of Walter Paepcke's "Aspen Idea": opera, ballet, and festivals celebrating music, film, and design attract internationally acclaimed performers and enthusiastic audiences.

In this Chapter

How and Where 160 • Sources 160 • Arts Venues 161 • Dance 163 • Film 164 • Kids' Stuff 165 • Music 167 • Opera 167 • Readings and Talks 167 • Theater 168

By Brent Gardner-Smith and Jeanne McGovern

cultural activities

IN 1949 CHICAGO INDUSTRIALIST WALTER PAEPCKE decided to commemorate the 200th birthday of German poet and philosopher Johann Wolfgang von Goethe by bringing together an eclectic mix of philosophers, musicians, and scientists and celebrating the humanities against a backdrop of great natural beauty. Today, Paepcke's "Aspen Idea" lives on, and cultural activities continue to take center stage in Aspen, especially during the summer. Leading the cultural parade is the Aspen Music Festival and School, which offers over 170 performances of chamber music, opera, and classical concerts. In June and over the Labor Day weekend, classical musicians make room for legendary jazz performers at the renowned Janus Jazz Aspen at Snowmass.

Summer also awakens Aspen's other cultural institutions, including the Aspen Center for Physics and the Aspen Institute, both of which offer free weekly lectures, Aspen Ballet Company, Aspen Theatre in the Park, the International Design Conference at Aspen, and the Anderson Ranch Arts Center.

And thanks to Aspen's generous base of patrons, much of the summer culture has found a winter home, be it classical music concerts at Harris Hall, theater and film at the Wheeler Opera House, readings from best-selling authors presented by the Aspen Writers' Foundation, exhibits at the Aspen Art Museum, or the annual Shortsfest presented by Aspen Filmfest.

New events continue to join the roster. The annual U.S. Comedy Arts Festival in Aspen brings the best comedians and actors to town for a week of performances and tributes, adding some mirth to the dark days of winter. And old standbys get better with age. Aspen's Crystal Palace has been serving up some of the funniest dinner theater entertainment in America since 1957, and the show is as fresh, and the cast as talented, as ever.

From the start, Walter Paepcke saw Aspen not just as a ski resort but as a year-round artistic and intellectual community. Today, visitors and residents continue to profit from his vision.

How and Where

While cultural opportunities abound in Aspen, taking advantage of the line-up can take some planning. Many cultural events are benefits for one good cause or another, and increasingly, many are either very high-priced or are closed altogether to the general public. Nevertheless, there is still a smattering of free public performances. Check with the presenting organization about these and other last-minute ticket deals or passholder opportunities. Keep in mind that "Aspen casual" is the way to dress for almost all events, which means blue jeans, a blazer, and boots (for men or women) is fine.

Sources

The epicenter of cultural information in Aspen is the box office and visitor center at the **Wheeler Opera House** (970/920–5770 box office). The box office sells tickets to virtually every event in Aspen or Snowmass Village, and the visitor center is staffed with knowledgeable and helpful people. It's open 9 to 5 every day of the year. Local radio station KSPN at 97.7 FM offers the most promotions and information on area concerts. Aspen's public radio station, KAJX at 91.5 FM, plays highlights of the Aspen Music Festival each afternoon and is a good source of information regarding classical music performances. Aspen's two free daily newspapers—the *Aspen Daily News* and the *Aspen Times*—offer good daily calendars. The weekly edition of the *Aspen Times* has comprehensive arts coverage. The Thursday edition of the *Aspen Daily News* has entertainment listings, as does the free *Roaring Fork Sunday* in its "GO!" section. On-line, www.aspen.com provides event information and a community calendar.

ARTS VENUES

The new **Benedict Music Tent** (tel. 970/925–9042 to Music Festival ticket office) is billed as the world's first concert facility combining the openness and romance of a tent with the acoustic integrity of a concert hall. The new $15 million, 2,050-seat tent opened in the summer of 2000 with a performance of Mahler's Symphony No. 2. It features a permanent teflon-coated fiberglass roof similar to that used at Denver International Airport. And while the lawn around the tent has shrunk a bit, it is set aside in perpetuity for the public to enjoy as the David Karetsky Memorial Lawn. A low chair, the Sunday *Times*, and a bottle of wine are all fair game. Inside, reserved seating was introduced in 2000, along with more comfortable seats. The tent also hosts occasional concerts by the likes of Lyle Lovett or Judy Collins. Bring a sweater to any cool summer evening event at the tent. Tickets are available in advance at the Music Festival ticket office, in the gondola building at the base of Aspen Mountain. The Benedict Music Tent is also the home of Aspen's **International Design Conference** (Box 664, Aspen 81612, tel. 970/925–2257, www.idca.org), held in Aspen each June.

The **Harris Concert Hall** opened in 1993 to rave reviews. It was called "acoustically perfect" and likened to being "inside a cello." Located next to the Benedict Music Tent in Aspen's West End, the 500-seat hall is tucked mostly underground and is the winter answer to the music tent. Designed by Aspen architect Harry Teague, Harris Hall's acoustical excellence makes it an ideal place to appreciate a chamber music performance. Run by the Aspen Music Festival and School, the hall hosts the Winter Music Series, which includes approximately 15 performances a year as well as the Music Vox performances, which highlight less traditional classical music. *980 N. 3rd St. Ticket office tel. 970/925–9042, fax 970/925–8077.*

Paepcke Auditorium (1000 N. 3rd St., tel. 970/925–7010) is located inside the Aspen Institute's main building, next to the Music Tent. Talks and films are presented here in both summer and winter. The popular lecture series run by the Aspen Institute takes place here in the summer.

School District Theater (0135 High School Rd., off Maroon Creek Rd.), home to the Aspen Ballet Company (ABC), is located on the campus of Aspen's elementary, middle and high schools. A high-tech theater designed specifically to host professional dance and theatrical performances, this 548-seat theater is light years away from a normal school auditorium. With steeply racked seats, the sight lines and acoustics are excellent. Bring a sweater, as it always seems chilly inside.

The 489-seat **Wheeler Opera House** (320 E. Hyman Ave., tel. 970/920–5770) was built in 1889 during Aspen's silver boom, and it's still a thriving opera house today. Meticulously restored in 1984, the four-story redbrick opera house hosts dance, theater, music, opera, film, lectures, and virtually any other performance that needs a stage. Architecturally, it is a cornerstone of downtown Aspen, and no buildings taller than the Wheeler are allowed in Aspen. It is a true community theater: any group can rent it for a night or two, and it is a community gathering spot where locals are sure to see one another on the grand staircase or near the bar in the comfortable intermission lobby on the second floor. The theater's balcony conjures up all the romance of an old moviehouse balcony, and the sight lines and acoustics are excellent throughout the venue. In the summer, the theater is home to the Aspen Music Festival's fully staged opera productions, which seem more profound when produced in a true opera

Benedict Music Tent

Aspen as modern cultural mecca can trace its heritage to the first time the "music tent" was put up for a summer concert in the meadow above the Roaring Fork River in 1949. The music tent, updated in 1964 by Bauhaus architect Herbert Bayer and his brother-in-law, Aspen architect Fritz Benedict, became a summer sanctuary for thousands of visitors and locals. Concertgoers got a thrill and a chill when afternoon thunderstorms came rattling down on the white canvas. Enjoying the Sunday afternoon concerts on the lawn, in the shade of quaking aspen trees, became a hallmark Aspen pastime.

The tent was put up each summer until 1999, when it was taken down for the last time to make way for a new tent designed by Aspen architect Harry Teague, who also designed winter's answer to the music tent, Harris Concert Hall. The new tent has a permanent Teflon-coated fiberglass roof that resembles the old white canvas while offering improved acoustics.

house. During the winter, an offbeat film series is held on nights when the endless variety of performances take a break. The Wheeler may be Aspen's most treasured cultural institution.

DANCE

Aspen Santa Fe Ballet Company (110 E. Hallam St., tel. 970/925–7175) entered into a co-venture with the Santa Fe Ballet Company in 1999, and this rising young company will now be performing a classic and contemporary repertory in both cities. Recent performances included works by Balanchine and Dwight Rhoden, in addition to the perennial favorite, The Nutcracker.

FILM

The **Aspen Filmfest** (110 E. Hallam, St., tel. 970/925-6882, www.aspenfilm.org) actually comprises three separate events. A five-day **fall festival** in late September brings to Aspen feature films, documentaries, special events, and discussions with directors and producers. At the end of December, the **Aspen Academy Screenings** attract Hollywood regulars, and after-screening parties often bring out the celebrities who call Aspen home. **Aspen Shortsfest** in April is a visual delight with animation, documentary, comedy, and drama all explored in short doses. "Independent by nature," the nonprofit Aspen Filmfest was started in 1979.

The **Wheeler Film Series** offers an ongoing program of foreign films as well as highlights from the current crop of Hollywood movies. The films are shown at the Wheeler Opera House, which can seem opulent and formal during a concert, yet feels spacious and relaxed during a movie. The theater's big screen helps make going to a movie an event. During the summer, there's a special nine-week film program in conjunction with the Aspen Music Festival. These movies are usually shown in **Paepcke Auditorium** (☞ Arts Venues, *above*) which is on the Meadows "campus" next to the Music Tent in Aspen's West End. Paepcke's not the best place in the world to see a movie, but if you stroll there and back from town, it provides the foundation for a good date.

In addition to these special film offerings, Aspen also has several standard movie houses. **Stage Three Theatres** (625 E. Main St., tel. 970/925-2050) offers first-run movies in a multiplex arrangement of three theaters. The old **Isis Theater** (406 E. Hopkins Ave., tel. 970/920-3456) has been refurbished and now offers five screens with stadium seating. Snowmass Village used to have a movie theater, but now it's conference meeting space.

KIDS' STUFF

In the winter, ski school is the best bet for kids, and the children's ski school at the **Aspen Skiing Company** (P.O. Box 1248, Aspen 81612, tel. 970/925-1220) is excellent, with programs offered primarily at Snowmass and Buttermilk. In the summer, almost every one of Aspen's cultural organizations has programs for kids and the **Red Brick Arts and Recreation Center** (110 E. Hallam St., tel. 970/920-7477), in a former elementary school, is a logical and convenient place to go to pick up the latest program schedules, as many nonprofit arts organizations have offices there. In Snowmass, the **Anderson Ranch Arts Center** (5263 Owl Creek Rd., tel. 970/923-3181, www.andersonranch.org) offers week-long workshops in photography, printmaking, ceramics, woodworking, and painting in June and July for kids from ages 6 to 17. Tuition ranges from $110 to $250 and scholarships are available. The funky and intriguing collection of wooden buildings, studios and artist's residences is set on a former sheep ranch—the Anderson Ranch—at the upper end of the Brush Creek valley. A homey cafeteria offers a nourishing breakfast or lunch, making it convenient and fun for families to spend a week at the ranch together in different workshops.

ASPEN BALLET COMPANY (☞ Dance, *above*) has summer programs for kids, such as "A Children's Rainforest Odyssey," as well as a ballet school run by former Joffrey Ballet dancers.

Each summer, the **Aspen Center for Environmental Studies** (100 Puppy Smith St., tel. 970/925-5756) has daily educational programs for kids ages 5 to 7 or ages 8 to 10, including arts-and-crafts classes based on observations made at the center's pristine Hallam Lake just behind the Aspen post office. Programs also include a naturalist field school for kids, with courses such as "Maps and Mountains: Kid's Orienteering," "Fangs, Talons and Claws," and "What Lurks in the Pond?" In the winter, guided naturalist snowshoe tours at the top of Aspen

Mountain or at Two Creeks in Snowmass are offered for children ages 8 to 19. ACES also has a "Winter Wild Things" program in conjunction with the Ski Schools of Aspen, "Naturalist Nights" every Thursday from 7 to 8:30 January through March, slide shows during "Potbelly Perspectives" on winter Wednesdays from 7:30 to 8:30 PM, and self-guided walks around Hallam Lake both winter and summer.

For kids with a literary spark, the **Aspen Writers' Foundation** (110 E. Hallam St., tel. 970/925–3122) offers a summer writing camp with workshops held in either morning or afternoon sessions. The **Aspen Historical Society** (620 W. Bleeker St., tel. 970/925–3721) offers programs for kids ages 8 and up on topics such as Silver Miners, Ancient Peoples of Colorado, and the Ashcroft Ghost Town. There are also "hands-on history" programs for preschoolers in July and August. **Aspen Theatre in the Park** (tel. 970/925–9313) performs a children's play each summer. Held in a spacious tent next to the Rio Grande Park, the productions are filled with creative costumes, classic stories such as *Rapunzel*, and lively music and songs.

Even if your kids don't enroll in a class, there are still plenty of entertaining and educational sights and sounds in Aspen. **The Aspen Music Festival** may not have intended it this way, but its Sunday concerts at the tent provide an opportunity to expose kids to a taste of classical music and then let them either toddle about outside on the public lawn, or wander off and explore the ponds, grassy mounds, and paths surrounding the Aspen Meadows.

More outdoor fun can be had at the computer-programmed **fountain** on the brick mall across from the Wheeler Opera House. Kids delight in skipping across the fountain before the 10-ft-high jets of water bubble up in seemingly random fashion. Another favorite practice: placing balloons on top of the jets as they rise up and then suddenly drop down. It's kind of like playing the market.

MUSIC

Aspen. Music. The words go together and mostly when the **Aspen Music Festival and School** (tel. 970/925–9042) is mentioned. For over 50 years, summers in Aspen have been filled with the sound of 170 musical events performed by the 875 students, 150 faculty members, and scores of guest performing artists. The school's campus is set right on Castle Creek, in a narrow valley just outside of town. But it's the Benedict Music Tent and the Harris Concert Hall where most people enjoy the fruits of years of studious labor and practice. The nine-week summer festival includes orchestral performances, chamber music, lavish operas, contemporary music concerts, lectures, master classes, and children's concerts.

But Aspen's musical repertoire does not end with the classical music performances orchestrated by the Aspen Music Festival and School. The **Janus Jazz Aspen at Snowmass** (tel. 970/920–4996) is a festival that's held in late June and again on Labor Day weekend. Legendary performers such as Natalie Cole, Wynton Marsalis, B. B. King, and Bonnie Raitt have appeared.

OPERA

As part of the Aspen Music Festival and School, the **Aspen Opera Theater Center** presents fully staged, professionally produced operas in the Wheeler Opera House. Some of the country's most talented vocalists, including Renée Fleming, Susanne Mentzer, and Sylvia McNair, perform each year during the nine-week summer festival. Recent operas include Puccini's *Il trittico*, Mozart's *Così fan tutte*, and the world premiere of Bernard Rands' *Belladonna*.

READINGS AND TALKS

The Aspen Institute (tel. 970/925–7010) holds a popular free lecture series on Tuesdays and Thursdays during the nine-week peak summer season. Held at Paepcke Auditorium next to the

Music Tent in Aspen's West End, the lectures feature notable figures from the fields of media, politics, government and international relations. Jonathon Alter of *Newsweek*, David Gergen of *U.S. News & World Report*, and author William Bennett are frequent speakers. The lectures are increasingly popular and the auditorium is often filled early. One of Aspen's oldest institutions, the **Aspen Center for Physics** (tel. 970/925–2585), presents winter and summer lecture series with topics relating to the origins of the universe and the nature of subatomic particles. Locations vary, but they are frequently held at the Wheeler Opera House.

The **Given Institute of the University of Colorado** (tel. 970/925–1057, www.giveninstitute.org) conducts a public lecture series both winter and summer on topics relating to human health. **The Aspen Center for Environmental Studies** (tel. 970/925–5756, www.aspen.com/aces) holds a Potbelly Lecture every Wednesday night at 7:30 during the winter. Local and visiting adventurers give slide slows in the cozy lodge at Hallam Lake just below the Aspen Post Office.

THEATER

Set literally in a park just two blocks from downtown Aspen, the **Aspen Theatre in the Park** (Box 8677, Aspen 81612, tel. 970/925–9313) is a professional theater and school that adds zest to Aspen's cultural mix. Produced in a small tent below Rio Grande Park, the shows may include a musical, two plays, and a children's production. High-caliber actors join local talent to perform both classical and new works. Recent productions include *I Do! I Do!* and *Wait Until Dark*. Performances are held from June through August; the educational programs are offered year-round.

One of Aspen's most enduring, and endearing, institutions is the **Crystal Palace** (300 E. Hyman Ave., tel. 970/920–1455). Located two doors down from the Wheeler Opera House, the

Palace has been entertaining Aspen visitors since 1957 with good food and after-dinner songs and skits. Founder Mead Metcalf still holds court on the piano and oversees a talented group of waiter/singer/actors, who delight in skewering just about everyone with satiric turns on national news. The red velvet atmosphere adds to the experience, and long-time Aspen visitors never let a season go by without a visit. There are two nightly seatings.

Aspen Community Theater (Box 743, Aspen 81612, tel. 970/544-9294) produces both a spring and fall musical, taking advantage of the large number of talented New York and Los Angeles refugees living in Aspen. A true community theater group, ACT tackles big productions such as *The King and I* and *Jesus Christ Superstar*. If you're in Aspen during a production, you'll be pleasantly surprised by the quality of the acting, the singing, and the stagecraft. Productions are either held at the Wheeler Opera House or the School District Theater.

Aspen and Snowmass have a wide variety of lodging options, from historic inns and charming bed-and-breakfasts to luxury condos and hotels. The single most arresting aspect of your accommodations may, however, be the price. Rates are generally astronomical during peak season, but with a little research, flexibility, and luck, you may still be able to find somewhat affordable digs.

In this Chapter

Prices 172 • Aspen Lodging 173 • $$$$ 173 • $$$ 180 • $$ 183 • $ 189 • Snowmass Lodging 194 • $$$ 194 • $$ 194 • $ 195

By Cindy Hirschfeld

where to stay

WHETHER YOU PREFER FULL-ON LUXURY OR A FAMILY-RUN SKI LODGE, you'll have no trouble finding accommodations to suit your taste in the Aspen/Snowmass area. The two resorts offer an unparalleled variety of hotels, motels, and condominiums. Many properties draw their inspiration from the town's mining past and skiing present.

The problem may not be finding a place to stay but actually paying for it. It's not without reason that Aspen regularly tops magazine lists of the "most expensive places to live in the U.S.," and that characterization extends to many of the lodging properties. If the latest Internet IPO has paid off handsomely for you, the sky's the limit as to the luxury you can enjoy. But if you're more apt to cruise the Internet in search of bargains, you can still find something "affordable" in Aspen. Just remember that you're paying to be in a top-notch resort.

Lodging runs the gamut from large luxury hotels, such as the St. Regis, to small inns to condominiums and private-house rentals. What you won't find are chain motels. Though many in Aspen have bemoaned the ongoing closure of the old-time small ski lodges, you'll still find the camaraderie and personal touch that characterized such lodges at places like the Chalet Lisl, Skiers Chalet, or the Boomerang.

Since Aspen is first and foremost a town, very few accommodations are ski-in/ski-out. As the town is relatively compact, however, most are just a few blocks from the gondola or Lift 1A. Frequent buses and shuttles mean that you'll never have far to walk. Slopeside accommodations are more prevalent in Snowmass Village, which was built as a resort.

During the Christmas–New Year's week and weekends in summer and winter, lodgings are often completely booked, so making reservations well in advance is a must. The "off-seasons"—from about mid-April until the beginning of June and from October until Thanksgiving—are the best time to find readily available lodging as well as discounted prices; however, many of the smaller hotels are closed during part or all of these periods.

Prices

The price categories used in this guide are based on the rack rate (the room cost that hotels print in their brochures and quote over the phone) of a standard double in winter high season, which runs from about the second week in February through March. Summer prices are generally slightly lower. When looking at the prices given for each property, keep in mind that they don't take into account the Christmas–New Year's week, when prices rise to the level of the 14,000-ft peaks that surround Aspen and Snowmass.

For easy comparison shopping, contact **Aspen Central Reservations** (tel. 800/262–7736) or **Snowmass Central Reservations** (tel. 800/766–9627). If your travel plans are flexible, you may be able to obtain lower-priced lodging by checking out the "Virtual Hostel" section of the Aspen Central Reservations Web site (www.aspen4u.com). New listings in this section are posted on Mondays. You must commence your stay within the two weeks that follow.

CATEGORY	COST*
$$$$	over $400
$$$	$275–$400
$$	$175–$275
$	under $175

All prices are for a standard double room, excluding 8.2% city, county, and state taxes in Aspen; 11.8% in Snowmass.

ASPEN LODGING

$$$$ THE BRAND. A stay in the Brand's one- or two-bedroom apartment-style suites lets you experience the high-profile side of Aspen both past and present. The downtown Brand building, constructed of native peachblow sandstone, dates to 1891 and once housed the offices of two of Aspen's largest mining companies. Today the building is owned by local magnate Harley Baldwin and also houses Baldwin's art gallery and an array of super-chic shops. The apartments, once featured in *Architectural Digest*, have been meticulously decorated by New York–based interior designer Peter Kunz, with looks that range from southwestern to English country to Soho loft. Sophisticated urbanites will feel right at home. The moderately sized bathrooms are done up in luxe marble; kitchens, on the other hand, have condo-style cabinetry and appliances. The staff will go to great lengths to meet any request, and niceties such as champagne, flowers, and fruit baskets are standard at check-in. Guests, of course, get temporary membership to Baldwin's well-known, private Caribou Club restaurant and nightclub during their stay. Minimum-night stay requirements apply year-round. *205 S. Galena St., 81611, tel. 970/920–1800, fax 970/920–3602. 6 suites. In-room data ports, in-room safes, in-room VCRs, baby-sitting, dry cleaning, laundry service, concierge, airport shuttle, free parking. AE, MC, V. Closed early Oct.–Thanksgiving and mid-April–Memorial Day. www.aspentimes.com*

$$$$ HOTEL JEROME. At the opulent Jerome, built in 1889 and now on
★ the National Register of Historic Places, guests experience the trappings of another era while enjoying comforts that late-19th-century travelers could never have envisioned. Victorian grandeur oozes from the lobby's dazzling array of vintage furnishings, crystal chandeliers, intricate woodwork, and gold-

laced floor tiling. Only an ascetic could fail to find comfort in the extra-large rooms, individually decorated in the jewel tones, patterned rugs and wallpaper, substantial drapes, and carved wood furniture (some antique) that typify Victorian style. Decidedly non-Victorian amenities include king beds and deluxe bathrooms with oversized marble tubs, separate showers, and, often, a Jacuzzi. In addition to two well-regarded restaurants, the legendary J-Bar is one of Aspen's best-known watering holes. A free shuttle conveys skiers to Aspen Mountain several blocks away. An on-site outlet of Aspen Sports makes ski rental and tuning convenient. *330 E. Main St., 81611, tel. 970/920–1000 or 800/331–7213, fax 970/925–2784. 76 rooms, 16 suites. 2 restaurants, 2 bars, outdoor café, air-conditioning, in-room data ports, in-room safes, in-room VCRs, kitchenettes (some), minibars, no-smoking floors, room service, pool, outdoor hot tub, massage, exercise room, ski shop, ski storage, baby-sitting, dry cleaning, laundry service, concierge, business services, meeting rooms, airport shuttle, parking (fee). AE, DC, MC, V. www.hoteljerome.com*

$$$$ ★ **LITTLE NELL.** To its loyal clientele, nothing compares with the discreet elegance and impeccable service of the Little Nell, a member of the Relais & Châteaux association of small luxury inns. Each generously sized room (starting at 600 square ft) at the slopeside hotel has a gas-burning fireplace and down sofas or lounge chairs that complement the warm neutral decor; the cavernous marble bathrooms are as big as some Aspen apartments. Suites also have European steam showers and Jacuzzis. Thoughtful touches include large-size Crabtree & Evelyn toiletries, magnifying mirrors in the bath, steam irons, and a ski concierge who provides storage, tuning service, and a complimentary wax. The Nell pampers its littlest guests, too, providing children with toys and books on check-in. Overstuffed couches in front of the large wood-burning lobby fireplace make a cozy venue for a drink; the newly renovated bar hosts one of Aspen's most fashionable après-ski scenes. And the Nell's

Hotel Jerome

No matter where you're staying in Aspen, make sure to include a stop at the historic Hotel Jerome as you stroll through town. Now one of Aspen's finest restored buildings, the hotel has gone through ups and downs over the past century. If buildings could speak, this one would have some incredible tales to spin.

Opened in 1889, the hotel was envisioned by two innkeepers from Kansas and financed by Jerome B. Wheeler, the former president of Macy's department store in New York and an influential figure in Aspen's mining boom. The three men intended to build a rival to the Ritz in Paris, and the design included such novelties at the time as indoor plumbing, steam heat, and an elevator. Living up to its promise, the Jerome attracted wealthy travelers from across the United States.

After silver was demonetized in 1893, Wheeler's fortune plummeted along with Aspen's, and he lost title to the Jerome in 1909. The hotel was bought in 1911 by Mansor Elisha, who managed to keep it going during Aspen's "quiet years." The Jerome got a second wind in the 1950s, when it was leased by modern town father Walter Paepcke and received a face-lift from Bauhaus designer Herbert Bayer. Stars like Gary Cooper and Lana Turner became visitors.

In the 1960s, the Jerome fell into neglect and was closed for a few years. When it was bought again in the late '60s, its former grandeur was all but gone, and beds could be had for about five dollars a night. The hotel's great renaissance began in 1985, thanks to Aspen real-estate magnate Dick Butera. A series of photos adjacent to the Jerome lobby documents all stages of the painstaking renovation. A collection of photos of old-time Aspen also graces the walls, providing a visual link between the grand hotel and the era in which it evolved.

revamped restaurant continues to receive accolades from guests and locals. 675 E. Durant Ave., 81611, tel. 970/920–4600 or 888/843–6355, fax 970/920–4670. 77 rooms, 15 suites. Restaurant, lobby lounge, piano bar, in-room data ports, in-room safes, in-room VCRs, minibars, room service, pool, outdoor hot tub, massage, steam room, health club, ski storage, bookstore, shops, baby-sitting, dry cleaning, laundry service, concierge, business services, meeting rooms, airport shuttle, parking (fee). AE, D, DC, MC, V. www.thelittlenell.com

$$$$ **THE RESIDENCE.** One of Aspen's most novel places to stay is The Residence, a boutique hotel with just seven suites and apartments on the second floor of the centrally located Aspen Block building, which dates to 1886. Owner Terry Butler, an avid collector, has decorated the rooms with a cornucopia of antique furniture, museum-quality art, upholstered walls and ceilings, Ralph Lauren linens, and objets trouvés from around the world. In comparison to the rooms, most bathrooms are small (though also highly decorated) and the kitchens have rather basic appliances. Guests rave about the personalized service; though The Residence doesn't offer many on-site amenities, the staff will procure just about anything one could desire, including a private chef for meals "at home." Continental breakfast is served in the small but airy reception area, reminiscent of an Italian palazzo courtyard. Guests have access to the private Caribou Club restaurant/nightclub and the Aspen Athletic Club. 305 S. Galena St., 81611, tel. 970/920–6532, fax 970/925–1125. 7 suites. Air-conditioning, in-room VCRs, baby-sitting, dry cleaning, laundry service, concierge, parking (fee). AE, DC, MC, V. www.aspenresidence.com

$$$$ **ST. REGIS ASPEN.** Given the St. Regis's size and array of amenities, you could vacation without ever leaving the premises. The hotel began life as a Ritz-Carlton, and many locals still refer to it as such, though the changeover took place in 1998. In fall 1999 much of the hotel underwent an extensive facelift, replacing the trademark Ritz chandeliers and pastels with a look billed as

"casual mountain elegance": overstuffed leather chairs, suede pillows, leather-topped tables, and rawhide lamp shades in the lobby lounge; dark-wood furniture, muted colors, and vintage Aspen photos in the guest rooms. The hotel's massive redbrick, château-style exterior remains the same. Signature touches include ultracomfortable "Heavenly" beds, a fruit bowl and bottled water in all rooms at check-in, and Bijan toiletries in the large baths. A stay on the restricted-access club level includes a continually changing buffet of food and beverages. The house restaurant is Olives, a venture of celebrity chef Todd English; Whiskey Rocks, a cousin to L.A.'s Sky Bar, is the chic place to imbibe. *315 E. Dean St., 81611, tel. 970/920–3300 or 888/454–9005, fax 970/925–8998. 231 rooms, 26 suites. Restaurant, 2 bars, lobby lounge, 2 outdoor cafés, air-conditioning, in-room data ports, in-room safes, minibars, no-smoking rooms, room service, pool, beauty salon, indoor/outdoor hot tubs, massage, sauna, spa, steam room, health club, ski shop, ski storage, shops, baby-sitting, dry cleaning, laundry service, concierge, concierge floor, business services, meeting rooms, parking (fee). AE, D, DC, MC, V. www.stregisaspen.com*

$$$–$$$$ ASPEN ALPS. These condominiums, built in the early 1960s and spread among several buildings at the eastern edge of Aspen Mountain, are a good choice for location and available amenities. Because condominiums start at two bedrooms, however, they're not the most economical choice for two people (though summer rates can be significantly lower than those in winter). About one-third of the condos are true ski-in/ski-out. All have fireplaces, either wood-burning or gas, and balconies. Amenities include free in-town shuttle service, a health club, and a bell staff that will pick up and deliver take-out orders from restaurants in Aspen. *700 Ute Ave., 81611, tel. 970/925–7820 or 800/228–7820, fax 970/920–2528. 66 2-bedroom condominiums, 17 3-bedroom condominiums. In-room VCRs, no-smoking rooms, room service, pool, outdoor hot tub, massage, sauna, steam room, health club, baby-sitting, coin laundry, dry*

aspen lodging

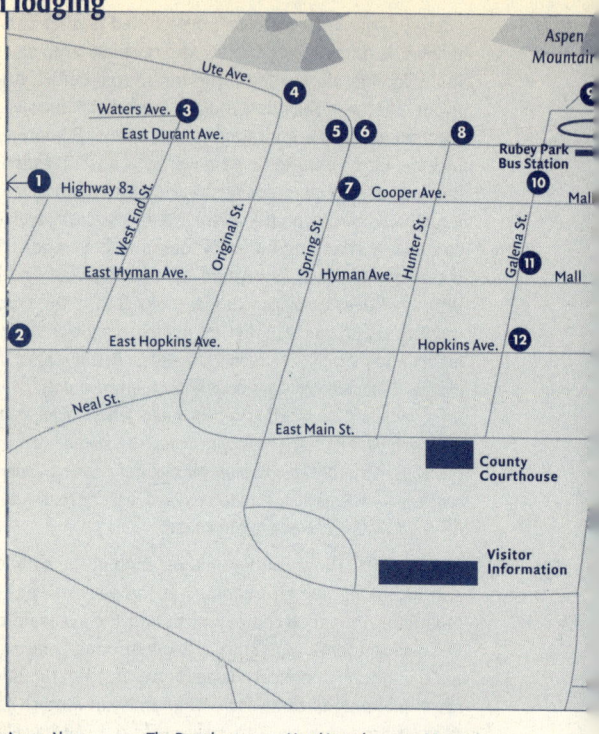

Aspen Alps, 4
Aspen Club Lodge, 5
Aspen Meadows, 34
Aspen Mountain Lodge, 31
Aspen Square, 7
Beaumont Inn, 1
Boomerang Lodge, 33
The Brand, 12
Chalet Lisl, 22
Christmas Inn, 29
The Gant, 3
Hearthstone House, 23
Holland House, 17
Hotel Aspen, 9
Hotel Durant, 20
Hotel Jerome, 25
Hotel Lenado, 24
Independence Square, 10
Inn at Aspen, 35
Innsbruck Inn, 30
Little Nell, 6
Lift One, 19
Limelite Lodge, 15
Molly Gibson Lodge, 27
Mountain Chalet, 14
Mountain House, 2
North of Nell, 8
The Residence, 11
St. Moritz Lodge, 32
St. Regis Aspen, 13
Sardy House, 26
Skiers Chalet, 18

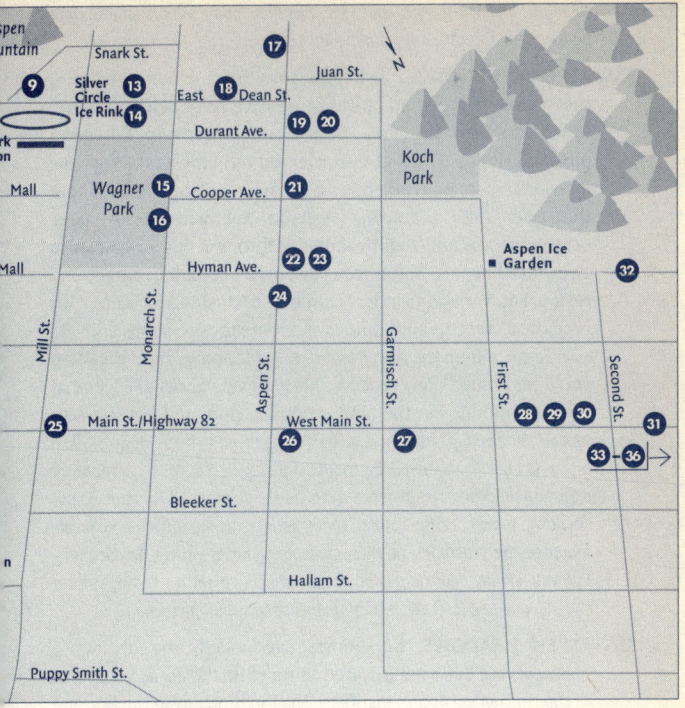

Snowflake Inn, 16

Snow Queen
Victorian Bed &
Breakfast, 21

T Lazy 7 Ranch, 36

Tyrolean
Lodge, 28

cleaning, laundry service, concierge, meeting room, airport shuttle, free parking. AE, DC, MC, V. www.aspenalps.com

$$$ ASPEN CLUB LODGE. Just steps away from Aspen Mountain, this luxurious lodge underwent extensive remodeling in 1999, which changed the look from Southwestern to European mountain lodge. The slightly pricier rooms in the west wing have interior access, pine beams and furnishings, and French doors that open onto a balcony or patio. East-wing rooms have exterior access and slightly larger bathrooms but no balconies or exposed beams. Suites also have fireplaces and Jacuzzis. The restaurant, Variations, offers continental cuisine and is open for breakfast, lunch, and dinner. An on-site ski shop and ski concierge eliminate any hassle of schlepping skis, meaning you'll be immediately ready to hit the lively après-ski scene at the bar or lounge in the always popular pool and hot tub with waterfall. *709 E. Durant Ave., 81611, tel. 970/925–6760 or 800/882–2582, fax 970/925–6778. 84 rooms, 6 suites. Restaurant, bar, outdoor café, air-conditioning, in-room data ports, in-room VCRs (some), no-smoking rooms, refrigerators, room service, pool, outdoor hot tub, massage, exercise room, ski shop, ski storage, baby-sitting, dry cleaning, laundry service, concierge, business services, meeting room, airport shuttle, parking (fee). AE, MC, V. www.aspenclublodge.com*

$$$ ASPEN MEADOWS. Sometimes overlooked, the distinctive Meadows is a Bauhaus-inspired complex on the 40-acre campus of the renowned Aspen Institute. The location along the Roaring Fork River has exceptional views of the mountains, and courtesy vans depart every half hour for town. The Music Tent, site of a summer-long music festival, is a short stroll away. The rooms, which start at 500 square ft, are capacious, with floor-to-ceiling windows, ultra-streamlined furniture (e.g., Eero Saarinen–designed tables and Harry Bertoia webbing and chrome chairs), and balconies or patios. Neutral color schemes are intended to inspire creative thoughts. A full-service, well-regarded restaurant and health club (complimentary for guests), as well as extensive conference facilities, round out the amenities. It's truly a serene oasis. *845 Meadows Rd., 81611, tel. 970/925–4240 or 800/452–4240, fax 970/925–7790. 40 rooms, 58 suites. Restaurant, bar, outdoor café, in-room data ports, in-room VCRs, minibars, no-smoking rooms, room service, pool, outdoor hot tub, massage, sauna, steam room, 6 tennis courts, health club, bicycles, library, coin laundry, dry cleaning, concierge, business services, convention center, airport shuttle, parking (fee). AE, D, DC, MC, V. www.aspenmeadows.com*

$$$ **ASPEN SQUARE.** This conveniently located condominium hotel (across from the gondola, one block from the supermarket) attracts a high percentage of repeat guests who appreciate its relative value. All units are individually owned, so furnishings and decor vary widely, but most are modern and attractive, and all have wood-burning fireplaces and balconies. The spacious studios (some with Murphy beds) are more than adequate for two people. Après-ski cookies and hot cider are served in the cozy lobby area with an antler chandelier and a gas fireplace. *617 E. Cooper Ave., 81611, tel. 970/925–1000 or 800/862–7736, fax 970/925–1017. 70 studios, 25 2-bedroom condominiums, 6 1-bedroom condominiums. In-room data ports, in-room VCRs, no-smoking rooms, pool, outdoor hot tub, exercise room, ski storage, coin laundry, concierge, meeting room, free parking. AE, MC, V. www.aspensquarehotel.com*

$$$ **THE GANT.** This condominium complex near the base of Aspen
★ Mountain is a great find for families or groups who want a little luxury, more than the standard amount of space, and proximity to the action without breaking the bank. The one- to four-bedroom units, among eight buildings, are generously sized, with one-bedrooms beginning at 800 square ft. Decor varies according to owner taste, but all have wood-burning fireplaces and private patios or balconies. A full menu of amenities includes concierge service, free shuttle vans within Aspen, and tennis courts. *610 W. End St., 81611, tel. 970/925–5000 or 800/345–1471, fax 970/925–6891. 115 condominiums. Fans, in-room data ports, in-room safes, in-room VCRs, no-smoking rooms, 2 pools, 3 outdoor hot*

tubs, sauna, 5 tennis courts, exercise room, ski storage, coin laundry, concierge, business services, convention center, airport shuttle, free parking. AE, D, MC, V. www.gantaspen.com

$$$ **HOTEL LENADO.** On first impression, this small luxury inn
★ seems more Southern California beach hotel than ski lodge, with its airy, contemporary lobby and three-story concrete-and-stone fireplace. The rooms, however, bespeak mountain comfort, with rustic bed frames of carved applewood or hickory, spacious closet armoires, Ralph Lauren linens, and roomy blue-and-white-tiled baths. The larger, deluxe rooms come with wet bars and Jacuzzi baths; some have woodburning stoves and balconies. Rates include a full gourmet breakfast, served in the urbane bar area. Room service is available from the Sardy House hotel, a block away. *200 S. Aspen St., 81611, tel. 970/925–6246 or 800/321–3457, fax 970/925–3840. 19 rooms. Bar, air-conditioning (some), fans, in-room data ports, in-room VCRs (some), outdoor hot tub, ski storage, library, dry cleaning, laundry service, concierge, meeting room. AE, DC, MC, V. Closed late Oct.–mid-Nov.*

$$$ **LIFT ONE.** The Lift One condominiums are priced slightly lower than those at other condo hotels in town yet have a great location one block from Aspen Mountain's Lift 1A. The one- to three-bedroom condominiums all have private balconies and fireplaces, and some enjoy south-facing views of Aspen Mountain. Though decor varies according to owner, most are stylish and contemporary. *131 E. Durant Ave., 81611, tel. 970/925–1670 or 800/543–8001, fax 970/925–1152. 30 condominiums. In-room data ports, in-room VCRs, pool, outdoor hot tub, sauna, ski storage, meeting room. MC, V. www.liftone.com*

$$$ **NORTH OF NELL.** The North of Nell condos offer a great location within steps of the Aspen Mountain gondola and, considering the generous square footage and the often luxurious decor, prices are not extravagant. The shopping-mall aura of the ground floor belies the contemporary look of the rest of the building. All condos have gas fireplaces and balconies; as

they're individually owned, furnishings vary greatly. There's no pool or hot tub on site, but during the winter guests have free access to the Aspen Athletic Club, several blocks away. *555 E. Durant Ave., 81611, tel. 970/925–1510 or 800/481–1510, fax 970/925–1550. 17 2-bedroom condominiums, 16 3-bedroom condominiums, 7 1-bedroom condominiums. Air-conditioning (some), fans, in-room VCRs, no-smoking rooms, shops, coin laundry, concierge, free parking. AE, MC, V. Closed mid-April–early June and early Oct.–Thanksgiving. www.lfoa.com/northnell*

$$$ **SARDY HOUSE.** Each December, Aspenites gather for the
★ holiday lighting of a towering spruce tree in front of the Sardy House, a meticulously restored brick 1893 Victorian. The genteel rooms, split between the original house and a newer wing (virtually indistinguishable from the original) include Victorian-style furniture in wood and wicker, mauve floral carpeting, Laura Ashley bedding, and many bay windows. Top-floor rooms evoke the feel of a luxurious attic with their vaulted, wood-paneled ceilings. Heated towel racks add an element of pampering to the black-and-white-tiled baths; all but two have Jacuzzis. A hearty breakfast at the intimate Jack's Restaurant is gratis for guests; dinner is available nightly. The outdoor pool and patio, ringed by huge spruces, is especially inviting. *128 E. Main St., 81611, tel. 970/920–2525 or 800/321–3457, fax 970/920–4478. 14 rooms, 6 suites. Restaurant, bar, air-conditioning (some), fans, in-room data ports, in-room VCRs (some), refrigerators (some), room service, pool, outdoor hot tub, sauna, ski storage, dry cleaning, laundry service, concierge, meeting room, free parking. AE, DC, MC, V. Closed mid-April to early May.*

$$ **ASPEN MOUNTAIN LODGE.** Just a few blocks from downtown on Main St., the lodge provides comfortable, moderately priced accommodations. Rooms on four floors ring an internal courtyard, highlighted by a 40-ft river-rock fireplace. The three deluxe rooms have Jacuzzi bathtubs; all rooms have wet bars. A continental breakfast is served each morning. *311 W. Main St.,*

81611, tel. 970/925–7650 or 800/362–7736, fax 970/925–5744. 38 rooms. Breakfast room, air-conditioning, in-room VCRs, no-smoking rooms, refrigerators, pool, outdoor hot tub, ski storage, free parking. AE, D, DC, MC, V. Closed mid-April–late May. www.aspenmountainlodge.com

$$ BEAUMONT INN. The Beaumont, a few blocks east of downtown Aspen, looks more motel than hotel from the outside but offers some nice amenities, such as European featherbeds, a full sit-down breakfast, and complimentary shuttle service to anywhere in town. "Deluxe" rooms are spacious, with pine furniture; "superior" rooms have not been as recently redone. The suite, with a log-framed queen bed and ample closet and bath, is a good value, comparatively. Guests can get discount passes to the Aspen Athletic Club in town. *1301 E. Cooper St., 81611, tel. 970/925–7081 or 800/344–3853, fax 970/925–1610. 29 rooms, 1 suite. Bar, breakfast room, no-smoking rooms, pool, outdoor hot tub, ski storage, coin laundry, dry cleaning, laundry service, airport shuttle, free parking. AE, D, DC, MC, V. Closed mid-April–late May. www.thebeaumont.com*

$$ BOOMERANG LODGE. One of Aspen's oldest lodges, the
★ unique Boomerang provides comfort, sophistication, and personal service at a moderate price. Owner Charlie Paterson originally built a small log cabin on the site in 1949; the cabin is still there, surrounded by the much larger structure that Paterson designed and built after studying with Frank Lloyd Wright. Wright's influence is evident in the multitude of glass and angled floor plans. The top-floor luxury rooms are the cream of the crop, with sleek furnishings, Southwestern decor, gas fireplaces, and huge granite and marble baths. The wonderful log cabin feels like the vacation retreat that's been in your family for years. Studios and multi-bedroom suites with full kitchens are also available. All rooms look out onto the quiet courtyard, with a secluded pool area. Continental breakfast is provided in the airy upstairs lounge. A capacious lower lounge has a large-screen TV, fireplace, and a sunken seating area with

an underwater view of the pool. 500 W. Hopkins Ave., 81611, tel. 970/925–3416 or 800/992–8852, fax 970/925–3314. 28 rooms, 6 suites. Breakfast room, in-room data ports, kitchenettes (some), no-smoking rooms, refrigerators (some), pool, outdoor hot tub, sauna, car rental, free parking. AE, D, DC, MC, V. Closed mid-April–mid-May. www.boomeranglodge.com

$$ HEARTHSTONE HOUSE. ★ Though short on amenities, the Hearthstone offers good value in a sophisticated setting. Guests return year after year to the unobtrusive structure, designed in 1961 by a student of Frank Lloyd Wright to look more like a house than a hotel. The furnishings throughout—Stickley mission-style in public areas, 1960s contemporary in the rooms—take their style cues from Wright's aesthetic. Standard rooms run small, while rooms with king beds are fairly spacious. Some baths are equipped with whirlpool tubs. Guests tend to congregate in the upstairs living room—with fireplace, books, games, and a computer for checking e-mail—or the adjacent balcony for afternoon wine and cheese. Continental breakfast is also included. 134 E. Hyman Ave., 81611, tel. 970/925–7632 or 888/925–7632, fax 970/920–4450. 17 rooms. Breakfast room, no-smoking rooms, steam room, free parking. AE, D, DC, MC, V. Closed mid-April–end May and late Oct.–Thanksgiving. www.hearthstonehouse.com

$$ HOTEL ASPEN. The Hotel Aspen's most striking feature is the upstairs lounge and breakfast room, lined with huge windows that take full advantage of a view of Aspen Mountain. Rooms are comfortably furnished and generously sized. All are equipped with microwaves; some have wood-burning stoves (for heat, not cooking!) An appealing, though pricier, choice would be one of the Jacuzzi rooms, with pine furniture and a killer hot tub located on a private balcony. A video library at the front desk helps you put those in-room VCRs to use. Continental breakfast is included, as is après-ski wine and cheese in winter. 110 W. Main St., 81611, tel. 970/925–3441 or 800/527–7369, fax 970/920–1379. 37 rooms, 8 suites. Breakfast room, air-conditioning, in-room data ports, in-room VCRs, kitchenettes (some), no-smoking rooms, minibars, pool, outdoor hot tub, free parking. AE, D, DC, MC, V.

$$ HOTEL DURANT. A couple of blocks from Aspen Mountain's Lift 1A, the petite Hotel Durant offers small but thoughtfully decorated rooms and personalized service. The decor varies from room to room and may include pinkish-beige or sage-green painted walls, knotty-pine ceiling beams, botanical prints, and down comforters with floral duvet covers. Most rooms have microwaves, and a continental breakfast is served downstairs. The lobby, with its modern country style furnishings, wall-length fireplace, and pillow-laden couches, is a comfortable venue for late-afternoon wine and cheese in winter; a small wood patio provides a warm-weather hangout. 122 E. Durant St., 81611, tel. 970/925–8500 or 877/438–7268, fax 970/925–8789. 17 rooms, 3 suites. Kitchenettes (some), no-smoking rooms, refrigerators, outdoor hot tub, free parking. AE, D, MC, V. www.preferredlodging.com

$$ INDEPENDENCE SQUARE. Housed in a late-19th-century brick building, Independence Square has a prime location on Aspen's downtown pedestrian mall. The completely renovated interior is modern and well lit. Rooms can be on the snug side and, more often than not, the queen beds are Murphy-style. As units are individually owned, specific decor differs, but most are accented with contemporary, light-wood furniture and tasteful decor. Plus you won't find a better-situated hot tub in town—the rooftop Jacuzzi is a stone's throw from the skiers on Aspen Mountain's Little Nell run and has views to Independence Pass on the Continental Divide. Continental breakfast is included, as are passes to the massive Aspen Club fitness and wellness center east of town (free shuttle service is available). 404 S. Galena St., 81611, tel. 970/920–2313 or 800/633–0336, fax 970/925–1233. 27 rooms. Breakfast room, air-conditioning, in-room VCRs (some), minibars, no-smoking rooms, outdoor hot tub, ski storage, concierge, airport shuttle. AE, MC, V. www.friasproperties.com

$$ INN AT ASPEN. ★ For those who plan to ski at both Aspen and Snowmass and want a full-service hotel, the Inn at Aspen may be the perfect choice. It's situated about halfway between the two resorts, at the base of Buttermilk Mountain, which itself offers premier beginner and intermediate terrain. Not having a car may be a potential drawback, but the inn runs complimentary shuttle service into Aspen, and it's also on the bus route. Rooms run the gamut from adequately sized to spacious junior suites. Knotty-pine furniture, wrought-iron lamps, and marbled wallpaper give warmth to the decor. The two royal suites are definitely high class. The restaurant closes during the spring and fall. *38750 Hwy 82, 81611, tel. 970/925–1500 or 800/925–1515, fax 970/925–9037. 117 rooms, 5 suites. Restaurant, bar, air-conditioning, in-room data ports, in-room VCRs, kitchenettes (some), no-smoking rooms, refrigerators, room service, pool, outdoor hot tub, massage, steam rooms, exercise room, ski storage, coin laundry, dry cleaning, laundry service, concierge, business services, meeting rooms, airport shuttle, car rental, free parking. AE, D, DC, MC, V. www.innataspen.com*

$$ INNSBRUCK INN. Located a few blocks from Aspen's downtown core, the Innsbruck, as its name might imply, attracts a steady stream of European guests who are drawn to this small hotel's basic but bright rooms with homespun touches, such as Bavarian-style furniture, down comforters, and spa-size toiletries. The small lobby, with fireplace, is a model of gemütlichkeit. Be sure to admire the dark, scalloped-edged beams throughout the hotel, which were painstakingly hand carved by a previous owner. A continental breakfast that includes homemade muesli and—in a nod to the European clientele—cold meats and cheeses is served in the airy breakfast room overlooking Main Street. In winter wine and cheese, cookies, and warm drinks are served après ski. *233 W. Main St., 81611, tel. 970/925–2980, fax 970/925–6960. 30 rooms. Breakfast room, air-conditioning (some), no-smoking rooms, refrigerators (on request), pool, outdoor hot tub, free parking. AE, MC, V. www.preferredlodging.com*

$$ MOLLY GIBSON LODGE. ★ You're sure to find something to suit your preference at the laid-back Molly Gibson, with nine types of rooms in two buildings and a full slate of amenities. Spacious deluxe rooms come with four-person Jacuzzis (some right out in the room), sitting areas, fireplaces, and skylights. On the other end of the spectrum are the diminutive courtyard rooms, which may be fine if you plan on being outdoors most of the day. One- and two-bedroom apartments with full kitchens are a good choice for families. Decor is contemporary classic, with generous use of mirrors. Transportation options include a courtesy van shuttle and—in summer—cruiser bikes for loan. A large continental breakfast is included. *101 W. Main St., 81611, tel. 970/925–3434 or 800/356–6559, fax 970/925–2582. 44 rooms, 6 condominiums. Bar, breakfast room, air-conditioning (some), in-room data ports, in-room VCRs, no-smoking rooms, refrigerators, 2 pools, 2 outdoor hot tubs, ski storage, laundry service, meeting room, airport shuttle, free parking. AE, D, DC, MC, V. www.mollygibson.com*

$–$$ MOUNTAIN CHALET. Since 1954 the same couple has owned and operated this property, providing clean, comfortable, and affordable accommodations in the heart of Aspen. Depending on your budget, you could get anything from no-frills economy rooms on up to more modern and bright deluxe rooms with fireplaces. Other options include several four-bunk rooms in which beds can be reserved individually and two-bedroom apartments with full kitchens. A "skier's breakfast" (eggs, pancakes, etc.) is included for winter guests; in summer continental breakfast is served buffet style. *333 E. Durant Ave., 81611, tel. 970/925–7797 or 800/321–7813, fax 970/925–7811. 37 rooms, 4 2-bedroom condominiums, 3 4-bedrooms. In-room VCRs (some), no-smoking rooms, refrigerators (some), pool, hot tub, sauna, steam room, exercise room, ski storage, coin laundry, meeting room, free parking. D, DC, MC, V.*

$–$$ ST. MORITZ LODGE. The friendly St. Moritz, tucked in Aspen's West End near Shadow Mountain, is popular with Aspen newcomers, who take advantage of low rates in the hostel rooms until they find permanent housing. Also available are motel-style standard rooms—bare-bones basic but clean—and several one- and two-bedroom condos that retain that beloved 1970s-style ski-lodge decor. Eight condos with kitchenettes are slated for addition in the next year. Continental breakfast is served in winter and summer, and free shuttles to the ski areas are a couple of blocks away. *334 W. Hyman Ave., 81611, tel. 970/925–3220 or 800/817–2069, fax 970/920–4032. 13 rooms, 11 3-bed rooms, 4 condominiums. Refrigerators, pool, outdoor hot tub, coin laundry. AE, D, DC, MC, V. www.stmoritzlodge.com*

$–$$ SNOWFLAKE INN. The motel has a prime downtown location, but the smallish rooms, with rough-wood paneling and older furniture, are in need of a face-lift. Nevertheless, this could be an acceptable choice for a family on a budget, as many of the rooms are suites. All have either kitchenettes or full kitchens, and a few are available with fireplaces. Continental breakfast is available in winter only. *221 E. Hyman Ave., 81611, tel. 970/925–3221 or 800/247–2069, fax 970/925–8740. 14 rooms, 21 1-bedroom suites, 3 2-bedroom suites. Air-conditioning (some), kitchenettes (some), refrigerators, pool, outdoor hot tub, sauna, coin laundry, free parking. AE, D, DC, MC, V. www.snowflakeinn.com*

$ CHALET LISL. Chalet Lisl is a vintage Aspen lodge, built in the 1960s. Moderately sized rooms have one queen and one twin bed each, full kitchens, and nicely remodeled bathrooms. Furnishings are clean but not modern. Some of the wood paneling in the rooms has been salvaged from barns, lending the feel of an old miner's cabin. For skiers and snowboarders, an old tuning bench has proven a popular amenity. In the summer, guests can use the grill and eat at picnic tables in the yard—and even make salads from the homegrown greens. *100 E. Hyman Ave., 81611, tel. 970/925–3520, fax 970/925–3580. 4 studios, 4 1-bedroom suites. Picnic area, air-conditioning (some), fans, no-smoking rooms, outdoor hot tub, ski storage, library, free parking. MC, V.*

Condo 101

If you're traveling in a group of four or more, a condominium may provide the most bang for your rental buck. Expect to pay about $350 on up for a two-bedroom condo in high season (mid-February through March).

Alpine Property Management, tel. 970/925–1100 or 800/542–7736, www.alpineproperty.com

Aspen Classic Properties, tel. 970/925–1100 or 800/542–7736, www.aspenclassic.com

Aspen Lodging Co., tel. 970/925–2260 or 800/321–7025, www.aspenlodgingco.com

Aspen Resort Accommodations, tel. 970/925–4772 or 800/727–7369, www.aspenreservations.net

Coates, Reid & Waldron Property Management, tel. 970/925–1400 or 800/222–7736, www.aspencrw.com

Laurelwood and Interlude Condominiums (Snowmass), tel. 970/923–3110 or 800/356–7893, www.destinationsnowmass.com

Exclusive Vacation Properties (ResortQuest), tel. 970/925–8667 or 877/387–8664, www.aspenrqirentals.com

First Choice Properties, tel. 970/923–4488, 800/759–3686, www.fcprentals.com

Frias Properties, tel. 970/920–2000 or 800/633–0336, www.friasproperties.com

McCartney Property Management, tel. 970/925–8717 or 800/433–8465, www.mccartneyprop.com

Snowmass Home Rentals, tel. 970/923–3636 or 800/999–0816, www.snowmasshomes.net

Snowmass Lodging Company, tel. 970/923–3232 or 800/365–0410, www.snowmasslodging.com

Top of the Village Condominiums (Snowmass), tel. 970/923–3673 or 800/525–4200, www.destinationsnowmass.com

$ CHRISTMAS INN. The inn, with its cheery red, white, and green exterior, offers very basic motel rooms at reasonable prices—for Aspen, that is. New owners purchased the property in 1999, so expect some updates to the tired-looking furnishings. A continental breakfast with a hot entrée is included. *232 W. Main St., 81611, tel. 970/925–3822 or 800/625–5881, fax 970/925–3328. 24 rooms. No-smoking rooms, outdoor hot tub, sauna, free parking. AE, D, DC, MC, V.* www.christmasinn.com

$ HOLLAND HOUSE. Family-owned and -operated since 1950, the Bavarian-style Holland House enjoys a slopeside location next to Lift 1A. Bright, cozy rooms, almost half of which have shared baths, are enhanced by knotty-pine ceilings and hardwood floors. Many rooms have king beds, and some have balconies. Rates include a full breakfast. A one-bedroom apartment with kitchen is also available. The front desk is usually unstaffed, so don't plan on extensive service requests. In summer, the lodge is given over entirely to students attending the Aspen Music Festival. *720 S. Aspen St., 81611, tel. 970/925–7361. 20 rooms, 14 with bath; 1 1-bedroom condominium. Breakfast room, no-smoking rooms, outdoor hot tub, ski storage, free parking. AE, MC, V. Closed mid-April–early June and mid-June–Thanksgiving.* www.hollandhouseskilodge.com

$ LIMELITE LODGE. The Limelite earns kudos for affordable price,
★ good comfort level, and central location. The large rooms, in two buildings, are done up with colonial-style furniture, patterned wallpaper, and plush carpeting. Continental breakfast is served in the cheery lobby with fireplace. Nine apartments with full kitchens are also available at the neighboring Deep Powder, an older ski lodge now owned by the Limelite; the two log cabin–style units have the most atmosphere. *228 E. Cooper St., 81611, tel. 970/925–3025 or 800/433–0832, fax 970/925–5120. 60 rooms, 9 condominiums, 3 suites. Air-conditioning (some), in-room VCRs (some), no-smoking rooms,*

refrigerators, 2 pools, 2 outdoor hot tubs, sauna, ski storage, coin laundry. AE, D, DC, MC, V.

$ MOUNTAIN HOUSE. ★ The Mountain House is a quiet little affordably priced refuge in a residential neighborhood in Aspen's east end. The small scale allows highly personalized service, too. Despite the lodge's bed-and-breakfast atmosphere, rooms have standard motel-style furnishings, but all are amply sized, with vaulted ceilings in upper-level units, and most have balconies. The suites are an especially good deal. In winter, the continental breakfast includes a hot entrée. *950 E. Hopkins Ave., 81611, tel. 970/920–2550, fax 970/544–0090. 21 rooms, 3 suites. Breakfast room, no-smoking rooms, refrigerators, hot tub, ski storage, coin laundry, free parking. AE, D, DC, MC, V. Closed late April–late May. www.mountainhouselodge.com*

$ SKIERS CHALET. An Aspen classic, the chalet opened in 1952, with a second building added in 1965, and not much has changed since. Come here for the location and reasonable price. Lift 1A is just out the back, and the heated swimming pool occupies a prime slopeside location. Rooms are simple, with double beds, dark-wood furniture, and dark-wood beams overhead. Continental breakfast is served in winter in the cozy, European-tinged lobby. A steakhouse restaurant is also on the premises. *233 Gilbert St., 81611, tel. 970/920–2037, fax 970/920–6504. 16 rooms. Restaurant, refrigerators, pool, free parking. MC, V. Closed mid-April–mid-June and late Oct.–Thanksgiving.*

$ SNOW QUEEN VICTORIAN BED & BREAKFAST. This seven-room bed-and-breakfast, in an 1886 Victorian, was in operation long before B&Bs became synonymous with Laura Ashley bedding and quaint decor. But what the Snow Queen lacks in fancy furnishings it makes up for in hospitality and tradition, as the guest letters posted in the front hallway attest. All rooms have private baths; some have a phone and TV. Breakfast is strictly continental. From about mid-June to mid-August, the

B&B primarily houses students attending the Aspen Music Festival. Three studio apartments at the neighboring Cooper Street Lofts are also available for rental. *124 E. Cooper St., 81611, tel. 970/925–8455 or 970/925–6971, fax 970/925–7391. 7 rooms. Kitchenettes (some), no-smoking rooms, outdoor hot tub. MC, V. Closed mid-April–mid-May.*

$ ★ T LAZY 7 RANCH. One of Aspen's most atmospheric places to stay is the T Lazy 7 guest ranch, located partway up the beautiful, glacially sculpted Maroon Creek valley. Set on 400 acres owned by the Deane family since 1938, the ranch offers horseback rides and fishing in summer, snowmobile tours and sleigh rides in winter (except on Sundays and Mondays). Accommodations are in cabins crafted out of the original outbuildings, which can lead to some funky layouts. Nevertheless, the cabins, all with full kitchens, are cozy and clean, with Western decor; some, like the recently redone studios and the Lou Deane cabin in the main lodge, are downright luxe. Many have vaulted ceilings and hardwood floors, and almost all have fireplaces. It's best to have a car so you can come and go as you please, especially since the ranch has no regular food service. Phoneaholics should be aware that there are no phones in the cabins, and cell phone reception is marginal. *3129 Maroon Creek Rd., 81611, tel. 970/925–7254, fax 970/925–5616. 17 cabins. Bar, pool, outdoor hot tub, horseback riding, fishing, sleigh rides, snowmobiling. D, MC, V. Closed mid-April–late May and mid-Oct.–Thanksgiving. www.tlazy7.com*

$ ★ TYROLEAN LODGE. The first thing you'll notice about the family-run Tyrolean—one of the most popular economy-priced accommodations in Aspen—is the distinctive eagle made of chrome bumpers perched atop the roof. Generously sized rooms all have one twin and two queen beds and furnishings of more recent vintage than other motels in the same price range. Top-floor rooms are the nicest, with sloped ceilings and funky—though somewhat useless—hanging adobe fireplaces. There's a long list of repeat clientele, so reserve far in advance during high seasons. *200 W. Main St., 81611, tel. 970/925–4595, fax 970/925–4598. 16 rooms. Kitchenettes, free parking. AE, MC, V.*

SNOWMASS LODGING

$$$ SILVERTREE HOTEL. This is the only full-service hotel in Snowmass, and it's ski-in/ski-out to boot. With a three-story atrium lobby and lots of steel-and-glass accents, the large Silvertree feels more urban hotel than mountain lodge. Rooms are of average size—though closets with built-in dressers and shelves are ample—and furnishings are comfortable, though not ultra-luxurious. Prices vary according to view. The slopeside pool has hosted the always amusing Ski Splash contest during recent January Wintersköl celebrations. With an on-site ski shop, health club, two restaurants, and the Snowmass Village mall right out the door, you won't lack for much. *100 Elbert La., 81615, tel. 970/923–3520 or 800/525–9402, fax 970/923–5192. 252 rooms, 8 suites. 2 restaurants, lobby lounge, in-room data ports, in-room VCRs (some), no-smoking rooms, refrigerators, room service, 2 pools, beauty salon, outdoor hot tub, massage, sauna, steam room, ski shop, ski storage, shops, baby-sitting, coin laundry, dry cleaning, laundry service, concierge, business services, meeting rooms, airport shuttle, parking (fee). AE, D, DC, MC, V. www.silvertreehotel.com*

$$ STONEBRIDGE INN. The Stonebridge, slightly removed from the hustle and bustle of the Village Mall, is one of the nicer hotel options in Snowmass. The lobby and bar areas are streamlined and elegant; the window-ringed Stonebridge Restaurant offers regional cuisine as well as outdoor dining in summer. Rooms, all with two queens, are not fancy but they're comfortably appointed and up-to-date. A continental breakfast, with hot items in winter, is included. The Stonebridge also rents out the adjacent two- and four-bedroom Tamarack Townhouses. *300 Carriage Way, 81615, tel. 970/923–*

2420 or 800/922-7242, fax 970/923-5889. 87 rooms, 5 suites. *Restaurant, bar, fans, no-smoking rooms, refrigerators, pool, outdoor hot tub, sauna, ski storage, coin laundry, meeting rooms, airport shuttle. AE, D, DC, MC, V. Closed mid-April–early June and mid-Sept.–Thanksgiving.* www.stonebridgeinn.com

$$ WILDWOOD LODGE. The Wildwood is the lower-priced, smaller-scale sibling of the Silvertree Hotel. Guests, however, can enjoy many of the Silvertree's amenities, including access to the health club, business services, and signing privileges at the two restaurants. Rooms are similar in size to those of the Silvertree but have exterior access. Decor tends toward dark wood furniture and plaid fabric accents, and a few rooms have fireplaces. As the location is adjacent to the Silvertree, it's still only steps to the ski slopes. The Village Steakhouse is the in-house restaurant; continental breakfast is complimentary in winter. 100 Elbert La., 81615, tel. 970/923-3550 or 800/471-9407, fax 970/923-4844. 144 rooms, 6 suites. *Restaurant, bar, in-room data ports, in-room VCRs (some), no-smoking rooms, refrigerators, pool, outdoor hot tub, ski storage, coin laundry, airport shuttle, parking (fee). AE, D, DC, MC, V. Closed mid-April–mid-May and late Oct.–Thanksgiving.* www.wildwood-lodge.com

$ POKOLODI LODGE. This low-key, no-frills motel-style lodge adjacent to the Village Mall provides all of the basics at basic prices. Comfortable, clean rooms can accommodate four close friends or a small family. Continental breakfast is served in the lobby. 25 Daly La., 81615, tel. 970/923-4310 or 800/666-4556, fax 970/923-2819. 50 rooms. *No-smoking rooms, refrigerators, pool, outdoor hot tub, coin laundry, airport shuttle. AE, D, MC, V.* www.pokolodi.com

$ SNOWMASS INN. Under the same management as the Pokolodi Lodge next door (where check-in is), the Snowmass Inn is one of the original properties in the village. Rooms are slightly larger, though the furnishings are not as up to date.

snowmass lodging

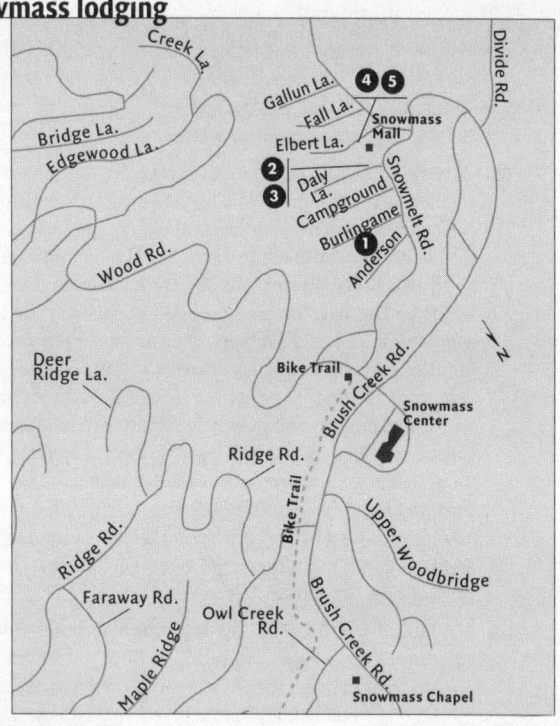

Pokolodi Lodge, 3
Silvertree Hotel, 5
Snowmass Inn, 2
Stonebridge, 1
Wildwood Lodge, 4

Continental breakfast is available at the Pokolodi, and the two motels share a pool and hot tub. 25 Daly La., 81615, tel. 970/923-4202 or 800/635-3758, fax 970/923-2819. 39 rooms. No-smoking rooms, refrigerators, pool, outdoor hot tub, coin laundry, airport shuttle. AE, D, MC, V. www.snowmassinn.com

PRACTICAL INFORMATION

Air Travel

Denver International Airport is about 200 mi from Aspen. United Express, America West Express, and Northwest Jet Airlink have daily flights into Aspen's Sardy Field Airport, which is 3 mi from Aspen and 8 mi from Snowmass. American, America West Express, Continental, Delta, Northwest Jet Airlink, and United Express fly daily nonstop from 11 U.S. cities into Eagle County Regional Airport, 70 mi northeast of Aspen. Daily direct van and limousine service to Aspen is available. Colorado Mountain Express runs trips from Denver and Vail. High Mountain Taxi provides prepaid charter service to and from Denver International Airport for groups of up to seven people.

From the U.K., British Airways has daily direct flights from London to Denver. Air Canada offers daily direct flights from Toronto, Montreal and Vancouver to Denver. In Denver, catch a connecting flight to Aspen, or take one of the van services listed above.

➤ AIRPORTS: **Denver International Airport** (tel. 303/342–2200 or 800/247–2336). **Eagle County Regional Airport** (tel. 970/524–9490). **Sardy Field Airport** (tel. 970/920–5385).

➤ AIRPORT TRANSFERS: **Colorado Mountain Express** (tel. 970/949–4227 or 800/525–6353). **High Mountain Taxi** (tel. 970/925–8294 or 800/528–8294).

BOOKING

When you book **look for nonstop flights** and **remember that "direct" flights stop at least once.** Try to avoid connecting flights, which require a change of plane.

CARRIERS

You'll most likely fly into the hub city of Denver. During ski season, Aspen has increased service and direct flights available, notably on United Express.

➤ **AIRLINES: Air Canada** (tel. 888/247–2262). **American** (tel. 800/433–7300). **America West** (tel. 800/225–9292). **British Airways** (tel. 800/247–9297). **Continental** (tel. 800/525–0280). **Delta** (tel. 800/221–1212). **Northwest** (tel. 800/225–2525). **TWA** (tel. 800/221–2000). **United** (tel. 800/241–6522). **US Airways** (tel. 800/428–4322).

CHECK-IN & BOARDING

If you're traveling during snow season, **allow extra time for the drive** to the airport. Weather conditions can slow you down more than you may have predicted. If you'll be checking skis, arrive early for your flight.

Assuming that not everyone with a ticket will show up, airlines routinely overbook planes. When everyone does, airlines ask for volunteers to give up their seats. In return, these volunteers usually get a certificate for a free flight and are rebooked on the next flight out. If there are not enough volunteers, the airline must choose who will be denied boarding. The first to get bumped are passengers who checked in late and those flying on discounted tickets, so **get to the gate and check in as early as possible,** especially during peak periods.

Always **bring a government-issued photo I.D. to the airport**. You may be asked to show it before you are allowed to check in.

FLYING TIMES

All times are approximate. Flight time from New York to Denver is four hours. Flight time from Chicago to Denver is 2½ hours. Flight time from Los Angeles to Denver is 2¼ hours. Flight time to Denver is 3½ hours from Toronto, 4 hours from Montreal, and 2¾ hours from Vancouver. Flight time from London to Denver is 10 hours. It's a 45-minute flight from Denver to Aspen.

Bus Travel

Greyhound Bus Lines runs five trips daily from Denver to Glenwood Springs, 40 mi from Aspen. The Roaring Fork Transit

Agency (RFTA), whose main station is at Rubey Park Transportation Center on Durant Street in downtown Aspen, offers hourly service between Glenwood Springs and Aspen and Snowmass. Within Snowmass there's free shuttle service; five colored flags denote the various routes.

FARES & SCHEDULES

There are both fare and free buses in Aspen. The shuttles within the City of Aspen and the Town of Snowmass Village are free. There are fare buses between Aspen and Snowmass and the "downvalley" towns such as Basalt, Carbondale, and Glenwood Springs. Buses on most routes run every 15, 20, or 30 minutes. Convenient discount punch passes and seasonal bus passes are available. Exact change is required; dollar bills are accepted.

➤ Bus Information: **Greyhound Bus Lines** (tel. 970/945–8501 or 800/931–2222). **The Roaring Fork Transit Agency (RFTA)** (tel. 970/925–8484).

Business Hours

A faded Aspen reality is the "gone skiing" signs hung in downtown shop windows on powder mornings. Aspen now functions like a little Manhattan in the mountains when it comes to business, complete with morning and afternoon commutes.

Throughout Colorado, most retail stores are open from 9 AM or 9:30 AM until 6 PM or 7 PM daily in downtown locations and until 9 or 10 in suburban shopping malls. Downtown stores sometimes stay open later Thursday night. Normal banking hours are weekdays 9–5; some branches are also open on Saturday morning.

Car Rental

Rates in Denver begin at about $35 a day and $180 a week for an economy car with air-conditioning, an automatic transmission, and unlimited mileage. This does not include tax on car rentals, which is 11.3%.

➤ **MAJOR AGENCIES: Alamo** (800/327–9633; 020/8759–6200 in the U.K.). **Avis** (800/331–1212; 800/331–1084 in Canada; 02/9353–9000 in Australia; 09/525–1982 in New Zealand; 0870/606–0100 in the U.K.). **Budget** (800/527–0700; 0144/227–6266 in the U.K.). **Dollar** (800/800–4000; 0124/622–0111 in the U.K., where it is known as Sixt; 02/9223–1444 in Australia). **Hertz** (800/654–3131; 800/263–0600 in Canada; 020/8897–2072 in the U.K.; 02/9669–2444 in Australia; 09/256–8690 in New Zealand). **National Car Rental** (800/227–7368; 0845/722–2525 in the U.K., where it is known as National Europe).

➤ **LOCAL AGENCIES: Eagle Rent-A-Car** (tel. 800/282–2128). **Rocky Mountain Rent-A-Car** (tel. 800/525–2880). **Thrifty Car Rental** (tel. 800/367–2277).

INSURANCE

When driving a rented car you are generally responsible for any damage to or loss of the vehicle as well as for any property damage or personal injury that you may cause. Before you rent see what coverage your personal auto-insurance policy and credit cards already provide.

For about $15 to $20 per day, rental companies sell protection, known as a collision- or loss-damage waiver (CDW or LDW), that eliminates your liability for damage to the car. In most states you don't need a CDW if you have personal auto insurance or other liability insurance. However, **make sure you have enough coverage to pay for the car.** If you do not have auto insurance or an umbrella policy that covers damage to third parties, purchasing liability insurance and a CDW or LDW is highly recommended.

REQUIREMENTS & RESTRICTIONS

In Colorado you must be 21 to rent a car, and rates may be higher if you're under 25. You'll pay extra for child seats (about $3 per day), which are compulsory for children under five, and for additional drivers (about $2 per day). Non-U.S. residents will need a reservation voucher, a passport, a driver's license, and a travel policy that covers each driver, in order to pick up a car.

SURCHARGES

Before you pick up a car in one city and leave it in another, **ask about drop-off charges or one-way service fees,** which can be substantial. Note, too, that some rental agencies charge extra if you return the car before the time specified in your contract. To avoid a hefty refueling fee, **fill the tank just before you turn in the car,** but be aware that gas stations near the rental outlet may overcharge.

Car Travel

Before setting out on any driving trip, **make sure your vehicle is in top condition.** It's best to have a complete tune-up, but at the least, you should check the following: lights, including brake lights, backup lights, and emergency lights; tires, including the spare; oil; engine coolant; windshield-washer fluid; windshield-wiper blades; and brakes. For emergencies, take along flares or reflector triangles, jumper cables, an empty gas can, a fire extinguisher, a flashlight, a plastic tarp, blankets, and coins for phone calls.

Make sure your gas tank is full, since distances between gas stations could make running on empty (or in the reserve zone) a not-so-pleasant memory of your trip. Deer, elk, and even bears may try to get to the other side of a road just as you come along, so **watch out for wildlife on the highways.** Exercise caution, not only to save an animal's life, but also to avoid possibly extensive damage to your car.

EMERGENCIES & SAFETY

Follow the posted speed limit, and **drive defensively.** Note that right turns on red lights (after making a stop) are legal in Colorado.

Four-wheel drive vehicles are better at going through snow than they are at stopping on ice and snow. **Give extra space and use extreme caution during blizzard conditions.** Most rental cars are not equipped with snow tires. Many locals employ studded snow tires on their cars for a better grip. If you're planning to drive into high elevations, be sure to **check the weather forecast** beforehand. The mountain passes even on main highways can be forced to close because of snow conditions.

Be prepared for stormy weather. Take food, water, a can with a candle, extra blankets or a sleeping bag, and tell someone your destination, if possible. It's also good to carry a cellular phone. Be aware, however, that because of the mountains cell phones don't work everywhere. If you become stranded **never leave your vehicle.** Instead wait (running the engine only when needed) until someone comes looking for you. Most roads are routinely patrolled and plowed.

➤ EMERGENCY CONTACTS: **Call 911 to be connected to all emergency services. For 24-hour towing and roadside assistance, contact Al's Ajax Towing** (tel. 970/920–3950). **Also available for towing and roadside assistance is D and D Towing** (tel. 970/925–1329). **Or try Palazzi Towing** (tel. 970/925-3549).

GAS STATIONS

The Aspen Store Texaco, at Main and Galena streets in Aspen, is open 24 hours. The Aspen Amoco Tire & Service Center, on the corner of Main and Monarch, has the most convenient air hose for car tires or bikes. The The Aspen Airport Amoco is across from the airport and has a car wash next door. The Snowmass Resort Conoco is the only gas station in Snowmass Village and usually has the gas prices to prove it.

ROAD CONDITIONS

Given the high cost of housing in Aspen, there is a traditional urban weekday commuter traffic jam coming "upvalley" into

Aspen between 8 AM and 9:30 AM and "downvalley" between 4:30 PM and 6 PM. Ongoing construction on the main valley route, Highway 82, also slows traffic.

In the summer, there are many spectacular drives in the area, and modern highways make mountain driving safe and generally trouble free even in cold weather. Although road maintenance is good and plowing is prompt, winter driving can present some real challenges. Aspen and Snowmass are both above 8,000 ft and subject to sudden and intense winter road conditions.

➤ ROAD CONDITION INFORMATION: **Colorado Road Condition Information** (tel. 303/639–1111 within a two-hour drive of Denver, 303/639–1234 statewide).

PARKING

A paid parking policy is enforced on the streets of downtown Aspen from 7 AM to 6 PM every day of the week except Sunday. The cost is 50¢ per half hour with a two-hour maximum. Make payments at the meters, marked with a blue parking sign, located on every block. You can park at the **Rio Grande Parking Plaza** (tel. 970/920–5430) for 75¢ per hour, with a maximum of $7.50 per day. This is the only parking garage in town, and it is located just below the Pitkin County Library.

In summer, parking in the Snowmass Village Mall area is generally free (although there are two time-limit lots). In winter, parking here is by permit. Ask your hotel or condo for a permit.

The cost to park at the base of the local ski areas varies. At Snowmass Mountain, the base area lots cost between $1 and $8, depending on the day. Free parking is available at the rodeo lot, a five-minute shuttle ride to the mountain, or for cars with five or more people. The cost to park at the Aspen Highlands base lot is $5, with free parking for cars with three or more people. Parking at Buttermilk Mountain is always free. Parking at the base of Aspen Mountain falls under the same restrictions as parking in the town of Aspen proper.

Children in Aspen

Aspen in the winter is fun for kids and simple for parents. There are ski-school programs on Highlands, Buttermilk, and Snowmass, as well as slopeside day care for infants and toddlers. In the summer, trails and meadows abound and the weather is great for outdoor play, but there are far fewer day care options.

If you are renting a car don't forget to **arrange for a car seat** when you reserve.

BABYSITTING

Year-round babysitting services are available in Aspen. Get details from your hotel concierge, or try any of the agencies listed below.

➤ AGENCIES: **The Agency** (tel. 970/544–3800). **Aimee's Angels** (tel. 970/923–2809). **Aspen Babysitting Company** (tel. 970/948–6849). **Aspen Day Trippers** (tel. 970/920–1769). **Kid's Club** (tel. 970/925–3136). **Mom's Day Off** (tel. 970/925–8448).

FLYING

If your children are two or older, **ask about children's airfares.** As a general rule, infants under two not occupying a seat fly at greatly reduced fares or even for free. When booking, **confirm carry-on allowances** if you're traveling with infants. In general, for babies charged 10% of the adult fare you are allowed one carry-on bag and a collapsible stroller; if the flight is full, the stroller may have to be checked or you may be limited to less.

Experts agree that it's a good idea to use safety seats aloft for children weighing less than 40 pounds. Airlines set their own policies: U.S. carriers usually require that the child be ticketed, even if he or she is young enough to ride free, since the seats must be strapped into regular seats. Do **check your airline's policy about using safety seats during takeoff and landing.** And since safety seats are not allowed just everywhere in the plane, get your seat assignments early.

When reserving, **request children's meals or a freestanding bassinet** if you need them. But note that bulkhead seats, where you must sit to use the bassinet, may lack an overhead bin or storage space on the floor.

LODGING

Most hotels in Colorado allow children under a certain age to stay in their parents' room at no extra charge, but others charge for them as extra adults; be sure to **find out the cutoff age for children's discounts.**

RESERVATIONS & DRESS

Reservations are always a good idea: we mention them only when they're essential or are not accepted. Book as far ahead as you can, and reconfirm as soon as you arrive. We mention dress only when men are required to wear a jacket or a jacket and tie.

Disabilities & Accessibility

➤ LOCAL RESOURCES: **Denver Commission for People with Disabilities** (tel. 303/640–3056). **Wilderness on Wheels** (3131 Vaughn Way, Suite 305, Aurora, CO 80014, tel. 303/751–3959).

LODGING

When discussing accessibility with an operator or reservations agent, **ask hard questions.** Are there any stairs, inside or out? Are there grab bars next to the toilet *and* in the shower/tub? How wide is the doorway to the room? To the bathroom? For the most extensive facilities meeting the latest legal specifications, **opt for newer accommodations.**

➤ COMPLAINTS: **Disability Rights Section** (U.S. Department of Justice, Civil Rights Division, Box 66738, Washington, DC 20035-6738, tel. 202/514–0301 or 800/514–0301; TTY 202/514–0383 or 800/514–0383, fax 202/307–1198, www.usdoj.gov/crt/ada/adahom1.htm) **for general complaints. Aviation Consumer Protection Division** (☞ Air Travel, *above*) **for airline-**

related problems. Civil Rights Office (U.S. Department of Transportation, Departmental Office of Civil Rights, S-30, 400 7th St. SW, Room 10215, Washington, DC 20590, tel. 202/366–4648, fax 202/366–9371) **for problems with surface transportation.**

TRAVEL AGENCIES

In the United States, the Americans with Disabilities Act requires that travel firms serve the needs of all travelers. Some agencies specialize in working with people with disabilities.

➤ TRAVELERS WITH MOBILITY PROBLEMS: **Access Adventures** (206 Chestnut Ridge Rd., Scottsville, NY 14624, tel. 716/889–9096), **run by a former physical-rehabilitation counselor. Accessible Vans of the Rockies** (2040 W. Hamilton Pl., Sheridan, CO 80110, tel. 303/806–5047 or 888/837–0065, fax 303/781–2329, www.access-able.com/avr/avrockies.htm). **Flying Wheels Travel** (143 W. Bridge St., Box 382, Owatonna, MN 55060, tel. 507/451–5005 or 800/535–6790, fax 507/451–1685, www.flyingwheels.com). **Hinsdale Travel Service** (201 E. Ogden Ave., Suite 100, Hinsdale, IL 60521, tel. 630/325–1335, fax 630/325–1342).

EMERGENCIES

Call 911 to be connected to all emergency services.

➤ DOCTORS/DENTISTS: **Aspen Valley Hospital** (☞ *below*) can refer you to a local doctor or dentist, or check the local Yellow Pages.

➤ HOSPITALS: **Aspen Valley Hospital** (0401 Castle Creek Rd., tel. 970/925–1120).

➤ HOT LINES: **Aspen Counseling Center 24-hour hot line** (tel. 970/920–5555).

➤ 24-HOUR PHARMACIES: There are no 24-hour pharmacies in Aspen/Snowmass Village. **Carl's Pharmacy** (306 E. Main St., tel. 970/925–3273) is open from 8 AM to 10 PM daily.

Gay & Lesbian Travel

Aspen and Snowmass Village are quite friendly to gay and lesbian travelers. In fact, Aspen's Gay and Lesbian Ski Week, held in late January, is one of the nation's largest gay and lesbian gatherings. For information, call the **Aspen Gay and Lesbian Community Fund's hotline** (tel. 970/925-9249).

➤ GAY- & LESBIAN-FRIENDLY TRAVEL AGENCIES: **Different Roads Travel** (8383 Wilshire Blvd., Suite 902, Beverly Hills, CA 90211, tel. 323/651-5557 or 800/429-8747, fax 323/651-3678). **Kennedy Travel** (314 Jericho Turnpike, Floral Park, NY 11001, tel. 516/352-4888 or 800/237-7433, fax 516/354-8849, www.kennedytravel.com). **Now Voyager** (4406 18th St., San Francisco, CA 94114, tel. 415/626-1169 or 800/255-6951, fax 415/626-8626, www.nowvoyager.com). **Skylink Travel and Tour** (1006 Mendocino Ave., Santa Rosa, CA 95401, tel. 707/546-9888 or 800/225-5759, fax 707/546-9891, www.skylinktravel.com), **serves lesbian travelers.**

Holidays

Major national holidays include New Year's Day (Jan. 1); Martin Luther King Jr. Day (3rd Mon. in Jan.); President's Day (3rd Mon. in Feb.); Memorial Day (last Mon. in May); Independence Day (July 4); Labor Day (1st Mon. in Sept.); Thanksgiving Day (4th Thurs. in Nov.); Christmas Eve and Christmas Day (Dec. 24 and 25); and New Year's Eve (Dec. 31).

Lodging

The lodgings we list are the cream of the crop in each price category. We always list the facilities that are available—but we don't specify whether they cost extra. When pricing accommodations, always ask what's included and what costs extra.

Assume that hotels operate on the **European Plan** (EP, with no meals) unless we specify that they use either the **Continental**

Plan (CP, with a Continental breakfast), **Breakfast Plan** (BP, with a full breakfast) or the **Modified American Plan** (MAP, with breakfast and dinner) or are **all-inclusive** (including all meals and most activities).

➤ **GENERAL INFORMATION: Colorado Hotel and Lodging Association** (999 18th St., Suite 1240, Denver, CO 80202, tel. 303/297–8335).

APARTMENT RENTALS

If you want a home base that's roomy enough for a family and comes with cooking facilities, **consider a furnished rental.** These can save you money, especially if you're traveling with a group. Home-exchange directories sometimes list rentals as well as exchanges.

B&BS

➤ **RESERVATION SERVICES: Montana Bed & Breakfast Association** (5557 U.S. 93 S, Somers, MT 59932, tel. 800/453–8870). **Bed & Breakfast Inns of Utah** (Box 2639, Park City, UT 84060, fax 801/595–0332).

CAMPING

Camping is invigorating and inexpensive. Colorado is full of state and national parks and forests with sites that range from rustic (pit toilets and cold running water), to campgrounds with bathhouses with hot showers, paved trailer pads that can accommodate even jumbo RVs, and full hookups. Fees vary, from $6 to $10 a night for tents and up to $21 for RVs, but are usually waived once the water is turned off for the winter.

Sometimes site reservations are accepted, and then only for up to seven days (early birds reserve up to a year in advance); more often, they're not. Campers who prefer a more remote setting may camp in the backcountry; it's free but you'll need a permit, available from park visitor centers and ranger stations. If you're visiting in summer, plan well ahead. *The National Parks: Camping*

Guide, published by the U.S. Government Printing Office and available for $3.50, may be helpful.

The facilities and amenities at privately operated campgrounds are usually more extensive (swimming pools are common), reservations are more widely accepted, and nightly fees are higher: $7 and up for tents, $23 for RVs.

➤ INFORMATION: **U.S. Government Printing Office** (Superintendent of Documents; U.S. Government Printing Office, Washington, DC 20402, tel. 202/738-3238).

HOME EXCHANGES

If you would like to exchange your home for someone else's, **join a home-exchange organization,** which will send you its updated listings of available exchanges for a year and will include your own listing in at least one of them. It's up to you to make specific arrangements.

➤ EXCHANGE CLUBS: **HomeLink International** (Box 650, Key West, FL 33041, tel. 305/294-7766 or 800/638-3841, fax 305/294-1448, www.homelink.org; $98 per year). **Intervac U.S.** (Box 590504, San Francisco, CA 94159, tel. 800/756-4663, fax 415/435-7440, www.intervac.com; $89 per year includes two catalogs).

HOSTELS

No matter what your age, you can **save on lodging costs by staying at hostels.** In some 5,000 locations in more than 70 countries around the world, Hostelling International (HI), the umbrella group for a number of national youth-hostel associations, offers single-sex, dorm-style beds and, at many hostels, rooms for couples and family accommodations. Membership in any HI national hostel association, open to travelers of all ages, allows you to stay in HI-affiliated hostels at member rates; one-year membership is about $25 for adults; hostels run about $10-$25 per night. Members have priority if the hostel is full; they're also eligible for discounts around the world, even on rail and bus travel in some countries.

➤ **Organizations: Hostelling International—American Youth Hostels** (733 15th St. NW, Suite 840, Washington, DC 20005, tel. 202/783–6161, fax 202/783–6171, www.hiayh.org). **Hostelling International—Canada** (400–205 Catherine St., Ottawa, Ontario K2P 1C3, tel. 613/237–7884, fax 613/237–7868, www.hostellingintl.ca). **Youth Hostel Association of England and Wales** (Trevelyan House, 8 St. Stephen's Hill, St. Albans, Hertfordshire AL1 2DY, tel. 01727/855215 or 01727/845047, fax 01727/844126, www.yha.org.uk). **Australian Youth Hostel Association** (10 Mallett St., Camperdown, NSW 2050, tel. 02/9565–1699, fax 02/9565–1325, www.yha.com.au). **Youth Hostels Association of New Zealand** (Box 436, Christchurch, New Zealand, tel. 03/379–9970, fax 03/365–4476, www.yha.org.nz).

HOTELS
Many properties offer special weekend rates, sometimes up to 50% off regular prices. However, these deals are usually not extended during ski season, when hotels are normally full. All hotels listed have private baths unless otherwise noted.

INNS
Charm is the long suit of these establishments, which generally occupy a restored older building with some historical or architectural significance. They're generally small, with fewer than 20 rooms, and located outside cities. Breakfast may be included in the rates.

➤ **Information: Distinctive Inns of Colorado** (Box 10472, Colorado Springs, CO 80932, tel. 800/866–0621).

Media

NEWSPAPERS & MAGAZINES
Aspen has two daily newspapers, the *Aspen Daily News* and the *Aspen Times*, and two weekly newspapers, the *Aspen Times Weekly* and the *Roaring Fork Sunday*. The weekly *Snowmass Sun* covers happenings in Snowmass Village. *Aspen Magazine* is published

six times a year, and *Sojourner Magazine* is published in winter and summer. Look for seasonal travel guides, gallery guides, and restaurant guides at newsstands around town.

RADIO & TELEVISION

Aspen has four television stations with local programming. Channel 12 covers community events and government meetings; channel 11 is a community bulletin board; channels 8 and 16 mix national and local programming, including *Aspen Today* at 8 AM every day on channel 16. Local radio stations KSPN at 97.7 FM, KSNO at 93.5, and KNFO at 95.3 offer a mix of music and local news. Public radio stations KAJX at 91.5 FM and KDNK at 90.5 FM feature National Public Radio syndications.

Money Matters

Aspen is not known for its bargains. During ski season, first-class hotel rooms in Aspen can cost over $400 a night. However, discounts are often available outside of ski season. Prices throughout this guide are given for adults. Substantially reduced fees are almost always available for children, students, and senior citizens. For information on taxes, *see* Taxes, *below*.

ATMS

➤ **ATM LOCATIONS: Cirrus** (tel. 800/424–7787). **Plus** (tel. 800/843–7587).

CREDIT CARDS

Throughout this guide, the following abbreviations are used: **AE**, American Express; **D**, Discover; **DC**, Diner's Club; **MC**, Master Card; and **V**, Visa.

National Parks

Look into discount passes to save money on park entrance fees. The National Parks Pass ($50) gets you and your companions free admission to all parks for one year. (Camping and parking are extra.) Both the Golden Age Passport ($10), for those 62 and older, and the Golden Access Passport (free), for travelers with disabilities, entitle holders to free entry to all national parks, plus 50% off fees for the use of many park facilities and services. You must show proof of age and of U.S. citizenship or permanent residency (such as a U.S. passport, driver's license, or birth certificate) and, if requesting Golden Access, proof of disability. The Golden Age and Golden Access passes are available at all national parks wherever entrance fees are charged. The National Parks Pass, and Golden Access passes are available by mail or through the Internet.

➤ PASSES BY MAIL: **National Park Service** (National Park Service National Office, 1849 C St. NW, Washington, DC 20240-0001, tel. 202/208–4747, www.nps.gov).

National Parks Pass (27540 Ave. Mentry, Valencia, CA 91355, tel. 888/GO–PARKS, www.nationalparks.org).

Outdoors & Sports

Opportunities abound in Aspen. Contact national forests, parks, or the U.S. Forest Service for details. The Bureau of Land Management also has information on Colorado's sterling trekking opportunities. The Mountaineers and Sierra Club Books are among the leading publishers of hiking guides for the Rockies. Topographical maps may be available in well-equipped outdoor stores (REI or Eastern Mountain Sports, for example). Maps are also available from the U.S. Geological Survey. Be specific about the region you're interested in when ordering.

Fishing is legal year-round, but you must obtain a license. Fees for nonresidents are $40.25 annually, $18.25 for a five-day period, and $5.25 for a single day. For more information, including the "Fishing Hotspots" and "Watchable Wildlife" booklets, contact the Colorado Division of Wildlife.

➤ CLIMBING: **American Alpine Institute** (1515 12th St., Bellingham, WA 98225, tel. 360/671–1505). **Colorado Mountain School** (Box 1846, Estes Park, CO 80517, tel. 970/586–5758).

➤ **Cycling: Adventure Cycling Association** (Box 8308, Missoula, MT 59807, tel. 406/721–1776).

➤ **Fishing: Colorado Division of Wildlife** (6060 Broadway, Denver, CO 80216, tel. 303/297–1192).

➤ **Golf: Colorado Golf Association** (5655 S. Yosemite, Suite 101, Englewood 80111, tel. 303/366–4653). ***Colorado Golf magazine*** (559 E. 2nd Ave., Castle Rock 80104, tel. 303/688–8262). **Colorado Golf Resort Association** (2110 S. Ash St., Denver 80222, tel. 303/699–4653).

➤ **Hiking: Bureau of Land Management** (tel. 970/947–2800). **The Mountaineers** (300 3rd Ave. W, Seattle, WA 98119, tel. 206/284–6310). **Sierra Club Books** (85 2nd St., 4th floor, San Francisco, CA 94105, tel. 415/977–5600). **U.S. Forest Service** (Box 25127, Lakewood 80225, tel. 303/275–5350; Arapahoe, tel. 970/498–1100; Medicine Bow/Routt, tel. 970/879–1722; White River, tel. 970/945–2521). U.S. Geological Survey (Distribution Center, Denver, CO 80225).

➤ **Mountain Biking: Colorado Plateau Mountain Bike Trail Association** (Box 4602, Grand Junction 81502, tel. 970/249–8055). **Colorado State Office of the U.S. Bureau of Land Management** (Dept. of the Interior, 2850 Youngfield St., Lakewood 80215, tel. 303/239–3600). **International Mountain Bike Association** (1121 Broadway, Suite 202, Boulder 80304, tel. 303/545–9011).

➤ **Rafting: Colorado River Outfitters Association** (730 Burbank St., Broomfield 80020-1658, tel. 303/280–2554).

➤ **Skiing: Colorado Ski Country USA** (1560 Broadway, Suite 2000, Denver 80202, tel. 303/837–0793). **Heli-Trax** (Box 1560, Telluride 81435, tel. 970/728–6990).

➤ **Snowmobiling: Colorado Snowmobile Association** (Box 1260, Grand Lake 80447, tel. 800/235–4480).

Packing

If you plan to spend much time outdoors, and certainly if you go in winter, **choose clothing appropriate for cold and wet weather.** Cotton clothing, including denim—although fine on warm, dry days—can be uncomfortable when it gets wet and when the weather's cold. A better choice is clothing made of wool or any of a number of new synthetics that provide warmth without bulk and maintain their insulating properties even when wet.

In summer, you'll want shorts during the day. But because early morning and night can be cold, and high passes windy, pack a sweater and a light jacket, and perhaps also a wool cap and gloves. Try layering—a T-shirt under another shirt under a jacket—and peel off layers as you go. For walks and hikes, you'll need sturdy footwear. To take you into the wilds, boots should have thick soles and plenty of ankle support; if your shoes are new and you plan to spend much time on the trail, break them in at home. Bring a day pack for short hikes, along with a canteen or water bottle, and don't forget rain gear, a hat, sunscreen, and insect repellent.

In winter, prepare for subzero temperatures with good boots, warm socks and liners, long johns, a well-insulated jacket, and a warm hat and mittens. Dress in layers so you can add or remove clothes as the temperatures fluctuate.

Remember that sunglasses and a sun hat are essential at high altitudes; the thinner atmosphere requires sunscreen with a greater SPF than you might need at lower elevations.

In your carry-on luggage, **pack an extra pair of eyeglasses or contact lenses** and **enough of any medication you take** to last the entire trip. You may also ask your doctor to write a spare prescription using the drug's generic name, since brand names may vary from country to country. In luggage to be checked,

never pack prescription drugs or valuables. To avoid customs delays, carry medications in their original packaging. And don't forget to carry with you the addresses of offices that handle refunds of lost traveler's checks.

CHECKING LUGGAGE

How many carry-on bags you can bring with you is up to the airline. Most allow two, but not always, so make sure that everything you carry aboard will fit under your seat or in the overhead bin, and get to the gate early. Note that if you have a seat at the back of the plane, you'll probably board first, while the overhead bins are still empty.

If you are flying internationally, note that baggage allowances may be determined not by piece but by weight—generally 88 pounds (40 kilograms) in first class, 66 pounds (30 kilograms) in business class, and 44 pounds (20 kilograms) in economy.

Airline liability for baggage is limited to $1,250 per person on flights within the United States. On international flights it amounts to $9.07 per pound or $20 per kilogram for checked baggage (roughly $640 per 70-pound bag) and $400 per passenger for unchecked baggage. You can buy additional coverage at check-in for about $10 per $1,000 of coverage, but it excludes a rather extensive list of items, shown on your airline ticket.

Before departure, **itemize your bags' contents** and their worth, and label the bags with your name, address, and phone number. (If you use your home address, cover it so potential thieves can't see it readily.) Inside each bag, **pack a copy of your itinerary.** At check-in, **make sure that each bag is correctly tagged** with the destination airport's three-letter code. If your bags arrive damaged or fail to arrive at all, file a written report with the airline before leaving the airport.

Rest Rooms

Public rest rooms can be found on the east side of Wagner Park in downtown Aspen, at both visitor centers (425 Rio Grande Pl. and at the Wheeler Opera House), and at the gondola building at the base of Aspen Mountain. In Snowmass Village, public rest rooms are located adjacent to the Village shuttle stop on the Mall. You can also use the rest rooms at many restaurants and retail shops, whether you're a customer or not.

Safety

Regardless of the outdoor activity or your level of skill, safety must come first. Remember: **know your limits!**

Many trails are at high altitudes, where oxygen is scarce. They're also frequently desolate. Hikers and bikers should **carry emergency supplies**: a flashlight, a compass, waterproof matches, a first-aid kit, a knife, and a light plastic tarp for shelter. Backcountry skiers should add a repair kit, a blanket, an avalanche beacon, and a lightweight shovel to their lists. Always **bring extra food and a canteen of water** as dehydration is a common occurrence at high altitudes. **Never drink from streams or lakes**, unless you boil the water first or purify it with tablets. Giardia, an intestinal parasite, may be present.

Always **check the condition of roads and trails, and get the latest weather reports** before setting out. In summer, **take precautions against heat stroke or exhaustion** by resting frequently in shaded areas; in winter, **take precautions against hypothermia** by layering clothing. Ultimately, proper planning, common sense, and good physical conditioning are the strongest guards against the elements.

ALTITUDE

You may feel dizzy and weak and find yourself breathing heavily—signs that the thin mountain air isn't giving you your accustomed dose of oxygen. Take it easy and **rest often for a few days until you're acclimatized.** Throughout your stay drink plenty of water and watch your alcohol consumption. If you experience severe headaches and nausea, see a doctor. It's easy to go too high too fast. The remedy for altitude-related discomfort is to go down quickly, into heavier air.

Taxes

Sales tax is 3% in Colorado. In Aspen and Snowmass, there are additional local sales and lodging taxes. Total sales tax in Aspen is 8.2%. In Snowmass Village the total sales tax is 9.8%.

Taxis

Taxis are metered at $5 for the first mile, plus $2.75 per additional mile and 60¢ per additional person (and don't forget the tip!).

➤ TAXI COMPANIES: **High Mountain Taxi** (tel. 970/925–8294) provides taxi service around Aspen. Look for the white cars and vans with blue signage parked at the corner of Galena Street and Cooper Avenue.

Telephones

The telephone area code for Aspen is 970. Pay telephones cost 25¢ for a local call. Charge phones, also common, may be used to charge a call to a telephone-company calling card or a credit card, or for collect calls.

Many hotels place a surcharge on local calls made from your room and include a service charge on long-distance calls. It may be cheaper for you to make your calls from a pay phone in the hotel lobby rather than from your room.

Time

Aspen and Snowmass are in the Mountain Time Zone. Mountain time is two hours earlier than Eastern time and one hour later than Pacific time. It is one hour earlier than Chicago, seven hours earlier than London and 17 hours earlier than Sydney.

Tipping

Aspen locals work hard to make a living in a town notorious for its high cost of living, which means they rely on tips to pay the rent. While 15% might be fine at restaurants in most of the United States, 20% is fairly standard in Aspen. For coat checks and bellmen, it's a minimum of $1 per coat or bag. Taxi drivers expect 15 percent. And don't forget about other service workers, such as ski technicians, coffee baristas, sandwich makers, and the like— a few dollars here go a long way toward improved service.

Train Travel

Amtrak has a scenic route from Denver to Glenwood Springs. Taxi and bus service to Aspen are available at the station.

➤ INFORMATION: **Amtrak** (tel. 800/872–7245).

Travel Agencies

A good travel agent puts your needs first. Look for an agency that has been in business at least five years, emphasizes customer service, and has someone on staff who specializes in your destination. In addition, **make sure the agency belongs to a professional trade organization.** The American Society of Travel Agents (ASTA), with 27,000 agents in some 170 countries, is the largest and most influential in the field. Operating under the motto "Integrity in Travel," it maintains and enforces a strict code of ethics and will step in to help mediate any agent-client disputes if necessary. ASTA also maintains a Web site that includes a directory of agents.

➤ LOCAL AGENT REFERRALS: **American Society of Travel Agents** (ASTA; tel. 800/965–2782 24-hour hot line, fax 703/684–8319, www.astanet.com). **Association of British Travel Agents** (68–71 Newman St., London W1P 4AH, tel. 0171/637–2444, fax 0171/

637–0713, www.abtanet.com). **Association of Canadian Travel Agents** (1729 Bank St., Suite 201, Ottawa, Ontario K1V 7Z5, tel. 613/237–3657, fax 613/521–0805). **Australian Federation of Travel Agents** (Level 3, 309 Pitt St., Sydney 2000, tel. 02/9264–3299, fax 02/9264–1085, www.afta.com.au). **Travel Agents' Association of New Zealand** (Box 1888, Wellington 10033, tel. 04/499–0104, fax 04/499–0827).

Visitor Information

➤ TOURIST INFORMATION: **Aspen Chamber Resort Association** (425 Rio Grande Pl., Aspen 81611, tel. 970/925–1940 or 800/262–7736; Wheeler Opera House, 328 E. Hyman St., tel. 970/925–5656). **Colorado Travel and Tourism Authority** (Box 22005, Denver 80222, tel. 303/832–6171 or 800/265–6723, fax 303/832–6174).

Web Sites

Do check out the World Wide Web when you're planning your trip. You'll find everything from current weather forecasts to virtual tours of famous cities. Fodor's Web site, www.fodors.com, is a great place to start your on-line travels. For more information specifically on Colorado, visit www.colorado.com.

When to Go

Aspen's ski season typically runs from Thanksgiving to mid-April. March has both the most sunshine and the best ski conditions. Late April and May are off-season in Aspen, although it can be beautiful. June, July and August are ideal, bringing clear days and cool nights, as well as a cultural explosion. There are fewer people in September and October but typically the weather is gorgeous. Late October and early November can be gray and cool and are quiet periods in town.

CLIMATE

Aspen's winters are drier and sunnier than most other ski resorts. The cold is not a "wet cold," so winter days are generally still pleasant. Snowstorms can be intense but generally last only a day or two. Spring and fall are cool and sometimes rainy. Summer brings mild temperatures, little humidity, cool mountain breezes, and crisp nights.

➤ **Forecasts: Weather Channel Connection** (tel. 900/932–8437), 95¢ per minute from a Touch-Tone phone.

What follows are the average daily maximum and minimum temperatures for the region.

ASPEN

Jan.	33F	1C	May	64F	18C	Sept.	71F	22C
	6	-14		32	0		35	2
Feb.	37F	3C	June	73F	23C	Oct.	60F	16C
	8	-13		37	3		28	-2
Mar.	42F	6C	July	80F	27C	Nov.	44F	7C
	15	-9		44	7		15	-9
Apr.	53F	12C	Aug.	78F	26C	Dec.	37F	3C
	24	-4		42	6		8	-13

INDEX

A

Air travel, 198–199, 205–206, 216
Ajax Tavern, 35–36, 149–150
Altitude sickness, 217–218
Anderson Ranch Arts Center, 142–143, 165
Antiques shops, 58
Apartment rentals, 209
Art galleries, 58–62
Artists' community, 142–143
Art museums, 130–131
Ashcroft Ghost Town, 129–130
Aspen Alps, 177, 180
Aspen Art Museum, 130–131
Aspen Center for Physics, 16, 168
Aspen Club Lodge, 149, 180
Aspen Highlands, 37, 87–92, 94
Aspen Historical Society, 131, 142, 166
Aspen Institute, 16, 141, 167–168
Aspen Meadows (hotel), 36, 38, 180–181
Aspen Meadows area, 131, 134
Aspen Mountain, 37, 81–87, 94
Aspen Mountain Lodge, 183–184
Aspen Music Festival, 16, 134–135, 166, 167
Aspen Square, 181
Aspen Underground, 41
ATMs, 212

B

Bagel Bites, 32
Ballooning, 117
Bars, 149–155, 157
Basalt, Colorado, 136
Beaumont Inn, 184
Bed and breakfasts, 209
Benedict Music Tent, 134–135, 161, 163
Benedict's, 39–40
Bentley's at the Wheeler, 29, 150
Bicycling, 117–118, 214
Big Wrap, 41–42
Blue Maize, 40
Boogie's Diner, 28, 140
Book shops, 63, 76
Boomerang Lodge, 184–185
Brand, The, 173
Business hours, 58, 200
Bus travel, 199–200
Butcher's Block, 41
Butch's Lobster Bar, 54
Buttermilk Mountain, 37, 92–93, 95–100

C

Cache Cache, 36, 150
Cafe Ink! (Aspen), 32
Cafe Ink (Snowmass), 143
Camping, 209–210
Campo De Fiori, 43, 150

Canoeing, 126–127
Cantina, 47, 150–151
Caribou Club, 33, 156
Car rentals, 200–202
Car travel, 202–204
Century Room at the Hotel Jerome, 33
Chairlift rides, 143
Chalet Lisl, 189
Charcuterie and Cheese Market, 41
Chart House, 47–48
Children, 165–166, 205–206
Christmas Inn, 191
Cirque Cafe, 51
Climate, 221
Clothing shops, 63–67, 76
Cloud Nine Cafe, 55
Compromise Mine, 138
Condominiums, 190
Conundrum, 33–34
Cooper Street Bar and Restaurant, 29, 151
Cowboys, 49, 157
Crafts shops, 63
Credit cards, 212
Crystal Palace, 48

D

Dance, 163
Dance clubs, 155–156
Dining, 23–55, 206
price categories, 24
Disabilities and accessibility, 206–207
Dog sledding, 114, 145

E

Emergencies, 202–203, 207
Explore Bistro, 49

F

Farfalla, 43
Film, 164
Finestra, 52, 54
Fishing, 14, 118–119, 214
Fitness clubs, 119–120
Freestyle Fridays event, 108
Fur shops, 67

G

Gant, The, 181–182
Gas stations, 203
Gay and lesbian travel, 208
Ghost towns, 129–130, 137
Gift shops, 68, 76–77
Given Institute, 16, 168
Glass shops, 69
Golf, 120, 214
Guido's, 48
Gwyn's, 39

H

Hallam Lake Nature Preserve, 135–137
Hang gliding, 121
Hard Rock Cafe, 28
Harry Vold Rodeo Company, 145
Hearthstone House, 185
High Alpine, 52
Hiking, 13–14, 121–123, 214
Holidays, 208
Holland House, 191
Home exchanges, 210
Home furnishings shops, 69–70

Horseback riding, 123–124
Hostels, 210–211
Hotel Aspen, 185–186
Hotel Durant, 186
Hotel Jerome, 137, 175
bars, 151–152, 153
dining, 28–29, 33, 38
lodging, 173–174
Hotel Lenado, 182

I

Ice climbing, 114
Ice skating, 114
Il Poggio, 52
In and Out House, 42
Independence Ghost Town, 137
Independence Square, 186
Inn at Aspen, 187
Inns, 211
Innsbruck Inn, 187

J

Jack's at the Sardy House Hotel, 36
Jacob's Corner in the Hotel Jerome, 38
Jewelry shops, 70, 72, 77
Jimmy's American Restaurant and Bar, 25, 28, 152
Johnny McGuire's Deli, 42

K

Kayaking, 14–15, 126–127
Kenichi, 44
Krabloonik (restaurant), 52
Krabloonik Kennel, 145

L

La Cocina, 46
Leather shops, 72–73

L'Hostaria, 42, 153
Library Bar at the Hotel Jerome, 153
Lift One, 182
Limelite Lodge, 191–192
Liquor stores, 53
Little Annie's, 28, 153
Little Nell
bar, 153
dining, 34
lodging, 174, 176
Little Ollie's, 32–33
Lodging, 171–197, 206–207
options, 208–211
price categories, 172
Lounges, 149–155, 157
Lucci's, 43

M

Magazines, 211–212
Main Street Bakery, 30, 137
Maroon Bells rock peaks, 138–139
Matsuhisa Aspen, 44
Meadows Restaurant, 36, 38
Medical assistance, 207
Mezzaluna, 40, 153–154
Milan's, 39
Mine tours, 138
Mirabella, 46
Molly Gibson Lodge, 188
Money, 212
Mother Lode, 42–43
Mountain adventures, preparation for, 127
Mountain biking, 124–125, 214
Mountain Chalet, 188

Mountain climbing, 125, 213
Mountain Dragon, 54, 157
Mountain environment, acclimating to, 111–112
Mountain House, 192
Musical instrument shops, 73
Music clubs, 155–156
Music festivals, 16–17, 134–135, 166, 167

N

National parks, 212–213
Nature preserves, 135–137
Newspapers, 211–212
New York Pizza, 47
Nightclubs, 156–157
Nightlife, 147–157
North of Nell, 182–183

O

Off-road driving, 125–126
Olives, 38, 154
Opera, 167

P

Pacifica Seafood Brasserie, 47
Packing, 215–216
Paesanos, 41
Paragliding, 121
Parking, 204
Perfume shops, 74
Pharmacies, 73, 207
Pine Creek Cookhouse, 55
Piñons, 34
Pokolodi Lodge, 195
Popcorn Wagon, 30
Poppies Bistro Cafe, 34–35
Poppycock's, 32

Price categories
dining, 24
lodging, 172

R

Radio stations, 212
Rafting, 14–15, 126–127, 214
R Bistro, 39
Readings and talks, 167–168
Red Onion, 29, 154
Renaissance, 35
Residence, The, 176
Rest rooms, 217
Road conditions, 203–204
Rodeo competitions, 145
Rusty's Hickory House, 30

S

Safety concerns, 217–218
Sage, 52
St. Moritz Lodge, 188–189
St. Regis Aspen, 176–177
Sardy House, 36, 183
Secondhand shops, 61
Shoe shops, 74
Shopping, 57–77, 200
ski equipment, 107–109
Silver Queen Gondola, 140
Silvertree Hotel, 194
Skiers Chalet, 192
Skiers Chalet Steak House, 48
Skiing
competitions, 105–107
cross-country, 12, 113
downhill, 9–12, 79–105
equipment and services, 107–109
extreme skiing, 94
visitor information, 214

Sledding, 115
Sled-dog kennels, 145
Sleigh rides, 115
Smuggler Mine, 138
Snowboarding
Aspen Highlands, 91–92
Buttermilk Mountain, 99–100
Snowmass, 104–105
Snowflake Inn, 189
Snowmass
dining, 37, 49–54
exploring, 142–145
lodging, 194–197
nightlife, 157
shopping, 76–77
skiing, 94, 100–105
supermarkets, 45
Snowmass Inn, 195, 197
Snowmobiling, 115–116, 214
Snow Queen Victorian Bed & Breakfast, 192–193
Snowshoeing, 106, 116
Sporting goods shops, 74–75, 77
Steak Pit, 48
Stonebridge Inn, 194–195
Stonebridge Restaurant, 51
Su Casa, 46, 154
Supermarkets, 45
Sushi Ya Go-Go, 44, 46
Syzygy, 35, 155

T

Takah Sushi, 44
Taxes, 58, 218
Taxis, 140–141, 218
Telephones, 218
Television stations, 212
Thai Tini, 49
Theater, 166, 168–169
Time, 218–219
Tipping, 25, 219
T Lazy 7 Ranch, 193
Tower Restaurant, 51
Toy shops, 75–76
Train travel, 219
Trattoria Toscana, 43–44
Travel agencies, 207, 219–220
Tyrolean Lodge, 193–194

U

Ultimate Taxi, 140–141
Ute City Bar and Grill, 38–39, 154–155

V

Variations, 40
Vinh Vinh, 49
Visitor information, 220

W

Weather information, 221
Web sites, 220
Wheeler Opera House, 141–142, 162–163
Wheeler-Stallard House, 142
When to go, 220–221
Wienerstube, 30
Wildcat Cafe, 51
Wildwood Lodge, 195
Woody Creek Tavern, 54

Z

Zane's Tavern, 51, 157
Zélé, 32

231

FODOR'S POCKET ASPEN AND SNOWMASS

EDITOR: Elizabeth Kugler

EDITORIAL PRODUCTION: Rebecca Zeiler Wintle

MAPS: Marcy Pritchard; Rebecca Baer

DESIGN: Fabrizio La Rocca, *creative director*; Tigist Getachew, *art director*

PRODUCTION/MANUFACTURING: Robert B. Shields

COVER PHOTOGRAPH: John P. Kelly/The Image Bank/PictureQuest

COPYRIGHT

Copyright © 2001 by Fodor's Travel Publications

Fodor's is a registered trademark of Random House, Inc.

All rights reserved under International and Pan-American Copyright Conventions. Published in the United States by Fodor's Travel Publications, a division of Random House, Inc., New York, and simultaneously in Canada by Random House of Canada, Limited, Toronto. Distributed by Random House, Inc., New York.

No maps, illustrations, or other portions of this book may be reproduced in any form without written permission from the publisher.

First Edition

ISBN 0-679-00774-1

ISSN 1531-2259

IMPORTANT TIP

Although all prices, opening times, and other details in this book are based on information supplied to us at press time, changes occur all the time in the travel world, and Fodor's cannot accept responsibility for facts that become outdated or for inadvertent errors or omissions. So **always confirm information when it matters,** especially if you're making a detour to visit a specific place.

SPECIAL SALES

Fodor's Travel Publications are available at special discounts for bulk purchases for sales promotions or premiums. Special editions, including personalized covers, excerpts of existing guides, and corporate imprints, can be created in large quantities for special needs. For more information, contact your local bookseller or write to Special Markets, Fodor's Travel Publications, 280 Park Avenue, New York, NY 10017. Inquiries from Canada should be directed to your local Canadian bookseller or sent to Random House of Canada, Ltd., Marketing Department, 2775 Matheson Boulevard East, Mississauga, Ontario L4W 4P7. Inquiries from the United Kingdom should be sent to Fodor's Travel Publications, 20 Vauxhall Bridge Road, London SW1V 2SA, England.

PRINTED IN THE UNITED STATES OF AMERICA

10 9 8 7 6 5 4 3 2 1